THE PLAGUE

AND I

BY

BETTY MACDONALD

A COMMON READER EDITION
THE AKADINE PRESS

The Plague and I

A COMMON READER EDITION published 1997
by The Akadine Press, Inc., by arrangement with
Joan MacDonald Keil and Anne Elizabeth Canham.

A COMMON READER EDITION and fountain colophon are trademarks
of The Akadine Press, Inc.

ISBN 1-888173-29-7

10 9 8 7 6 5

For Dr. Robert M. Stith, Dr. Clyde R. Jensen and Dr. Bernard P. Mullen without whose generous hearts and helping hands I would probably be just another name on a tombstone.

Contents

THE PLAGUE AND I

"O Captain! My Captain!"

The Captain of all these men of death that came
against him to take him away, was the Consumption,
for it was that that brought him down to the grave.
—Bunyan, *The Life and Death of Mr. Badman*

GETTING TUBERCULOSIS IN the middle of your life is like starting downtown to do a lot of urgent errands and being hit by a bus. When you regain consciousness you remember nothing about the urgent errands. You can't even remember where you were going. The important things now are the pain in your leg; the soreness in your back; what you will have for dinner; who is in the next bed.

By background and disposition some people are better suited to being hit by a bus than others. For instance Doris, who had worked in a Government office with me. Her mother had a little tumor, her father had a "bad leg," Doris had a great deal of "female trouble," and they all were hoping that Granny had cancer. Doris, her brothers and sisters, her aunts and uncles, her mother and father, her grandmother and grandfather, all of them, had begun life as barely formed, tiny little premature babies carried around on pillows and fed with eyedroppers. If they did manage to pull through the first year, and they often did, life from then on was one continuous ache, pain, sniffle and cough. When Doris or any member of her large ailing family asked each

11

other how they felt, it wasn't just a pleasantry, they really wanted to know.

They were so anxious to be sick that they prepared for colds days in advance of the actual germs, like training for the big game. Doris would say Monday morning at breakfast that she thought she felt as if she might be getting a cold. Instantly the whole household was *en garde*, and for the next week Doris was given hot tea, whiskey and lemon; a little sweater to wear under her blouse; many pills to take at the office, including nose drops which she administered by lying across her desk with her head hanging over the edge; a small screen to put around her desk to ward off draughts; sun lamp treatments on her back; mustard foot baths and plenty of encouragement.

By Saturday she usually had "the sniffles" as they called it, and during the next week she worked it into something big. To Doris and her family tuberculosis would have been anti-climactic but a definite asset. So of course it was not Doris but I who got tuberculosis, and the contrast between our families was noticeable.

In the first place our family motto was "People are healthy and anybody who isn't is a big stinker." In the second place there were five children in the family but not one little premature baby. We began life as large, plump, full time babies, filled with vigor and strength and all but one had bright red hair. My father, a mining engineer and a great admirer of health, spent much of his spare time and energy maintaining our good health. As soon as we were able, he made us run around the block every morning before breakfast in winter; hike for miles and miles in the mountains with mother and him in summer; go to bed every night at eight o'clock; drink ten glasses of water a day; and play out of doors (much against our wills) during all daylight hours.

For my sister Mary and my brother Cleve (sisters Dede and Alison were yet to come), this routine brought the desired results but as I grew out of infancy I turned thin and olive green and remained so no matter how many times I ran around the block, which was undoubtedly why I was Gammy's favorite child.

Gammy was my father's mother who lived with us and consistently undermined his health program. Gammy was a wonderful grandmother. She was a tireless reader-alouder, doll-clothes sewer, storyteller and walk-taker, but she was a pessimist, the kind of pessimist who gives every cloud a pitch black lining. With Gammy the state of being pessimistic was not a spasmodic thing induced by nerves or ill health, it was a twenty-four-hour proposition and she enjoyed it. She began her black premonitory remarks each morning as Daddy forced Mary and Cleve and me out the front door to run around the block.

We were living in Butte, Montana, the mornings were often bitterly cold, and we children, who were not exactly eager good sports about this morning exercise, would rush in from our rooms and sit down to breakfast, hoping that Daddy had forgotten about the morning run. But he never did. "Let's see some color in those cheeks," he would say heartily, unclamping our fingers from spoons and forks, stuffing us into our coats and rubbers and driving us out into the crisp morning air. Gammy would stand by the door waving her "apern" and wailing, "Darsie Bard, how can you drive those poor little cheeldrun out into this bitter cold?"

We'd hang around the steps blowing our hot breaths into the freezing air and watching them smoke and hoping that Gammy would soften Daddy, but he only laughed at Gammy and shut the door firmly and finally. We'd start out then moodily shuffling our feet and pushing each other off the sidewalk into the deep snow but about halfway down the block the natural childish spirit of competition would come bubbling up and we'd race each other the rest of the way and arrive back at the house with full circulating blood and, in the case of Mary and Cleve, rosy cheeks. The first one in the back door would always hear Gammy say, "Here come the poor little things now, I'll fix them some hot Potsum." (She always called Postum "Potsum.")

After she had fixed us some hot Potsum and had given us each a much too big helping of her gray, gluey, lumpy oatmeal, Gammy would pick up the morning paper and read aloud bad news. "I see that the Huns are cutting off all the Belgian women's breasts," she would remark pleasantly as she took a sip of Potsum. Or, "Well, here's a poor careless little child who played on the railroad tracks and the train came along and cut off both his legs at the hip. Poor little legless creature." Or, "Here's a little mountain girl who had a baby at thirteen. Well, I suppose we can't start too young to learn what life has in store for us." When she had exhausted all the sad news about people, she would read bad weather reports from all over the world. Blizzards, cyclones, droughts, floods, hurricanes and tidal waves were her pleasure. Mother pleaded with Daddy to stop taking the morning paper, but we children enjoyed it.

Like all children, we were bloodthirsty little monsters and relished Gammy's tales of brutality, death and violence. Our favorite stories, made up by Gammy, were about a little boy who put beans up his nose and grew a beanstalk through the top of his head with little pieces of his brain stuck to the branches; and a little girl who swallowed a peach stone and a peach tree grew inside her, the main branch finally forcing its way up into her throat and choking her to death. Our favorite books were *Slovenly Peter* and a cheery little thing left in one of our houses by a former tenant that told about some men who were trapped in a cave in the Yellowstone and ate each other up. The book described in detail the smell of the soup made out of Tom's leg and the sweet, porky taste of Ernest's roasted arms. We almost wore it out making Gammy read it to us, which she did willingly.

Gammy thought all of Daddy's efforts to keep us healthy were a ridiculous waste of time and no wonder, because according to Gammy childhood was a very hazardous time of life and if we children weren't bitten by rattlesnakes, eaten by wild animals, killed by robbers or struck by lightning, catarrh, consumption and leprosy were just around the corner. Gammy said that catarrh, consumption and leprosy were diseases very common to little children and were brought on by coasting too late; not making your bed; quarreling; not feeding the chickens; keeping bad company; not washing your hands; cheating at croquet; being impudent and eating too many eggs.

We learned first about catarrh and consumption. Leprosy came a little later. Gammy diagnosed anything wrong above the neck as "catarrh" and anything below as "consumption." We weren't afraid of catarrh. It was just an old thing that made our noses run and often presaged one of the less interesting children's diseases such as measles, scarlet fever or chickenpox. But consumption was different. It was vague in cause and effect but seemed very fatal and so easy to get. Look at "poor little Beth," Robert Louis Stevenson, Chopin, Keats, O. Henry, Elizabeth Browning, Thoreau and Paganini.

We knew about consumption because Gammy took great pleasure in reading aloud to us in a sepulchral voice about "the Captain of all these men of death that came against him to take him away, was the Consumption. . . ." Mary had a very bad cold when Gammy first read that part in *Mr. Badman* and I remember that Gammy used to look over at her a lot and say "poor little thing." We were so sure that Mary would get consumption that Cleve and I had a fight over who was to inherit her ice skates. When Gammy read us *Little Women* she explained to us mournfully that "poor little Beth" really died of consumption. She read us all of Robert Louis Stevenson's poems but dwelt morbidly on "When I was sick and lay a-bed . . . " and told us that "poor little

Robert Louis Stevenson" always had consumption and finally died of it.

Mary, Cleve and I had perilously achieved the ripe old ages of eight, six and five when leprosy entered our lives. One winter afternoon just after lunch, Gammy announced that she was taking us to see Charlie Chaplin. As this was to be our first moving picture show, we were immediately thrown into a frenzy of anticipation and paid little heed as Gammy hurriedly stuffed us into each other's clothes. To Gammy, clothes were mere coverings for the body as opposed to the sin of nakedness and she was completely indifferent to backs and fronts, rights and lefts and sizes. She matched garments and children by the simple expedient of grabbing the nearest at hand of each and forcing them to mesh.

That winter we were all wearing dark blue woolen leggings buttoned from the ankle to well above the knee with little slippery black buttons like licorice drops; dark blue chinchilla reefer coats; woolen mittens securely attached to each other by a long crocheted cord that was supposed to be threaded up one sleeve, around the neck and down the other sleeve but was more apt to be threaded through a legging leg and into somebody else's coat sleeve or up through one sleeve and down into the impenetrable depths of the lining; and shiny black rubbers that were impossible to tell apart or to get on or off but squeaked deliciously on the hard dry snow.

Mary and I were distinguished from Cleve by broad-brimmed dark blue beaver hats which Gammy clamped on our heads just as she finished forcing my hand into Mary's mitten and herding us out the front door and into the biting winter air. In the excitement, we creaked along in the snow for half a block before we became aware that Mary had on Cleve's leggings which were so tight in the crotch that she had to walk on tiptoe, that Cleve's coat was buttoned up the back leaving him red-faced and choking in the front and that he was further hampered by Mary's leggings which were so long for him that they dragged behind him in the snow like dark blue evening shadows; and that all of our rubbers seemed to be for the same foot.

We stopped short and demanded to be sorted out and re-assembled, but Gammy said there was no time and that any-way it could be done much more comfortably in the warm theatre. She grabbed me by the hand and started up the street again but Cleve and Mary didn't follow. They sat stubbornly down in the snow and began laboriously unbuttoning the slippery little black legging buttons with clumsy mittened fingers. Gammy finally had to go back and help them change clothes and though they were much more comfortable we missed most of the Charlie Chaplin picture.

Gammy said not to mind because they would show it right over again, which was where she was wrong and how leprosy entered our lives. Because when the movie started again instead of Charlie Chaplin there was a long depressing picture about leprosy. My memory of the story is vague but I do remember something about a man, obviously a fine scientist, working in his laboratory and suddenly looking up from his microscope right at the audience and with big scared eyes saying something. The word came on the screen next. All by itself and in black letters. LEPROSY! Gammy read it to us and explained comfortingly, "Leprosy is a dreadful disease. There is no cure for it. They always die!"

Subsequent scenes showed the fine scientist washing his hands thoroughly, many times. Then one morning he happened to be washing his hands and he looked at his wrist and there was a white spot the size of a fifty-cent piece. He rushed to another scientist and showed him. Then they both looked at the spot under the microscope and, sure enough, leprosy. The rest of the picture was devoted to the white spots, horrible sores, arms and legs dropping off, a beautiful girl getting leprosy and a man jumping off a building.

I don't remember whether or not we ever saw Charlie

Chaplin again but I do remember that we stopped under a street light on our way home, rolled up our sleeves and looked for the dreaded white spots, and that for weeks afterwards we examined our arms every morning and night looking for spots. Several times Cleve became very alarmed until he realized that the white spot on his dirty little arm was just a place where some water had dropped by mistake because, although we were scared, we hadn't yet reached that point of desperation where we washed thoroughly.

On the other hand, we figured that Daddy, being a mining engineer, was a kind of scientist and we pleaded with him constantly to wash his hands more thoroughly and every morning we examined his wrists. He finally wanted to know what in hell was the matter with us, so we told him about the moving picture. He immediately forbade our going to any more moving pictures, then got out the *Encyclopaedia Brittanica* and read us a long comprehensive article on leprosy and leper colonies. We listened carefully, as Daddy read aloud very well and then we compared Daddy's information with Gammy's and decided that Gammy knew the most because she had already added leprosy to catarrh and consumption as being ordinary ailments for small children. Leprosy, she told us, was the immediate and natural result of keeping bad company and not washing enough.

When we children were eleven, nine, eight and two we left Butte and moved to Seattle, Washington. Up to this time and in spite of Daddy's ministerings in the form of exercise and Mother's in the form of good food, we had had, to date, measles, mumps, chickenpox, pink eye, scarlet fever, whooping cough and tonsillectomies. It was after the last batch of German measles that Daddy began checking up on the health strains of both sides of the family. He found them excellent. Mother's ancestors were Dutch and had all lived actively for eighty-five or ninety years. Mother herself was never sick. Daddy's forebears were Scotch and terrifically healthy.

Daddy himself displayed the utmost in stamina by growing up to be tall, handsome and vital in spite of Gammy's cooking.

Daddy decided that all his children needed was a good toning up, so he bought a set of exercise records for the Victrola and made us get up at five a.m. to take cold baths and do exercises. He enrolled us in the YWCA and YMCA gymnasium classes. He started Mary and me taking ballet dancing. He had the ballroom in the basement of our house made into a gymnasium. He would not let us eat salt. He stopped our drinking water with our meals. He ordered us to chew each bite one hundred times. He bought apples by the carload and made us eat brick-hard toast and raw vegetables. He read us long dull articles on natural foods and the diets of the aborigines of different countries.

Evidently some tribe with good bone structure and sound teeth had eaten nothing but smoked fish because Daddy bought one hundred pounds of smoked herring and instructed us to gnaw on it after school. Fortunately for us he gave Mother the instructions and the herring just as he left on a mining trip, so she helped us shovel the whole hundred pounds of it into the furnace. When he came home a month or so later he had forgotten all about the herring and ordered an enormous canvas sack of hardtack for us to gnaw on after school. We ate the entire lot eventually because Gammy taught us to soften it by dipping it in hot cocoa or Taylor Tea (hot water with sugar and milk). He also bought one hundred pounds of peanuts, "a natural food high in protein," which we thought was more like it. We loved peanuts and filled our pockets with them morning and night. For weeks Mother said that she could follow our little peanut-shell trails to and from school and around the neighborhood. She could also follow them through the house, much to her annoyance.

When Daddy first started the cold baths he put us on our honor, so of course we cheated. We used to go into the bathroom fully dressed and run the cold water loud and force-fully. Then, when the tub was full, we'd lean over and splat our hands and scream as though we were jumping in. For one blissful week not a drop of cold water, in fact any kind of water, touched our innocent little bodies. Daddy didn't say anything. He merely watched speculatively as each morn-ing we lined up for our exercises, smiling blandly, very dry and obviously warm and tousled from our beds. Then he went downtown and bought some large, brown, rough, English towels and from then on personally supervised the torture.

We had to get in and immerse ourselves all but the head while he counted ten, slowly. Then, as we got out, shivering and baleful, he rubbed most of the skin off our little blue bodies with one of the big English towels. These towels must have been made of a very cheap grade of hemp for, in addi-tion to their terrible roughness, they had occasional little spikes, which brought loud screams from the victim.

Gammy used to get up every morning at five o'clock with us, not because she thought it was healthful, but so she could stand in the upper hall and moan, "Darsie Bard, you're driv-ing those poor little cheeldrun right into consumption," as Daddy herded us from our warm beds and into the icy bath. Perfect Health For All had become Daddy's goal, so Gammy had closed the lid on leprosy as being too unlikely and catarrh as being too common, and had taken out consump-tion, given it a good shaking and erected it over our heads again.

After the baths Mary and I put on middies and black bloomers while Cleve put on his knickers and shirt and then we all went sullenly downstairs. Our rooms were on the third floor. On the second floor we were joined by our sister Dede, who was too young for the cold baths, and Mother, who didn't care for any of it and was sleepy. Up the stairs from the first floor came the loud and sturdy rhythm of "Our

Director March." It was record No. 1 of the Victor Exercise Records. "Hurry up!" Daddy called from the front hall, where he and Gammy waited. We straggled into line just as the nasal-voiced man on the record began, "Hands on hips, feet together. Head up, shoulders back! At the count of one, raise the arms. . . ." The music began "Daaaaaaa, da da, dada, da . . . daaaaa, da, da, da. . . ." We were off.

Gammy watched us for a while, then with a "poor little things" went out to the kitchen to make either mush or batter cakes. It was a toss up which was the worst. The mush, always oatmeal, was gray and gluey, and the batter cakes, large and nicely browned on the outside, tasted as though they had been basted together over a wool batt. We could look forward to these delicacies as we ran around the block after the exercises.

On Saturday mornings after the cold baths Daddy substituted tennis for the exercises. Striding briskly ahead he led his reluctant children through the quiet early morning streets to a park, about ten blocks away, where there were tennis courts which were always free at that ungodly hour. Daddy taught us a good backhand stroke, to keep score, and to place our balls. He also taught us by means of a smart blow on the behind with his tennis racket that, even with Daddy as a partner, when playing doubles both partners play the game instead of one leaning heavily on the net with his mouth open and thoughts on the warm bed so recently left. Daddy grimly explained that beating each other over the head with our rackets after every set was not good sportsmanship either. He taught us to jump the net and to shake hands after the game. We often accompanied the handshake with a stuck-out tongue or vomiting motions, which Daddy, who had a sense of humor, ignored.

Two years later Mary and I were runners-up in the St. Nicholas School for Girls tennis championship matches and, though our tennis game left much to be desired, we created

a sensation with our good sportsmanship and our net jumping. Cleve is still a fine tennis player, but I'm not sure he
adheres to those old park manners.

After the tennis we had breakfast and then went down for
our gym and swimming classes. I think my innate hatred
for all exercise and all gym teachers was bred in those early
years at the YWCA. The teachers were always big mannish
women with short hair and sadistic tendencies. They made
us climb ropes clear to the ceiling and slide down again,
which burned our hands and put permanent scars on our
black sateen bloomers. They put the big brown leather horse
up so high that if we did manage to straddle it from a running
jump, we fell on our faces on the other side. They called
us awkward and lazy and slow. They roared "Higher!
HIGHER! *HIGHER!*" when we were jumping and scared
us so that we took off on the wrong foot and made little
wiggling hops instead of the long sweeping leaps they
demanded.

They made us line up for roll call with hands on hips, feet
together, heads to the left. As our names were roared we
had to step smartly out of line, face the front, say, "Here,"
step back and face left again. Somebody always made a
mistake and we would have to start over. There were about
fifteen little girls in the class and sometimes all we did for
two hours was to step smartly out, face the front and say,
"Here." We complained a lot to Gammy about the gym
teachers and she was a most sympathetic listener. "Young
Women's *Christian* Association, bah," Gammy would snort,
as she slipped us big strong cups of coffee.

Cleve didn't have much trouble with his gym classes for
the very simple reason that he never went. He dutifully
checked in every Saturday morning at the YMCA but not at
the gymnasium. He reported to the reading room where he
sat quietly looking at magazines until time for swimming.
After the swim he met us for lunch, unless he felt like walk-

ing on the waterfront, which he often did. Cleve was always like that. He did exactly as he pleased without any fuss.

When he was in the Fifth B he didn't like his teacher so he didn't go to school. We lived in the country then and rode to school on a bus and Cleve got up every morning and got on the bus but he wouldn't get off. He stayed on and rode back and forth with the bus driver for the entire semester. I guess the teacher thought we had moved away. The next semester he liked the teacher so he got off the bus and went to school.

We learned this from the bus driver some years later, when he had become our laundry man and used to spend hours in the kitchen drinking coffee and listening to Gammy tell about the waste that went on in our house. For proof she would show him big opened but uneaten jars of jam that she had made by dumping together all left-over fruit, jams, jellies, applesauce, honey, peanut butter and candy and boiling it into a dark brown gummy mass. "Gammy Jam" we called it and wouldn't touch it. When the bus driver told Gammy about Cleve not going to school Gammy said, "Everybody in this house does just as he pleases," and she held up a big jar of the uneaten jam. "Look at that, perfectly good jam but not a soul will touch it. Yes sir, we all do as we please in this house."

After eating lunch at the YWCA cafeteria, Mary and I took our dancing lessons and every Saturday we came home and told Daddy about our dancing teacher's legs. "Daddy, her legs are as hard as rocks," we told him. "You should come down and feel them." He always laughed at this and we didn't see why.

On Sundays we took bird walks. Daddy bought a book on Western birds with colored pictures and, armed with this, his field glasses, a notebook, several dogs and his quarreling disinterested children, he would walk for hours along the Lake Washington Boulevard. "There is a flicker," Daddy would say suddenly, looking through his field glasses into a densely wooded area. We would all stop short, bumping, jostling and stamping on each other's toes. After the shoving and slapping had subsided we took turns with the glasses, focusing them on the ground or on a distant leaf. We seldom saw anything, but we pretended we did because we moved along faster that way.

The bird walks had become part of the health program because of the walking, but they had originally been started as the last lap in a mental program, which had been in full swing since we were born. As soon as a baby was born Daddy would begin by holding objects in front of its eyes to see if and how they focused. At an early age we had all been tested for color blindness, balance, focusing, etc., and as soon as we could talk we began having intelligence tests. "What is the opposite of black?" Daddy would ask. "White," we'd snap back in unison. "Of high?"—"Low." "Of up?" —"Down." "Repeat these numbers after me," he would say, listing about twenty-seven numbers. "Give me a synonym for house." "Dwelling." "For woman." "Female." "For macaroni." "Spaghetti." "For beautiful." "Pretty." "If a boy is walking ten miles an hour and leaves the house at two o'clock. . . ."

Sometimes on the bird walks we would try to get him to play the old mental games. "Let's play numbers or what Johnny has in his pocket," we'd beg, but Daddy was no longer interested. Health was the thing now and he made us jump the logs that lay in our paths and grab branches and swing over streams.

The health program went on until Daddy died three years later. A year or so after he died I suddenly began to bloom and to turn into a large, fat, healthy girl, which just goes to show that either Daddy's health program brought results or a watched pot never boils.

This sudden swelling was a bitter thing for me and I feverishly thumbed through magazines and clipped out coupons and sent for books on reducing. Then, of a school morning I would push away the big bowl of lumpy oatmeal, which Gammy clunked down in front of me, and she would wail, "Reducing! Reducing! These fool girls. First thing you know, Betsy, you'll have consumption." What a pity that she wasn't alive when I did get tuberculosis. It would have been such a satisfaction to her!

When she slapped down a bowl of oatmeal in front of my brother Cleve, who wasn't reducing but hated oatmeal, Cleve would say defiantly, "I want eggs." At that time, as I remember, he was wearing, in the privacy of the home, a black silk stocking cap to keep his curly hair smooth. He wore it low on his forehead and it made him look like a torpedo. This torpedo look, coupled with his defiance, made him seem quite dangerous and Gammy usually broke down and fried him an egg. First, however, she gave him the treatment. "I am cooking your mother an egg," she would say impressively as she pushed the oatmeal back in front of Cleve. She acted as if she had laid the one egg herself and that it was the only thing that would sustain life in Mother.

"Miss Kurshible's Reducing Diet says that for breakfast I should have an egg, a thin slice of gluten bread and a small ripe pomegranate," I would read off importantly from my latest reducing diet. "I don't care what that old Miss Kurshible says, all I want's an egg and I'll cook it myself!" Cleve would shout, starting to get out of his chair. "No need for shouting," Gammy would say with tight lips. "I'll cook you and Betsy your eggs." Whereupon she would get out a frying pan, fill it half full of drippings, heat it until blue smoke filled the kitchen, then drop in the eggs, always managing to get in several pieces of shell. The eggs exploded when they hit the grease and Gammy would scream accusingly, as she moved the frying pan off the heat and covered it with a large lid. In a few minutes she would serve us on ice cold plates, the greasy, rubbery eggs, completely encased in a grayish white covering and resting uneasily on hard toast.

While we tackled this delicacy, Gammy would take a tablespoon of the oatmeal from one of the untouched bowls, put it on a saucer, pour skimmed milk on it and eat it. She always ate from saucers, and left-over food whenever possible. There was no reason for it except that she didn't think eating was healthy and some odd quirk in Gammy's nature enjoyed the frugality of such proceedings.

It was another quirk which made her so mean with her eggs. We lived in the country and had chickens and there were always pans of fat brown eggs sitting around the kitchen. But according to Gammy eggs were for supper and for *adults* and by eggs she meant one egg. Only "hawgs" ate two eggs. There was a charming man who lived near us who told Gammy unblushingly and quite casually, during one of her egg arguments with us children, that sometimes he ate ten eggs at a sitting. He was a delightful neighbor and very handsome but Gammy never forgave him. "There goes a perfect pig," she'd mutter as she watched him drive past in the morning. "Ten eggs," she'd mutter as he waved gaily to her.

As Gammy was always so much against "big eaters" with their "food eyes" I thought she would be delighted to have me go on a reducing diet, and I think she would have, if all of the diets hadn't required so many eggs. "An negg *every* morning for breakfast?" she read incredulously from the "Twenty Day Wonder Diet"—"And ANOTHER egg for lunch?" She was horrified. "Give it up, Betsy," she said pushing her glasses up on her forehead. "It's just a fad some fool woman thought up and it will end in consumption."

It did too but not for years and years and not from reducing, cold baths or cheating at croquet. I'm not sure about eggs.

➤➤II◄◄

I Have a Little Shadow—Who Don't?

I have a little shadow that goes in and out with me,
And what can be the use of him is more than I can see.
—Robert Louis Stevenson

IN ADDITION TO good health, my family possessed a great
capacity for happiness. We managed to be happy eating
Gammy's dreadful food or Mother's delicious cooking; in
spite of cold baths and health programs; with Gammy's awful
forebodings about the future hanging over our heads; in
private school or public; in very large or medium-sized
houses; with dull bores or bright friends; with or without
money; keeping warm by burning books (chiefly large thick
collections of sermons, left us by some of the many defunct
religious members of the family) or anthracite coal in the
furnace; in love or just thrown over; in or out of employment; being good sports or cheats; fat or thin; young or old;
in the city or in the country; with or without lights; with or
without husbands.

This enjoyment of life, no matter what, was Mother's idea
and she taught us early to despise "saddos" (sorry-for-them-
selves) and to make the best of things. How she managed
this with Gammy around busily making the worst of everything is beyond my powers of comprehension. It could have

been that Mother realized that as children's whole lives are made up of threats of one kind or another—"Just wait until Daddy gets home"; "Step on a crack and break your mother's back"; "Eat another piece of cake and you'll burst"—we wouldn't take Gammy's morbid prophecies very seriously, which we didn't.

When I finally got tuberculosis, thus achieving the goal Gammy had set for me so early in life, we were all being happy and making the best of things in a brown shingled house in the University district of Seattle, Washington. Mary and Cleve were married and Gammy had died several years before, so at that time "we" meant Mother, me, my ten- and nine-year-old daughters Anne and Joan, my younger sisters Dede and Alison, an adopted sister Madge and as many other people as we could jam inside the bulging walls.

During the seven years that Anne and Joan and I had lived in Seattle, people had arrived from Alaska with meagre letters of introduction from Cleve, who had made a trip there. Old mining friends of Daddy's had come and had stayed months. People had come to spend the night and had stayed weeks. One girl came for the weekend and stayed five years.

Madge was brought to the house one Sunday evening along with about forty other people, introduced as a friend of somebody's roommate. She played the piano, was instantly recognized as one of us and a week later moved in and was adopted permanently as a member of the family. Having no family of her own Madge was very grateful for our love and companionship but even more grateful that none of us were tone deaf or very neat and that we were all nasty in the morning and usually up when she got home from her work as a pianist with a dance band at two a.m. or thereabouts. Madge never got any sleep, moved through life in a perpetual fog, had a lovely slow deep voice and a dry biting wit, told dandy fortunes with cards, played the piano magnifi-

cently and through her work as a musician met many unusual
people, among whom was a shoplifter who showed Madge
her wedding dress and said, "Now tomorrow I gotta go down
and steal the veil."

Our casually increasing household was such a source of
amazement to a dear little neighbor who had a well-ordered
life and only one child, that she used to hurry over on Sunday mornings to count us and see who or what had been
added.

We still tease Mother about the time Mary tiptoed into
her room at two a.m. and hissed in the dark, "Move over,
Sydney, I'm going to sleep with you." Mother obligingly
moved over and then asked in her gentle voice, "Who is it,
please?"

In this friendly crowded house illness was unwelcome. We
were poor and had many bills and a glass of water and an
aspirin had to fix any ailment. "Thank God, we're all so
healthy!" we said during the depression when we had meatloaf three hundred and forty-two times running. "At least
we have our health," we used to say laughingly when the
Power Company turned off the lights.

Now I was ashamed because suddenly I didn't seem to
have my health. In January I began having a series of
heavy colds, one right after the other. They would begin as
head colds and I'd stay in bed and drink water and take
aspirin for a day. Then the cold would move down into my
chest and because my eyes and nose had stopped running I'd
decide I was well and go back to work.

At work I'd notice vague pleurisy pains in my back so I'd
move out of draughts and take more aspirin. If my cough
was deep and shattering I'd get some cough medicine from a
reliable druggist and after a while the cold would be gone.
For a few weeks I would be apparently all right and then
bang, another cold. I couldn't figure out where they were
coming from or why, but I did know that each one left me

thinner and tireder. In fact my tiredness became so constant that I ceased to notice it and thought that I felt well and had energy when actually I was merely not as tired as usual.

By spring I began getting up in the morning feeling dead tired and after dressing, drinking a cup of coffee and smoking a cigarette, I would feel like going back to bed instead of straining at the leash to begin the day's activities. By having another cup of coffee and a cigarette when I got to work and another cup of coffee and cigarette at ten o'clock, I managed to scoop up enough energy so that I felt quite brisk by noon. During the afternoon my energy receded rapidly until by four o'clock I used to be so tired that I would go out to the rest room and stretch out on a hard wooden bench for a blissful five minutes of rest.

I couldn't understand it. My job was hard but it was interesting and I liked the people I worked with, but every day I had to force myself to go to work. On weekends when I gardened, cleaned house and took the children for walks, I felt quite well so I reasoned that my lassitude had something to do with my job and everything would straighten out when I had my vacation.

From January on I noticed also that I had stars in front of my eyes when I bent over. Reaching down to get a file from a low drawer I would straighten up to a blinding kaleidoscope of stars, whirls, flashes and round black dots. Biliousness, I thought, and took calomel and tried not to bend over any oftener than I could help. I thought also that it was probably a combination of my tiredness, my job and the calomel that gave me the indigestion. People who are very nervous and eat so fast they rarely taste what they eat have indigestion but only big bores talk about it, so I ignored mine.

By the time I had gone through my sixth cold, I noticed that I seemed much more nervous, that I slept badly and that I had a heavy feeling over my heart and occasional sharp pains in my lungs. I attributed the heavy feeling and the pains to my indigestion and my indigestion to my nervousness and my nervousness to my job.

This sounds, I know, as though in addition to many symptoms of tuberculosis, I had also all the symptoms of a very retarded mentality. I hadn't. It was just that I was operating under the impression that I was healthy and I thought that everybody who worked felt as I did. It never occurred to me that my complaints were symptoms of tuberculosis. (Actually they all were.) From Gammy's training, the movies I had seen and the books I had read, I thought that the only real symptoms of tuberculosis were a dry hacking cough and a clean white linen handkerchief delicately touched to pale lips and coming away blood-flecked.

I was almost thirty years old, had been married and divorced, had two children, had raised chickens and seemed to have normal intelligence but what I knew about tuberculosis, its symptoms, its cause and its cure, could have been written on the head of a pin. It was just that nobody in our family had ever had tuberculosis. None of my friends had ever had tuberculosis, and it is not something that you read up on just for the pure joy of the thing.

The ironic thing is that, although I knew nothing about tuberculosis and never entertained the thought that I might have the disease, for two years I had been very concerned about a co-worker of mine in the Government service, who looked like a cadaver and coughed constantly, with a dry little hacking cough, much of the time in my face. "I think that man has tuberculosis," I finally told my boss excitedly. "Who don't?" was his laconic reply.

When I entered the sanatorium and filed a compensation claim against the Government, naming the cadaverous co-worker as a possible source of infection, he was sent through the t.b. clinic and found to have had active, communicable tuberculosis for nineteen years. He knew he had it and apparently liked it, for it was much against his will that he was finally sent to a sanatorium.

Four or five of us, who had worked with him, went to sanatoriums with t.b. but the Government paid none of the compensation claims. Whoever it was in charge of compensation claims in Washington had the same attitude as my boss. "All these girls have tuberculosis," read our claims. "Who don't?" came back the reply from Washington.

In March I still had January's cold so I surreptiously consulted an eye, ear, nose and throat specialist. Having had little to do with doctors and having been convinced since infancy that I was healthy, I was ashamed to tell him all the little things that seemed wrong with me so I limited my symptoms to his field and told him about the cold and the chest pains. He examined my eyes, my nose, and my throat and said that there was nothing wrong with me. He patted my shoulder and told me to try infra-red on my back. Sometime later the cold went away.

In May the attacks of indigestion became so frequent and so severe that I went to an internal medicine specialist. I gave him the symptoms which fitted his field. I told him about the indigestion and stars in front of my eyes. He examined my stomach and abdomen and said that there was nothing wrong with me. He patted my shoulder and told me to drink less coffee.

By July I coughed a lot. Also in July I had a complete physical examination for $5000-worth of life insurance. I told the examining physician about my cough and he said, "Cigarettes, haha, I have one too." I told him about the tiredness and he said, "You should have this job." I answered truthfully all the questions about who died of what and "has anyone in your family ever had tuberculosis, syphilis, Buerger's disease, large swelling of the spleen, a steady job, etc.," was considered a good risk and given the life insurance.

In spite of my increasing debility, there seemed to be nothing wrong with me. I was like the frail creatures in the olden days who for no apparent reason wasted away and died. I continued to take aspirin for the colds and chest pains; calomel for the stars and bismuth for the indigestion, and to attribute the other discomforts to my job, which was arduous in itself and, like all Government jobs, made more so by politics and conflicting personalities (chiefly my own).

In September I became afflicted with hemorrhoids (according to the dictionary you can have but one hemorrhoid—more than one are piles, which I consider an indelicate word). Hemorrhoids should not be glossed over or ignored, so I called my sister Mary, and she sent me at once to her husband, a pathologist. Inasmuch as the study of pathology seemed to embrace the entire human body, I told him all of my symptoms, even the nervousness and the insomnia. He listened gravely, examined my back and chest; tested my sputum, had my lungs x-rayed and sent me to a chest specialist.

I was at the chest specialist's all afternoon. He listened to my breathing and coughing, tested my sputum, examined my throat and fluoroscoped and x-rayed my lungs. He was showing me the x-rays when he gave me the diagnosis. He said, "This shadow is the tuberculous area in the left lung. You have pulmonary tuberculosis." I didn't know that pulmonary tuberculosis meant tuberculosis of the lungs. I thought it was some strange quick-dying type. He concluded, "You will have to go to a sanatorium."

Sanatorium, I knew what that meant. I had seen Margaret Sullavan in *Three Comrades* and I had read *The Magic Mountain.* Sanatoriums were places in the Swiss Alps where people went to die. Not only that but everyone I'd ever heard of who had had tuberculosis had died. I was undoubtedly going to be in excellent company but I didn't want to die.

For one who had just pronounced a death sentence the chest specialist seemed singularly untouched. He was whistling "There's a Small Hotel" and looking up a number in the telephone directory. He found his number and began to dial. I got up and went over to the window. It was nearly five o'clock and the September evening fog had begun to drift up from the waterfront. A car tooted its horn irritably in the street below. In the lighted windows of an office across the court I watched the girls jam things quickly into drawers, slam files closed and hurry into their coats and hats.

I said to the doctor, "What about my job?" He had hung up the phone and was leaning back in his chair. He was well tanned and very handsome. He said briskly, "Oh, you won't be able to work for a long time. Complete bedrest is what you must have. You're contagious too," he added comfortingly. I began to cough and he automatically reached down into the drawer of his desk and handed me a Kleenex. I covered my mouth as he had told me to do, and as I had not done for the four or five months I had been coughing, and felt neat and very sad. I said, "How much does a sanatorium cost?" He said, "Thirty-five to fifty dollars a week." My salary had just been raised to $115 a month. I said, "How long will I have to be in a sanatorium?" He said, "At least a year—probably longer." I picked up my purse and gloves and said goodnight. As I went through the waiting room I could hear him whistling "There's a Small Hotel."

Mary's husband was waiting for me in his office. In a shaky voice and close to tears I told him about the diagnosis, the sanatorium and the $35 to $50 a week. He said, "The Pines, one of the finest sanatoriums in the world, is an endowed institution and free to anyone who needs care and cannot pay. There is a waiting list of over two hundred but mothers with small children are usually taken right in. I'll write a letter to the Medical Director." He took a sheet of paper and began to write. His writing was scratchy and entirely illegible, but he seemed very satisfied with it and anyway it was going to another doctor. He folded the letter and handed it to me. He said, "Be at the clinic at eight-thirty tomorrow morning. Here is the address. Give them this letter and tell the doctor to call me. As soon as Mary gets here I'll drive you home." He also was very handsome but, more important, he was interested and he was kind.

Mary came in then and in five minutes told me so many big lies about tuberculosis, who had it, where they got it, and so forth, that I was immediately cheered up. She said that practically everyone on the street had tuberculosis, that she couldn't go to a party without seeing at least four far-gone cases, that actually it had gotten to a point where she was ashamed to admit she hadn't t.b. because everyone who was anyone—look at Robert Louis Stevenson and Chopin—had had t.b. Anyway with or without t.b. she wished someone would order *her* to go on complete bedrest—she hadn't had any sleep for so long that the muscles of her eyelids had atrophied. She thought a slight case of t.b. should be the aftermath of every pregnancy so that the poor mother could get a little sleep. She thought a lot of things and she thought them out loud, which was soothing and made it unnecessary for me to talk and so I didn't cough all the way home.

Instead I worried about how to tell the family and if I should tell the children. I toyed with dramatic little scenes in which I went quietly into the house as though nothing had happened, smiling often and bravely, and then Mary told them. I entertained the idea of telling just Mother and when I had gone upstairs, smiling often and bravely, she would gather them all together, preferably around her knee, and tell them about my "trouble."

I needn't have wasted the effort. When we stopped in front of the house the entire family, including the children and the dogs, came bursting out. They already knew. Mary had called them while I was at the chest specialist's office. I was to go right to bed in Mother's bed, the fourposter in which we had all been born, and had had all of our illnesses.

There was a fire in the fireplace. There was fresh hot coffee. There were infinite love and abundant sympathy. There may have been too much sympathy because after a while I became almost overcome with my own bravery, selflessness and power of mind over body. To think that for the whole past year I had been going my way, working, playing and laughing, while all the time I was seriously, perhaps fatally, ill. I wallowed in self-pity. Instead of admitting to myself that it was a great relief to know what was wrong with me and that I was really sick instead of ambitionless and indolent, I dripped tears on Mother's blue down quilt as I created doleful mental pictures of little Anne and Joan putting flowers on "Mommy's" fresh grave. I was a big, no-sense-of-humor saddo. I coughed all night long and enjoyed doing it.

⇶III⇷

"Good-bye, Good-bye to Everything!"

Crack goes the whip, and off we go;
The trees and houses smaller grow;
Last, round the woody turn we swing;
Good-bye, good-bye to everything!
—Robert Louis Stevenson

THE NEXT MORNING I was awakened by Anne and Joan who, instead of arising early to gather the flowers for my grave, came boiling into the room to involve me in one of their senseless quarrels. They demanded that I get right out of bed and go into their room and peer into the eaves trough outside their windows to determine by the number of pits, which were not supposed to be there, who had eaten the most of a large box of cherries sent them early in the summer.

My sister Dede coming in with my breakfast tray in the middle of the story said that she thought the best and fairest way to handle the thing would be to hold them out the window by their heels while they counted the pits one by one. Everyone in our family knows that Dede always means what she says so the children left, flashing us several withering looks over their shoulders and fighting all the way downstairs about who had the thickest arithmetic book. Dede called down that the one with the thickest book had the thickest head and we were rewarded with a stony silence.

"At least Anne and Joan are making themselves awfully

easy to say good-bye to," Dede said cheerfully sitting on the bed and lighting a cigarette. Then she offered to stay home from work and go to the clinic with me and I accepted eagerly for Dede has a very direct approach to life and has often been described as "having her feet on the ground." Sometimes her feet are so firmly planted that you can hardly see her ankles but this is most comforting in times of stress.

Dede is the only one of us who is small and quiet and hasn't red hair. She has dark curly hair, large gray eyes and a low voice. In one so slight and wistful-looking, great strength of character and immutability are unexpected qualities. Dede describes herself as merely being a person who faces facts. "The trouble with you," she used to tell Mary, Madge, Alison and me, "is that if you have a date with a short, dull man you pretend to yourself that his growth was stunted in early childhood and that he's not dull, he's tired. I face the fact that I'm going to spend the evening with a *little bore* and I plan to go some place where there will be other people and we can sit down."

We learned on arrival that The Pines Clinic shared a building with the police station, city jail, emergency hospital and venereal disease clinic. The dark, ancient elevator seemed to have caught some virulent ailment from its patrons for, when it was loaded, it coughed and wheezed, lost its breath entirely, dropped back a foot or two, bounced uncertainly for a while and finally by summoning every ounce of its strength managed to struggle up to the second floor. Because of the location and bad light, Dede and I were certain that all the other occupants of the elevator were crooks and prostitutes and were very disappointed when most of them filed out of the elevator and entered the t.b. clinic with us. In the strong daylight of the clinic they turned out to be just average people. A few better than average. All sad.

The clinic was a depressing place filled with golden oak benches, stale air and the other people with t.b. The nurse at the desk took my letter, read it and asked me suspiciously who had sent me down "there." She pointed with her pencil to the paragraph in the letter mentioning the name of the chest specialist. I told her, but I couldn't see what difference it made. It made a lot of difference apparently because it seemed that the chest specialist had his own sanatorium and the nurse gave me to understand that if I had been over there learning their methods there was no place for me on one of her benches. She also gave me to understand that tuberculosis was something just a little special and she wasn't sure she was going to let me have it.

Her tight-lipped, unsmiling, unfriendly attitude was a shock to me. I had thought, from my meagre previous experience in hospitals when Anne and Joan were born, that all nurses were unusually kind, gentle and friendly little ladies. That girls were originally chosen to be nurses because of these qualities and that their training enhanced them. I tried smiling at the desk nurse. She gave me a stony stare and motioned me to one of the benches. Apparently she hated people with tuberculosis the way some people hate liver. I slunk over to the bench and sat down beside Dede.

Immediately another unsmiling, hard-eyed nurse rustled over and stuck a thermometer in my mouth. She tried also to put one in Dede's mouth but Dede clenched her teeth and said that she wasn't sick. Either the nurse didn't hear her or didn't believe her because she made three attempts. After the last one Dede said quietly, "If you try that again I'll bite your hand off." The nurse looked startled and backed into the scales. Another nurse came by. She was a fat, motherly-looking woman but she was about as friendly as a halibut. She handed me two blue sputum specimen bottles. I started to say, "Thank you," but she held up her hand for silence. "Don't talk with the thermometer in your mouth," she said coldly and went away.

In about half an hour the rustling nurse removed the thermometer, took my pulse and weighed me. Then a very deaf old nurse gave me the Mantoux test, which is an injection of tuberculin serum in the forearm. She shouted questions at me and I shouted replies, which was very embarrassing owing to the nature of some of the questions. As each operation was completed we were moved forward a bench like playing Rock School. The benches were as hard as tombstones so the long intervals between each operation were not only dull but painful due to my hemorrhoids.

The next step was a Wassermann test, given in another part of the building. The man who took the blood out of my arm was very pleasant and very kind. As we left his department and walked down the hall toward the t.b. clinic, Dede said, "I'd choose syphilis."

After another longer wait I was given a throat and chest examination by a cheerful, red-haired young doctor. At last we reached the front bench and had only to wait for the Medical Director. While we waited we looked at the other patients and they looked at us. Some of the patients seemed to be old-timers and knew all the nurses and most of the other patients. Everyone but me was either very young or very old. Also I seemed to be the only one who coughed and each time I coughed three nurses and all the patients looked at me accusingly to see if I covered my mouth.

On the wall were several framed mottos. One said, "If you have nothing to do, Don't do it here." Another said "All that is not rest is exercise." Another, "Don't stand up if you can sit down. Don't sit down if you can lie down." After the third hour I felt as if the mottos were etched on one end of me and the grain of the wooden benches on the other.

The windows, very tall, very narrow and uncurtained, framed a bail bond office, an old rotting hotel with orange-crate coolers tacked on the windowsills, and the station clock. The hands of the clock slowly moved from 8:30 to 12:25. Dede discovered that by changing to the outside seats we could see into the little room where they showed the x-rays but when we got up to move we found that the benches had grown sticky from the long sitting and we had to peel ourselves off like adhesive tape.

Watching the x-rays was a tiny bit more interesting than the mottos or the station clock. The doctor slid the x-ray film into a little frame, turned on a light under the frame and pointed out to the patient the tuberculous area in his lung. The x-ray pictures were milky and the doctors, instead of saying, "This muddy area here is t.b.," said things like "exudative infiltrate in the middle of the left lung representing a bronchogenic extension from the cavity" or "infiltration of mixed exudative and productive character in the upper third of the right lung."

The patients shifted their feet and tried to look intelligent. The tuberculous males said, "Sure, Doc. I see, Doc." The tuberculous females swelled their nostrils to show understanding. One doctor showed the mother of a fourteen-year-old girl the infected areas and cavities in her daughter's lungs. He said, "Your daughter is a very sick girl. If you want her to get well you must send her to the sanatorium." The mother said, "I prefer to keep Arlene at home. She don't like hospital food." Arlene had pale tan hair, a pale tan face and a pale tan polo coat. She gazed disinterestedly out the window. The mother said, "They sent her home from school. They act like she's got smallpox." The doctor said, "Your daughter is very sick. She is contagious." He went over the x-rays again. He looked worried and grave but he would have been more forceful with something a little easier than "right bronchopulmonary lymph nodes." The pale tan girl turned to the window and said in a hoarse whisper, "I won't go to no hospital!" The mother said, "See, she don't like the food." They left soon after that and from the window Dede and I watched them walk down the street laughing and talking.

At last it was my turn for the Medical Director. I peeled myself off the bench and went into his office. He was sitting at a desk reading the letter from Mary's husband. He glanced up at me briefly and went on with the letter. On the wall back of him was a very large picture of a human eye. Reflected in the pupil of the eye was a pretty young woman with a pompadour and a very small waist. She was seated at her dressing table looking at herself in the mirror. Reflected in the mirror was her face with death peering over her shoulder. Underneath the picture was printed in large type, "Provided a man is not mad, he can be cured of every folly but vanity." I thought it could just as well have read, "She don't like hospital food."

The doctor finished the letter and looked up at me. He was bald and wore two pairs of glasses. His face was lined and severe—his eyes warm and kind. He said, "How old are your children?" I said, "Nine and ten years old." "Girls or boys?" "Girls," I said. "Who'll take care of them while you're at The Pines?" "My mother and sisters." He said, "We have a children's hospital at the sanatorium—you can have them there if you want to." I said, "Mother has taken care of them since they were small. I think they'd be happier with her."

He said, "Have your mother bring them down here to the clinic for a physical." Then he said, "You know we have a long waiting list for The Pines, more than two hundred people, all sick, all needing care but I'm going to put you ahead of them because you have children. When would you like to enter?" I said, "Immediately!" which seemed to surprise him. He said, "All right, you can go out Friday." This was Wednesday. I asked fearfully about payment. He said, "You'll have to give up your job won't you?" I said, "Yes." He said, "Someday when you make a lot of money, you can pay for someone else to get well." Then seeing that his kindness had brought tears, he changed and became very severe.

He said, "Taking the cure is going to be difficult for you. You have red hair—lots of energy, you're quick, active, impatient. All bad for tuberculosis. Discipline will be hard for you. The cure of tuberculosis is all discipline." I said that I would do anything. Anything at all to get well. He stood up and put his arm around me and said, "That is the spirit," which was very kind of him considering the fact that he had just written on my card, "Prognosis—doubtful."

When we got home Mother had her bed turned down for me and it was very comforting to lean back against the pillows and to know that the terrible lassitude and pointless fatigue were part of the disease and therefore excusable. For lunch I had chicken soup, fresh gingerbread and hot tea. Impaired appetite was never one of my symptoms. All afternoon Mother called people to say, "Have you heard about Betty?" and all evening long people called to say, "We have just heard about Betty." The children, not allowed to cross the threshold of my room, hurried home from school to stand in the doorway, look forlorn and reach for loose ends of the conversation.

Mary's husband called to say that everyone in the family must be x-rayed and have a Mantoux test. I explained importantly to the assembled family that the Mantoux test is an injection of tuberculin in the forearm. If it swells and turns red in the course of a few days, it is positive; if not, negative. That approximately eighty per cent of all Mantoux tests given to adults are positive but a positive Mantoux does not mean that the person has active t.b. It merely shows that at some time or another he has had tuberculosis in some form and that x-rays should be taken. Everyone was very happy over the prospect of staying away from school or work for the tests.

The next afternoon at three o'clock the entire family returned from the doctor's exultant over their fine health and flawless lungs. They were all on my bed drinking coffee and drawing smoke into their perfect lungs when the doorbell rang. "Come in, come in," they shouted, thinking it was some of Alison's high school friends. The doorbell continued to ring so they screamed, "Come in, fat head. We're upstairs in Betty's room." The front door opened carefully and a heavy contralto called, "Does Elizabeth Bard live here?"

We sent Anne down to see who it was. She came back immediately, glazed with excitement. "It's a nurse!" she said. "She's coming up." Madge, Alison and Dede were sitting on the bed. Mother was in a small rocking chair beside the bed. Joanie leaned in the doorway. The bedside tables, the bureau, the chest of drawers and the sewing machine were littered with coffee cups, ash trays, books, magazines, coats, hats and purses. The air was opaque with smoke.

At Anne's announcement everyone jumped up self-consciously and began picking things up and putting them in other places. A cup of cold coffee with a swollen cigarette floating in it and an ash tray with many cigarette stubs and two apple cores in it were overlooked on my bedside table. The nurse came in. She was a sturdy little woman with steel-rimmed spectacles, a flowing dark blue cape and a brown leather satchel. She strode over and threw up the windows, choking and clearing her throat. The family melted into the hallway. The nurse fanned the air around me and asked a lot of questions about my condition.

Then she unlatched her little satchel and took out: a brown paper bag, which she shook open and pinned with two safety pins to the mattress by the pillow; a stack of small square paper handkerchiefs; a little book called, "You Have Tuberculosis"; and a list of things I would need at the sanatorium. On the list were three pairs outing flannel pajamas;

one wool robe; one pair bedroom slippers; sweaters; three washcloths; soap; toothpaste; toothbrush; metal hot-water bottle; cosmetics as desired.

She bent over and shuffled around in her satchel some more and came up with the following information: I had pulmonary tuberculosis; I had positive sputum; I must not even clear my throat without first putting a paper handkerchief to my mouth; all handkerchiefs must be deposited in the brown paper bag; the children must not come near me; and drinking very hot water would help my cough.

As she talked, she eyed the overflowing ash tray and the coffee cup with the floating yellow cigarette in it. Finally she said, "You don't *smoke*, do you?" Her eyes were brimming with disappointment. I said, "I did smoke constantly until a few days ago but the doctor said I should stop so I did." I sounded like a coiled spring of will power. Actually it hadn't been too difficult because of the coughing.

As she gathered up her things and put them in her satchel, I asked her why the nurses at the clinic were so disagreeable, why nobody ever smiled. "Do they despise all people with t.b. or is it just me?" I asked. The nice little nurse hardened her eyes, compressed her lips and recited: "Complete impersonality between patients and nurses is the most strictly enforced rule of The Pines and The Pines Clinic."

Then she softened up again and went on to explain that at The Pines discipline was the most important factor in the cure of tuberculosis and as the nurses were the ones who had to enforce this discipline there had to be impersonality between patients and nurses. This certainly sounded reasonable and knowing it made my initiation into The Pines routine a little easier.

The little nurse was efficient and kind and as she talked she plumped the pillows, smoothed the sheets and left the room clean, well-aired and chilly.

After she had gone the family came surging back with the

kittens, the coffee, now hot and fresh, presents, flowers and new books. Soon the bed, the chairs, the bureaus, everything spilled over with people, coffee cups and ash trays and into the sterile brown paper bag on the side of the bed, went apple cores, candy wrappers, and still-smoldering cigarettes. The room was again as littered and cozy as an old saloon.

Outside the windows the evening sky gleamed palely through the cutleaf maple. Inside, the conversation flowed around me as warm and comforting as an old sweater. The dogs came upstairs, their toenails clicking on the bare steps, to find out what was the matter. Why there was no fire in the fireplace. No smells of dinner. Why we were all upstairs.

The telephone rang—it was a date for Alison. The doorbell rang—a neighbor wanted to borrow a cup of sugar. The telephone rang—it was a date for Dede. The children's radio changed to Hop Harrigan. The telephone rang—it was for Mother.

Mother stayed downstairs and soon there floated through the house the tingling smells of woodsmoke, garlic, and baking potatoes. Dinner and the fire were started. The dogs went downstairs. The children's radio changed to Jack Armstrong. The telephone rang—it was my last night at home.

⟫⟫IV⟪⟪

All New Patients Must First Be Boiled

BEING SENT TO an institution, be it penal, mental or tuberculous, is no game of Parchesi, and not knowing when, or if, you'll get out doesn't make it any easier. At least a criminal knows what his sentence is. I had been confidently counting on the chest specialist's guess of one year, when I remembered the rider he had tacked on of "or longer." "Or longer" could mean anything from one month to ten years. It was not comforting.

Instructions from the clinic were that new patients must arrive at The Pines between the hours of three and four-thirty in the afternoon, "after rest hours and before supper." Mary was to drive me out and Madge and Mother were going along. We had planned to leave about two o'clock. We had also planned to send the children to school and to keep everything very normal. People who "packed up their troubles in their old kit bag and smiled, smiled, smiled!" made us want to throw up and yet we were not of the "Let's Close Down the Lid of the Old Cof-fin and Bawl! Bawl! Bawl!" school of thought. Mother's philosophy embraced a middle track somewhere between the two and that middle-track attitude was what we intended to maintain on the day of my departure.

I awoke early to milky windows and foghorns. The hollow echoing footsteps of the paper boy followed by the thump

47

of the paper on the porch. A streetcar clanging past, high-spirited and empty on its first trip. A window slamming shut across the street. The thud of the front door and several sharp joyful barks as Mother let the dogs out. The complaining groans of the starter on a car somewhere down the alley. The rumbling thunder of another streetcar crossing the bridge over the park ravine two blocks away.

Finally Anne asked bluntly, "Are you going to die, Betty?" I said of course not. How ridiculous. Joan said, "Bessie had tuberculosis and she died." Bessie was a school friend of Alison's, and until this moment her illness and death had been tactfully kept from me. I said, "She must have been a great deal sicker than I am." Anne said, "Will you be home for Christmas?" I said that I didn't know and then Joan said, "Mr. Bartlett takes out his teeth and washes them in the hose." The good-byes were over. It was time to get up.

In spite of our good intentions, the children did stay home from school and everything was very abnormal but I managed somehow to tie up most of the odds and ends of my life, and to have a permanent wave and a very short haircut before two o'clock. Then the thin autumn sunshine and the rollicking dogs gave a picnicking air to the good-byes, but even so as I walked down the steps of the old brown shingled house I remarked morbidly to Dede that I felt like a barnacle that had been pried off its rock. Glancing briefly at my short, too-curly hair she remarked drily that I looked quite a lot like one too.

As we drove off I turned and waved and waved to the children. They stood on the sidewalk, squinting against the sun. Young, long-legged and defenseless. I loved them so that I felt my heart draining and wondered if I was leaving a trail behind me like the shiny mark of a snail.

The Pines was several miles out of the city and it was a lovely day for a drive but horrible little phrases such as "The

Last Mile" and "The Last Roundup" kept creeping drearily into my thoughts as I looked at gardens blazing with dahlias, zinnias, Michaelmas daisies and chrysanthemums. At lawns blatantly green from damp fall weather, lapping the edges of the sidewalks. At full-leaved Western trees hesitantly turning a little yellow on the edges, while imported Eastern trees blushed delicately as they dropped their leaves in the soft, warm autumn air. Mother in the front seat with Mary said tactfully, "Have you ever noticed that the ugliest flowers, like the ugliest people, are always the strongest. Look at those hideous dahlias over there." She pointed with her cigarette to some virulently purple dahlias exuding their uncompromising color against a red brick house.

After a while we left the city and drove along the shores of the Sound. As we progressed the autumn colors grew braver and so did I. The bloodless lukewarm sunshine, too weak to lift the fog from the silky gray water, at least made the greens and yellows of the trees clear and brilliant, my outlook less doleful.

A freight train, enveloped in its own smoke, racketed and panted along the shore. Occasional late-flowering dogwoods gleamed greenish white in the dark woods, like numbers on a luminous-dialed clock at night. The madroña trees, leaning down and twisting their trunks in an endeavor to see from under the suffocating firs, dripped with berries bright as blood. Their cinnamon brown bark curled back to show patches of chartreuse skin. Occasional pines stood alone, their branches stiff, their gray green skirts held high. The whole outdoors was fragrant and beautiful and grew more so as inexorably we drew closer and closer to The Pines and my incarceration.

We entered The Pines by a long, poplar-lined drive. On either side were great vine-covered Tudor buildings, rolling lawns, greenhouses and magnificent gardens. It might have been any small endowed college except that there were no laughing groups strolling under the trees. In fact, the only sign of life anywhere at all was a single nurse who flitted between two buildings like a white paper in the wind. We parked the car, distributed the luggage among us and went up the brick steps of the main building.

The entrance hall was large and dim with tall leaded windows, a tiled floor and dark woodwork. Feebly-lit mysterious corridors radiated from this central point and we all stood uncertainly wondering which to take. There was no one in sight anywhere. No sound. Mary said, "I didn't realize that your arrival would create such a sensation," and a nurse bobbed up from behind a high counter and said, "Shhhh!" This startled Madge so that she dropped the four large books she was carrying. They crashed to the floor and noise rolled along the corridors like spilled marbles.

The nurse swelled her nostrils and drew in her lips. I hurried over to the desk and explained that I was the patient. She said, "We were expecting you." Her voice held the same wild enthusiasm generally bestowed on process servers. She said, "What is your full name, Mrs. Bard?" I said, "It's Miss Bard. Miss Betty Bard. You see I have always used my maiden name in business and . . . "

The rest of what I was about to say went dribbling back down my throat for the nurse was looking at me with eyes that could have been taken out and used to replace diamond drills. She said, "You have children, haven't you?" "Yes," I said almost adding, involuntarily, "Mr. District Attorney." She said, "You're Mrs. Bard, then." I said, "If you want me to be Mrs. Something why not use my married name?" She gave me the look again for a full minute, then said, "It says here on this card," she tapped it with a long black pen, "Mrs. Bard. You'll be Mrs. Elizabeth Bard out here."

Then she took my history, probing deep, questioning all my answers and in general giving the impression that she was building up a case to prove that tuberculosis was really a venereal disease. When she had finished she gave me some papers to sign; a little book called, "Rules of the Sanatorium"; and some salient facts about visitors. She threw these facts into me like darts into a target.

They were: 1. The children could come to see me once a month for ten minutes only. 2. I could have three adult visitors on Thursdays and Sundays from two until four o'clock. 3. If my visitors came too early, stayed too late, were noisy, broke rules or exceeded the allotted three in number, my visiting privileges would be removed for an indefinite length of time.

Then Florence Nightingale leaned over the counter and directed us with her pen down one of the dark corridors to a waiting room. She undoubtedly was impersonal but she was also the most thoroughly disagreeable woman I had ever met and I didn't see why The Pines didn't rent her out to England to threaten India with.

The waiting room had large casement windows, a lovely view of the gardens, overstuffed furniture, a virginal fireplace with its firebricks washed and waxed clear up into the chimney, and no magazines, no ash trays. We put down the suitcases, chose places, sat down and were immediately engulfed in silence. The kind of all-embracing silence that makes the snap of a purse clasp sound like a pistol shot, the scratch of a match like the rasp of a hacksaw blade. Mary said at last, in a strained unnatural voice, "Napoleon Bonaparte had tuberculosis but I don't suppose you care. I certainly don't."

The silence settled down again like wet newspapers. Finally Madge, who was young and healthy but a terrific hypochondriac, said in her deep, slow voice, "God this is a depressing place! It would cheer me up just to hear somebody choking to death. I've got a pain in my chest, Sydney, do you think I've got t.b.?" Mother said, "Madge, you know that if this were an orthopedic hospital the pain would be in

your leg." Madge laughed and dropped all the books again.
The clatter was muted by the rug but we all looked guiltily
toward the door. No one came. Nothing happened. Just
the silence.

Like wax figures in a store window we sat motionless in
unnatural attitudes on the unyielding furniture, all facing
each other and the empty grate. The quality of the whole
scene was so dreamlike that I looked at Mother and Mary,
side by side on a mustard-colored love seat in front of the
window, and expected to see large cobwebs attaching them
to each other and to the casement back of them. I felt that
we had all been there forever.

Then from far off, down one of the dim passageways we
heard the creak of a wheelchair and the slap, slap of approaching footsteps. At once we came to life, stood up,
checked over the luggage, embraced each other tenderly and
said all the things we'd been trying so hard not to say for
the past thirty minutes. I said, "Only once a month for
ten minutes—I won't even know them." Mother, with tears
in her sweet brown eyes, said, "I can't bear to say good-bye
to you, Betsy." Mary said, "Don't worry about money."
Madge said, "I hope the rest of the place isn't as depressing
as this."

A nurse came in pulling a wheelchair behind her. She was
blond, cool and efficient. She said, "Which of you is Mrs.
Bard?" I stepped forward. She did not smile. She looked
at me, then at my luggage with expressionless granite eyes.
She said, "Get in the wheelchair. Don't bring any books,
you won't be able to read for a long time." She didn't
acknowledge the presence of Mary, Mother or Madge. She
merely piled my belongings in my lap and wheeled me out
the door and down the corridor. I turned to wave good-bye
but all I could see past her starched white uniform were
waving fingertips, pale and blurred against the dark walls.

We left the main building, crossed a little vine-covered

bridge, entered another building, took an elevator to the second floor and went creakily down a long, draughty, pale green hall, each side of which was partitioned off into rooms. Each room had two white-covered single beds in it and in each bed a head was raised as I went by.

At the end of the hall we went through a pair of swinging doors marked BATHROOM. Bathroom proved to be three rooms—a square center room with a single hospital bed in each corner, tall casement windows at the end and dark red block linoleum on the floor; a room to the left with three lavatories and two washtubs; and a room to the right, in which there was a large old fashioned bathtub. The nurse was busily filling this with boiling water. I explained to her that I had had a bath not three hours before but she didn't even look up. She said, "Makes no difference, rule of the Sanatorium is that all incoming patients must have a bath. Get undressed."

As I undressed she opened my suitcase and took out soap, washcloths, pajamas, slippers and robe and accompanied each movement with a rule. She acted as if she were reading them off the bottom of the soap, in my bathrobe sleeve, from the hem of the washcloth. "Patients must not read. Patients must not write. Patients must not talk. Patients must not laugh. Patients must not sing. Patients must lie still. Patients must not reach. Patients must relax. Patients must . . . " I was ready for the bath so I interrupted to ask if I might put a little cold water into the steaming tub or if there was a rule that patients must be boiled. She gave me the full impact of her granite eyes and let a little cold water into the tub.

While I bathed she unpacked my bags, holding up everything in two disdainful fingers and saying, "Why did you bring this?" I answered truthfully that some of the things, such as extra sweaters, I thought I would need; other things, such as a little sewing box made me by Anne and a calendar with the picture pasted on upside down, made me by Joan, some sachet bags and a little cactus plant, I had brought to remind me of home.

She put them all back in the suitcase with no comment but when she came to my bottle of cough medicine and box of aspirin, she exploded. "Patients must *never* take medicines without the Doctor's permission. No patient of the Sanatorium *ever has medicine* of any kind whatsoever in his possession. Patients are *never* allowed to choose own medicines. These," she held up the cough medicine and aspirin as if they were Home Cure for Syphilis and Quick Aborto, "will have to be sent home or *destroyed*. These extra sweaters, these bed jackets, all your clothes, books, writing materials and *handkerchiefs* [her disdain of this last filthy habit-forming article was tremendous] will have to go through fumigation and be sent home."

After I was well scrubbed and beet red from the boiling water which, I judged, was at least one third disinfectant, I was told to put on my pajamas and report to the washtub. Knowing that it would be wasted effort, I told Granite Eyes that already that morning I had had two shampoos, one before and one after my permanent wave.

She looked without interest at my hair, which had been painstakingly arranged in flat curls close to my head, and said, "It's a rule of the Sanatorium that all incoming patients must have their hair washed." This she proceeded to do, aided by a great deal of green soap, her own strong fingers, and more boiling water. "At least she didn't delouse me," I thought bitterly as she hauled out the drier. The drier was very hot and had enough force to strip the spring growth from any tree at fifty yards.

When my hair was as dry as excelsior the nurse handed me a comb and a mirror. One glance at my exploding head and I felt like breaking the comb in little pieces and throwing them over my shoulder. I made a few futile dabs but it was like trying to part and arrange a thistle. The nurse offered no suggestions. She put away the bath things, then wheeled me down the hall and into a four-bed ward.

The ward was large and square. The walls were a pale Oscar Wilde-ish green. The floor was dark red. Across the east end of the room were four casement windows, curtainless and blindless and opened wide. In each corner of the room were a bed, a bedside stand and a chair. Each bed had a white muslin slipcover, called a windshield, over the head, a white cotton spread and a folded dark green blanket on the foot. The bedside stands had white porcelain tops. In three of the beds there were patients. The fourth, in the southeast corner by the windows was turned down for me.

The nurse helped me off with my bathrobe and motioned me in. After the scalding bath and the hot blasts from the hair drier, reaching my legs down into the clammy depths of the bed was like pulling on a wet bathing suit. I asked for a hot-water bottle. The nurse had just put it, along with my clean pajamas and washcloths into the cupboard of the bedside stand. She didn't take it out and she didn't answer.

She put the bath powder, soap, toothpaste and toothbrush in the drawer. To a bar on the side of the stand she fastened, with large safety pins, a heavy brown paper bag neatly folded down at the top. Inside this she put a smaller brown paper bag, also neatly folded down at the top. "All used paper handkerchiefs must go into this bag," she said. "You must put in a clean bag every morning." Beside the used-napkin bag she pinned another heavy brown paper bag. Into this she put a large package of new paper handkerchiefs. She said, "Always cover your mouth when you cough. Use these handkerchiefs."

On the top of the stand she put two glasses of water on a neatly folded paper napkin. Also a waxed cardboard sputum cup. She said, "Keep nothing on your stand but your water glasses and sputum cup. Never keep pictures or flowers on your stand." She put extra brown bags, extra sputum cups and extra paper handkerchiefs in my stand drawer, saying, "Keep your stand neat and clean. An orderly patient is a helpful patient." Then pushing the wheelchair out of the way she stepped back and looked me over. Coolly, impersonally.

I said again, "May I please have my hot-water bottle filled?" Granite Eyes said, "It is a rule of the Sanatorium that hot-water bottles are never filled until October first." I said, "I'm cold. My teeth are chattering." She said, "October first," and left. This was September twenty-eighth. Three days to go. Well, I could hold out if my teeth would. I pulled the covers up to my chin and looked around.

Across from me was a woman apparently in her early thirties, thin to the point of emaciation, with thick short curly brown hair, a small triangular face, feverish cheeks and enormous luminous brown eyes. Her name was Sylvia Fletcher she told me. She was very sweet and very hoarse. She said in a whisper that sounded like walking on spilled sugar, "Don't worry about the cold. You'll warm up eventually. I know because I've had t.b. for twenty years." I said, "Why do we have to be so cold? Is it part of the cure?" "In a way," she said. "You see everything out here is governed by rules and the theory of the greatest good for the greatest number. Somebody decided that the average patient could keep warm in this temperature and with this number of blankets and if you can't then that is your problem." I said, "But how can I rest when I'm shivering?" She said, "You'll warm up. As your nervous tension lessens you'll get warmer."

In the southwest corner was a small, very pretty dark woman also in her early thirties and also very thin. Her name was Marie Charles and she informed me immediately that she hated everything about The Pines and everyone in The Pines. She said, "It kills me when I think how anxious

I was to get in this place. I had read too many books and I thought all sanatoriums were like those in the Swiss Alps. What a laugh! The only thing Alpine about this place is the attitude of the nurses." Sylvia said, "Now, Marie, you must be patient. The cure of tuberculosis is all discipline. Patience and discipline." Marie flounced over and turned her face to the wall.

In the northwest corner was a little Japanese girl with delicate pale brown hands folded demurely on her chest. Her name was Kimi Sanbo. She had thick straight black hair parted in the center and pulled severely back with two blue barrettes, sharp black brows that tilted toward her temples and large, very bright buttonhole-shaped black eyes. Her cheeks were pink and shiny. She said nothing.

At four o'clock we had supper. First an ambulant patient came around and propped up the beds so that we were sitting up; then nurses dealt out trays, set with silver, napkins, salad, bread and butter, dessert and little slips of paper with beautiful thoughts on them. Then the food carts were wheeled around, and we were served spaghetti, soup and tea by the Charge Nurse. The food was well seasoned and very good but cold. The beautiful thought on my tray said, "If you must be blue, be a bright blue."

While we were eating supper the Charge Nurse and House Doctor made a rapid tour of the room and asked us how we felt. I said that I felt cold and the Charge Nurse, who was Nordic and beautiful, said, "Hot water bottles October first," and they left. Half an hour after supper we took our temperatures. Temperatures seemed to be very important and as each of my wardmates took the thermometer out of her mouth she solemnly reported the results. Sylvia's was 102°, Marie's 101°, Kimi's 101.6° and mine was 99°.

At five o'clock the radio, which was controlled and set at the office, with a speaker in each ward, began drooling forth organ music. Organ music of any kind depresses me and added to that was the fact that I had no bed lamp. A bed lamp apparently was not considered a necessity and had not been on the list of requirements. My corner was dark. My thoughts gloomy.

It was hard to remember how anxious I had been to enter The Pines; how grateful I had been to the Medical Director for putting me ahead of the long waiting list; how wonderful it was that I was being cured and cared for for nothing. I was cold and lonely and I missed my children and my family. The ward was very quiet and little wisps of fog crept through the wide-open windows. If only I could read, or write, or talk or do anything but lie there and listen to that awful organ music.

The organist was playing "Hills of Home." I couldn't stand it. Large tears rolled out of the corners of my eyes, across my temples and into my ears. I looked at my three wardmates. They all seemed relaxed and contented. Sylvia said, "The first hundred years are the hardest," and a nurse, coming in just then to give us back rubs, said, "Patients are not allowed to talk. Roll over, Mrs. Bard."

At seven o'clock we had hot cocoa, hot milk or cold milk. At nine o'clock the lights were turned out by a main switch in the hall. The night nurse operated by flashlight. Up and down the halls she went with her flashlight like a firefly dancing over each bed, resting for a second on each face. When she left our room the darkness, silence and cold settled down again like a shroud.

The dark-haired woman coughed, drank water, reached in her stand for something, turned over and coughed again. Sylvia wheezed faintly. Her bed creaked and I heard the thump of her water glass on the stand. There was no sound at all from Kimi's corner. I drank some water and tried turning on my stomach but in so doing I missed the original slightly warmed place where I had been lying and hit virginal, ice cold, fog-dampened sheet. I almost screamed as I quickly turned back and snuggled down into my original lukewarm nest. The night went on and on and on and I grew progressively colder and sadder. "There's one thing to be said in favor of life at The Pines," I thought, as I tried futilely to warm a small new area at the bottom of the bed, "it's going to make dying seem like a lot of fun."

➤➤➤ V ⋘⋘

Oh, Salvadora! Don't Spit on the Floora

THE STAFF AT The Pines had but one motivating factor—to get the patients well. This motivating factor, like a policeman's nightstick, was twirled over our heads twenty-four hours a day. And by necessity too, because a tuberculosis sanatorium is a paradox. It should be a place where the patients are striving to get well, aided by the doctors and nurses, but is actually a place where the patients are trying to kill themselves but are prevented, in many cases, by the doctors and nurses.

In the beginning the staff at The Pines had undoubtedly been more sympathetic, more understanding, more interested in each patient as an individual, but years and years of working with people who clutched their tuberculosis to them like a beloved old shawl and dared the doctors and nurses to get it away from them, or took the attitude that the staff was secretly injecting them with tuberculosis to keep them on to perform small tasks like putting up beds or pushing tray carts, had finally worn off any little facets of sympathy and tenderness and left the system smooth, efficient and immutable. "We are going to make you well and the shortest distance between two points is a straight line," we were told. "Here is the line, either follow it or get out."

The shortest distance between two points in waking people up in the morning is to bong them on the head with something. The Pines had the next best thing, the wash-water girls. The washwater girls were female patients with eight hours up, who were testing their strength and endurance (and the bedrest patients' nerves and stamina) by doing a little work around the hospital.

That first morning, in the bleak, low vitality period between five-thirty and six, they suddenly came careening in our door, snapped on the overhead lights and brought their cart, loaded with basins and pitchers, to a crashing halt in the center of the room. The blare of light and the shattering noise were like being exploded.

I was jerked out of sleep and into wakefulness with one blow and sat up quivering, trying to bring the room into focus. A short, round girl with black curly hair and surprising, light blue eyes, slammed an aluminum basin down on the porcelain-topped stand with a resounding wham and told me in a loud cheerful voice to put one of my water glasses into the basin. I did and she filled the glass with hot water, putting a very small additional amount into the basin.

"What's the glass for?" I asked. "Teeth," she said. "Not hot water!" I said, horrified. "Sure," she said. But added generously, "You can brush your teeth in your drinking water and drink this if you want to." She smiled. "You're new, aren't you?" I told her I was and we exchanged names and information.

She told me that her name was Estelle Richmond and that she had been at The Pines for three years and was "real bad." As she was plump and pink cheeked and looked much healthier than most of my friends, I said, "But you look wonderful." She said, "Oh, I get along fine for a while and then I break down and back to bed I go. I've been in this ward five different times. Are you very bad?" I answered truthfully that I didn't know but that I hoped to go home in a year. "A year!" She was scornful. "Nobody gets out of here in a year. It even takes longer than that to die. You better plan on longer, kiddo." Kiddo didn't dare tell her that she had been secretly planning on six months, dead or alive.

The other washwater girl, a very thin young blonde with a gold tooth and a maroon sweater, was giving Sylvia, Marie and Kimi the news about the rest of the sanatorium. "Mary Haley had a hemorrhage and is back at Bedrest. Katherine Fay had a chest exam yesterday but the doctor told her she had to stay on three hours up. She's been on three hours for two years. Poor kid! Hazel Espey's going to have an operation and John Hennigan was caught smoking and lost his town leave, his first in two years."

I noticed two things: all the news was depressing and the patients spoke of two, three and five years with a casualness usually associated with minutes. But as I was still having difficulty coming face to face with the bald fact that I would be away from the children and the family for a year, this new business about two, three and maybe five years, made me feel as though I had just finished a hearty dinner and then been informed by my laughing hostess that she had canned those funny-tasting oysters herself.

I asked Sylvia if she knew how long the average patient stayed at The Pines but she was brushing her teeth and didn't answer, so I pushed the question to one side and took up a weightier one of whether to wet my hair first and wash in comby water, or to wash first and wet my hair with spit.

Always cross and irritable in the morning, I was now also sodden with fatigue and cramped with cold and when I had finished washing in the small puddle of already lukewarm water, my face felt as pulled and dry as though I had on a mud pack. I reached in my stand drawer for my bottle of rose water and glycerin and found that the nurse who admitted me had evidently considered it medicine and sent it home.

I took out my hand mirror and prepared to do something

with my hair but one look at my dry gray face and sphagnum moss hair made me want to bang my head against the back of the bed and scream. I took out my lipstick and Sylvia said immediately, "No, no, Betty, patients are not allowed to wear makeup except on visiting day." This made me want to bang her head against the back of the bed and scream. To make matters worse my blood was all crouched shivering in the vicinity of my heart instead of coursing warmly down into my icy extremities. I slammed the drawer of my stand shut and lay back and hated morning.

I have always hated morning. It is a horrible time of day. It is too early and it brings out the worst in everybody. My sister Dede and I used to keep from biting each other on our way to work by classifying morning types encountered on the seven-twenty streetcar.

There was "Bills, bills, bills!" a man who, having quite obviously just before boarding the streetcar, slapped his children and kicked his poor old mother down the cellar stairs, rode all the way downtown with chin on chest, pig eyes brooding, his thoughts quite naturally on "Bills, bills, bills!"

There was the Silent Hater, always a woman, who in spite of having gotten up extra-early to drink hot water, lemon juice and fruit salts, was still bilious and nasty at seven-twenty. She burped behind her hand, hated everybody, and glared at anyone who sat down beside her. Coming home on the five-thirty at night, the Silent Hater usually had a large square bakery box filled with rich dessert to make her more bilious and nastier the next morning.

Big Saddo, also usually a woman, was so busy feeling sorry for herself that every morning she forgot to get out her money, dropped the change on the floor, forgot to get a transfer and fought a tearful losing battle with the conductor all the way downtown.

The Non-Sleepers were usually men and so sensitive to noise that a celery seed carelessly brushed from the kitchen table by a callous wife would hurl them into another long sleepless night and another long dull story about it on the streetcar the next morning. The Sickos were women with voices like whistling teakettles, lots of "trouble" at night and retentive memories for all the boring details of tossing, turning, twitching, lurching and finally getting up and heating milk.

The Sighers sat and sighed dolorously and heavily like wind in the pines, all the way to town. The Chokers, for at least ten blocks after they got on, cleared their throats, made noises like a clogged drain, snorted, hacked, rasped, croaked and spit inexpertly out the window.

The Pretend-to-be-Cheerfuls were women who, laughing only with their mouths, said to seatmates in loud carrying voices, "Oh, I always feel wonderful in the morning. You'd feel better in the morning too if you didn't wear that green coat. People with sallow skin like yours [laugh, laugh] shouldn't ever wear green."

Marie and Sylvia were coughing, spitting and clearing their throats. It was only prescribed routine procedure to them but, in my nasty mood, it was willful, deliberate disgustingness. From all over the hospital came the same horrible noises. I shuddered and looked over at Kimi who was at least quiet. She was busily taking an entire, very lathery bath in the two scant cupfuls of water the washwater girls had given her, scrubbing with as much intensity and vigor as though she had been shoveling coal all night instead of lying perfectly still in a clean white bed. As she added more and more lather, I asked her how she intended to rinse it off. She said, "I will dry it off." I said, "I should think that would make you feel like you had been dipped in white of egg." She frowned at me and said, "It does but I do not care. Germ which might flourish on skin do not flourish on soap." I laughed. Laughing made me cough but it lifted the veil of my morning hatefulness.

After the washwater girls had collected the basins, we all removed the brown paper bags of used handkerchiefs from our stands, unfolded the edges, twisted the tops and threw them to the foot of the beds. Then we put in carefully folded clean bags, marked our sputum specimens with the name, date and whether it was an eight- or twenty-four-hour specimen, assembled our new sputum cups, tidied our stands and listened to Marie complain.

Marie had pains in her chest, gas on her stomach, aches in her joints, was sure she had bedsores, and was constipated. She thought all doctors were quacks because they hadn't diagnosed her tuberculosis while it was in its early stages, and though I learned that this complaint was common among all the t.b. patients and stemmed undoubtedly from the fact that too many doctors wouldn't know tuberculosis if it was coiled around their legs, in Marie's case picking early tuberculosis out from among her hundreds of other ailments would have been as difficult as picking one lone violet in a field of vetch.

Marie said that all patients were supposed to be moved out of the four-bed ward and up the hall into one of the cubicles at the end of one month, yet she had been at The Pines five weeks and they hadn't moved her. She said that all the other patients were allowed to read and write fifteen minutes a day and walk to the bathroom once a day at the end of the first month, but not she. The Charge Nurse didn't like her.

Marie was thirty-five years old and had worked in a law office for years and years but she reasoned like a ten year old. Everyone at The Pines was against her. They were keeping her in bed just to be mean. Sylvia told her that she hadn't been moved and hadn't been given her reading and writing time because she was running a temperature, so Marie said that she would shake her thermometer down. Sylvia said, "You would only be fooling yourself."

Kimi said, in her small high voice, "It has been my observation that, in all things in life, the man is favored. Here at The Pines, in the Men's Bedrest Hospital, which is one floor below this, a man may read all the daily paper from the day he enters." Sylvia said, "Men are stronger than women. They don't need such complete rest." Kimi said, "Nonsense, it is because the Medical Director is also a man. He thinks, 'The woman's mind is little. She can lie twenty-four hour a day for thirty day, a total of seven hundred and twenty hour, doing nothing. The man's mind is big. He must give it something to think about. I will let him read the paper immediately.'"

Marie said, "How did you get so smart in only seventeen years?" Kimi said, "I will be eighteen tomorrow and anyway I have not been popular. I have had plenty of time to observe and think." As Kimi was very beautiful, I was curious to know why she had not been popular. She said, "The Japanese are a race of small people. I am tall. I used to go to parties but I would spend the evening sitting alone on the couch. Like a giant Buddha I smiled and smiled as I watched the antics of the little people."

The night nurse came in bringing medicines. She was tall, slender, young and pretty. Her dark hair sparkled with night mist from the porches and her cheeks were pink from hurrying to finish her work before the day staff came on duty. She clicked the medicines down on the stands, smiled at us and started for the door but Marie stopped her. "Didn't you bring me anything for my constipation," she whined. The nurse said, "I'm sorry but the doctors prescribe the medicines." She turned off the overhead lights and was gone. Marie said, "My God, the way they act here you'd think constipation was a permanent thing like a birthmark." Sylvia said, "Shhhh."

It was time for the day staff to come on duty so we all leaned back on our pillows and closed our eyes. We had been lying perfectly still for about ten minutes when I opened my eyes a crack and saw the Charge Nurse materialize in the doorway. She walked without a sound and appeared in the doorway so suddenly it was as though she had been projected there by a machine from the main office. She looked us over quickly and moved on to appear in other doorways and maybe catch other patients talking or laughing or reaching or singing or scratching or twitching or any of the other things that did not come under the category of resting.

At twenty minutes past seven the same ambulant male patient who had come in the evening before, put up our beds for breakfast. The beds operated like lawn chairs and, after he had helped us to sit up, he adjusted the backs of the beds according to our comfort. The evening before he hadn't spoken a word so I presumed that talking to us was against the rules. Unfortunately it wasn't.

As he put up the back of my bed he said, "My name's Charlie Johnson. You're new here, ain't you?" I said yes, so he said, "Well, I been here five years and I seen 'em come and I seen 'em go. Some go out on their feet but most of 'em go out in a box. How bad are you?" I said that I didn't know but that I only expected to stay a year. "Ha, ha!" he laughed mirthlessly. "A year. That's what they all say when they first come. Ha, ha! The only one who ever got out in a year was a woman who had cancer of the lungs. They let her out in three months—feet first. Ha, ha!"

Laughing Boy's appearance was as morose as his outlook. His putty-colored cheeks had deep little gullies running from the bridge of his nose down past the corners of his drooping mouth, as if his face had been eroded by a constant flow of tears from his small watery eyes. His long sad-looking gray cardigan, obviously hand-knit on very large needles by trembling weak fingers, gave the appearance of being pulled down around his knees by the weight of its own sorrow. It was so long that when he reached in one of its gaping pockets for a handkerchief, he had to bend nearly to the floor. His wrinkled gray trousers poured down over his shoes and his shoes were so spread and shapeless they seemed to be melting on the floor.

Charlie moved slowly and resentfully, as though the little tasks he performed for the institution would be the death of him and he and the institution both knew it. It was our misfortune to be the last room to be served food, so Charlie was in no hurry. He lingered on and on as depressing as an open grave. At last the nurses came with the breakfast trays.

Breakfast, at seven-thirty, consisted of half a grapefruit, oatmeal and cream, toast, boiled eggs and coffee. It was very good and very cold. The Charge Nurse, who served the food, said, "You may have as many eggs as you wish, Mrs. Bard, and you may have them either hard- or soft-boiled." I chose two hard-boiled and when she had gone Marie whispered loudly. "That's a laugh. 'Choose what you wish.' All the eggs are hard-boiled and if you take less than two, old Gimlet Eyes will say you are not a cooperative patient and you'll get a warning letter from the Medical Director." She also said that the coffee was fifty per cent saltpeter and that if I didn't find a cockroach on my tray it was just beginner's luck. She wrinkled her nose with distaste, took one bite of the grapefruit, two sips of coffee and pushed the tray away.

After we had eaten breakfast, the Charge Nurse made rounds to see what we had eaten and to hear our complaints. As we were all as immobile as blobs of dough in rising pans when she flashed in our doorway, she was very pleasant to us. Sylvia complained about pains in her stomach and diarrhea, Marie complained about pains in her stomach and constipation, Kimi said nothing.

My only complaint was that I was cold. A dank shivery cold that lukewarm coffee had done nothing to dispel. I said so. The Charge Nurse smiled blandly and said, "October first we have hot-water bottles." I said, "How about an extra blanket?" She turned back my spread and saw that I had two woolen blankets and a night blanket. She said, "You should be warm, Mrs. Bard." I said, "I'd like to be but I'm not." She looked at me sternly for a few minutes, as though I were deliberately not circulating my blood, then went away. I could see what Marie meant about her constipation.

After she had gone Charlie came back to let down the beds and to tell us about two hemorrhages in the Men's Bedrest Hospital. "I'll probably be next," he finished gloomily. Like everyone else, I had heard that people with tuberculosis are characterized by over-optimism and a great sex urge. From my limited experience I had found that people with a great sex urge are usually over-optimistic but I hadn't learned why it characterized tuberculosis and watching Charlie shuffle morosely out the door didn't do anything to clear it up. If he was either overly optimistic or a bundle of taut desires, I was Clara Bow.

A nurse came in and put a thermometer on each bedside table. "Take your temperature in half an hour," she told me. "Put the thermometer under the tongue and leave it in the mouth five minutes." Another nurse came in with bedpans. Past the door went a parade of lucky month-or-more patients on their way to the bathroom. Their long housecoats, measured tread and serious demeanor made them look like bridesmaids. Occasionally the illusion was spoiled by a nurse helping a new patient on her first trip, or by some brave patient who waved and smiled at us.

When the bathroom parade was over we took our temperatures. They were low. A nurse came in to count pulses and collect the thermometers. I asked her if everyone's temperature was low in the morning but she didn't answer. Just looked at me blankly and wrote on her chart.

When she had gone Sylvia got out bath powder, towels, washcloth and soap. It was her bath day she explained. Baths were given once a week and bath days assigned on entering. Shampoos were given once a month, and judging from my still excelsior-like hair, even this was too often.

As the nurse helped Sylvia into her robe, I saw how frighteningly thin she was, realized for the first time how much too bright her eyes were, how flushed her cheeks. It gave me an unpleasant feeling, as though someone had hit me hard in the pit of the stomach. I felt my own body and noticed how tight the skin was on my ribs, how my pelvic bones stuck out like hooks in a coatroom. I wanted to ask about Sylvia but Kimi and Marie had their eyes closed.

I looked out the window. I could see sky and the tops of the poplars that lined the drive. The sky was gray and puffy with rain. The poplar trees were yellow and limp. It was not very stimulating. I looked out the door and saw a nurse wheel by a patient on a bed. The woman's eyes were closed. Her face as white as the pillow. I wondered why she didn't ride in a wheelchair like the rest of us. If she was dying. Where she was going.

Two nurses came in to change the sheets on Sylvia's bed and to make the rest of our beds. As they made my bed, they instructed me to cover my mouth with a handkerchief and to roll from side to side. They made the top of the bed then the bottom. I asked them why the woman had been wheeled by on a bed instead of in a wheelchair, where she was going. They didn't answer. They left me apprehensive, the bed plump, smooth and chilly.

A small withered man in a dirty white cap and clean blue coveralls came in to sweep the room. His name was Bill, he said. As he swept he sniffed loudly and looked longingly out the windows instead of at his pushbroom, which left wads of gray dust under the beds. I asked him if he were a patient and he turned his small sad face from the window and said,

"Patient, that's rich. I been a patient here off and on for nine years." Nine years! Dear God! Was there no limit?

When he had gone I asked Kimi if all the male patients were old and sad like Bill and Charlie. She said, "No, most of the male patient are young but because of sex the young virile men are not allowed in the Women's Bedrest Hospital and, vice versa, the young pretty nurse are not allowed in the Men's Bedrest Hospital." I asked her what the young men did and she explained that they worked in the greenhouse, laboratory, x-ray and shops where there was close supervision. I thought of Bill's yearning glances out the open window and wondered if he was longing for sex or work in the greenhouse.

At nine-thirty a nurse offered us either hot chocolate or cold milk. She explained that we did not have to take this nourishment but I was already hungry and still cold so I took hot chocolate gladly. So did Kimi. Marie and Sylvia had nothing. The nurse, coming back a little later to pick up the cocoa cups and to bring us clean, filled water glasses, explained that we must drink lots of water, as it was very important in the cure of tuberculosis.

At ten-thirty the Charge Nurse, with a wheelchair, appeared suddenly by my bed. Without a word, she helped me into my bathrobe, my slippers and the wheelchair and wheeled me out the door. I asked her where we were going but she only smiled, said, "Shhh," and took me down another corridor and into a small examination room where a young doctor gave me a chest examination. When I came back everyone was eager to know where I had gone and what they had done to me. They seemed disappointed that it had not been the removal of some large organ, something more exciting than a chest examination.

At eleven, Miss Hatfield, an assistant charge nurse and a gay friendly girl, brought medicines to cure the complaints of the morning. At eleven-fifteen Charlie came in, sagging with bad news, to put up the beds. At eleven-thirty we had dinner.

I was very hungry and the delicious, well-seasoned food, much to my surprise, was hot. There were roast pork, applesauce, bread-and-butter pickles, mashed potatoes and gravy, string beans, lettuce with French dressing, tomato soup, served for some strange reason after the main course, hot rolls and butter, baked custard and tea. Marie looked at her tray, said, "Ugh, pork again," and pushed it away. Sylvia said nothing. Kimi covered everything on her tray but the custard with shoyu sauce, a large bottle of which she kept in her bedside stand. When the Charge Nurse returned to offer us second helpings, I asked for more meat and applesauce and was immediately shamed by incredulous stares from Sylvia and Marie. Kimi asked for a "leetle soup, and some more hot roll."

While we were eating, a nurse brought in the mail. As this was the only reading matter allowed any of us, we were eager for a letter from anybody, no matter how boring. I was too new to have mail so the nurse informed me that I could read the little book of rules given me at the desk the day before, "but," she added sternly, "patients are not allowed to open or read mail until they have eaten their dinner." Thus assuring the Charge Nurse that if the news from home was sad, we would bawl on full stomachs.

The little book of rules began, "Everything that is not rest is exercise." The writer elaborated. . . . "If you had a broken leg you would not walk on it. The same applies to your lung. In order to heal, your lung must have rest. Talking, laughing, singing are all exercise which can be avoided." This all seemed very logical and easy to understand. The next part struck me as a trifle odd. "Please," the writer of the little book begged, "do not steal out of other patients' lockers and *please* do not spit on the floor." Apparently sex and over-optimism weren't the only characteristics of people with tuberculosis.

From twelve-thirty to two-thirty were rest hours. "The strictest rule of The Pines is observance of rest hours and any infraction of the rule for absolute rest during these two hours, means instant dismissal," it had stated in the book of rules. It also stated: "Getting well depends on the patient. Rest, fresh air, good food, and later, regulated and supervised exercise, all help but if the patient doesn't have the will power, honesty, and character to obey the rules, nothing will save him. . . . If you cannot pay the price and feel that you will not be a good influence on others, go home and give your bed to someone who will be of value."

During the rest hours, I lay in my clammy bed and looked at the pale green walls and tried to think about will power and honesty and how grateful I was to be there; about the two hundred people on the waiting list, who they were and what they were doing. Marie and Sylvia and Kimi slept. Everyone else slept too, apparently. There was not a sound. Occasionally, with terrifying suddenness, a nurse would appear at the door to see if we were resting. One time it was a cheerful nurse. She winked at me and disappeared. Through the windows I could just see the tip of one of the poplars. Its yellow leaves were motionless, like paper leaves hung by threads to an imitation tree. The sky was a dirty white now, the air steel blue with fog.

It seemed so strange, this stillness. It was daytime and there should at least have been the tapping of a distant hammer, the bark of a dog, the slam of a door. It was as though we were all dead. I took a drink of water and it had the acrid, slightly warm taste of bathroom water. I wondered why kitchen water and bathroom water never tasted the same. I moved my feet around to try and find a warm place in the bed. It was as futile as feeling around on a cement floor to find a soft place to lie down. I looked at my watch. One o'clock: an hour and a half to go.

I closed my eyes and tried to relax, joint by joint, muscle by muscle, according to an article I had recently read on charm. This relaxing was supposed to have been done by the hostess just before a dinner party and while the capon was roasting, the wild rice was steaming and the pistachio-nut ice cream cake was hardening. My reaction at the time had been that she should have had cheaper food and more help, but now I was grateful for her suggestions on how to relax.

There had been a picture of her lying on her bed in a negligee, with witch-hazel pads on her eyes. Lounging in the doorway was a rather unsavory-looking man, presumably her husband, and I remember thinking that she couldn't have been the nervous type if she could relax on a bed with pads over her eyes and him in the doorway. The article had said, "Think of your big toe. It is heavy. It is limp." I thought of my big toe but it was cold and stiff and there seemed to be a short circuit between my brain and my lower extremities. I tried my fingers, arms and shoulders. I was no more successful.

A girl in the next room began to cough. Her cough was deep and resonant and was a welcome relief from the silence. It was like a signal, for immediately up and down the corridors there were more coughs. Small dry coughs, loose phlegmy coughs, short staccato coughs, long whooping coughs. The hospital began to seem peopled and cheerful.

A nurse flashed in the doorway. She said to me, the others being asleep, "Patients must control their coughs. A cough can be controlled." I didn't say anything because I hadn't coughed and I knew if I spoke I would. She looked at me penetratingly for a minute and then flashed away again. I noticed that the coughing had ceased. Apparently she had stopped at each door and turned it off, like the radio.

I looked at the green ceiling again and tried to be honest and grateful. I thought of that terrible evening when the chest specialist had told me that I had tuberculosis; that if I wanted to get well I would have to go to a sanatorium; that sanatoriums cost $35 to $50 a week. I remembered how I had stood and looked at him, feeling like a mouse in an apple barrel—no way out. Around and around—no way out—no way out—no way out.

Now here I was in a hospital, being cared for, being fed, being watched over, being cured, I hoped. Yet the institution had to remind me to be grateful. I had to remind myself to be grateful because my instinct was to be resentful. Resentful of the rules, resentful of the nurses who enforced the rules. What was the matter with me? Was that what the Medical Director had meant when he said the cure would be hard for me, or were all tuberculosis patients the same way? I would ask Kimi when she woke up. When the rest hours were over. I looked at my watch. It was one-seven.

I looked back at the ceiling and tried to relax my fingers but my heart was pounding and I felt like a skyrocket about to explode into a million jagged stars. I turned my pillow over and took another drink of the tepid water. I closed my eyes and pressed my fingers against the eyeballs. Brilliant, blinding kaleidoscopic pictures appeared. It was infinitely more interesting than the green ceiling but according to the little book, not very honest or grateful.

I reached out and got my damp cold washcloth and put it over my eyes. That was better. I thought, "That is my big toe. It is heavy." But all I could see was that pistachio ice cream cake. I'll bet it was heavy. I took the washcloth off and turned over so I could see the poplar tree again. While I watched, one small leaf let go and dropped limply through the misty air. Compared to the hospital it seemed like an act of hysterical activity. I watched for a long time but no other leaves fell off the tree.

The girl in the next room began to cough again. It was muffled as though she were trying desperately not to cough but I heard the low murmur of the nurse and "Patients must control their coughs." My heart began to pound again, senselessly, as though I were climbing a steep hill. I turned over and lay on it and could feel its thudding clear to the top of my head. Thump, thump, thump, thump. I turned back again and it pounded harder.

When the nurse looked in I motioned to her. She came quickly to the bed on soundless feet. I said, "My heart's pounding." She looked at my chest and held my wrist for a minute then said, "Palpitations. Very common with t.b. Go to sleep," and left. I turned on the right side and my heart quieted a little. I closed my eyes but my thoughts, like a skidding car toward the railing of a bridge, immediately veered toward home and the children. I quickly opened them again.

Marie coughed and turned over. Her pale face blended into the sheet. Her black hair looked like an ink blot on the white bed. Her mouth was turned down petulantly even in sleep. Kimi slept gracefully, one flushed cheek on a slender palm. She was either very well adjusted or imbued with Oriental fatalism. Sylvia had her back to me. She snored faintly like a fly buzzing behind a curtain.

I drank some more water and thought, "I haven't even been here a full twenty-four hours yet and I have at least a year yet to go." Again my thoughts careered dangerously toward home. Keeping away from homesickness was like walking across a rock slide. Every step was insecure and the very next one might bring the whole mountain down on me. If only I had a hot-water bottle. How long could people stay dank and cold without mildewing? How long was two hours anyway? Was being cold all the time part of the cure or was it the easiest way to keep patients quiet and under the covers? Why weren't frail little creatures like

Sylvia cold? She said she was always warm. Maybe that was the fever.

I reached under the covers and tried massaging some warmth into my feet. It was as unproductive as trying to get sparks by rubbing two wet sponges together. I made up my mind that before that day ended I was going to have a talk with the Charge Nurse. I was going to ask her if keeping the patients half frozen was part of the cure; what the term "taking the cure" meant; what tuberculosis was; what the germ looked like; what its effect on the lung was; what rest had to do with the cure; if t.b. was actually curable; why some people, like the man in my office, could have t.b. for twenty years and live normal lives while others, like me, in less than one year became completely incapacitated; why I couldn't rest during rest hours; why I was so nervous; if, as time went on, I would become more restless or more well-adjusted. There were hundreds more questions I could ask but these would do for a start and would give me something to go on. Give me a basic understanding of the disease, The Pines and the cure. I was sure that I could be more intelligently cooperative if I knew what I was doing.

Trying to memorize the questions I wanted to ask took up the last long dragging minutes of the rest hours and at last there was a gentle clink-clank down the hall and in the door came a nurse with the nourishment cart. "Thank God," I thought. "Hot cocoa!" But the choice was ice cold milk or ice cold buttermilk. "What, no fans?" I said bitterly under my breath, as I chose ice cold buttermilk. Kimi took plain milk, Sylvia and Marie nothing.

After nourishment a nurse filled our water glasses again, another nurse took orders for supplies, such as toilet paper, paper handkerchiefs, sputum cups, etc., and told me to order enough for a week, as supplies were only given out on Saturdays.

After she had gone a nurse came in and asked us questions

and wrote the answers down on a chart. She asked us how we slept; how our appetites were; if our bowels were regular; if we coughed; if we raised; how much; color of sputum. The frequent detailed discussions of sputum, its amount and color, often made me wish for a more dainty ailment like diabetes or brain tumor. After she had gone the nurses brought wash water and in a little while Charlie put up the beds and it was time for supper.

Except for rest hours the day had gone by quickly. The long spaces of time had been well broken by small activities. For supper we had cold beef, scalloped potatoes, vegetable soup, banana salad, bread and butter, cookies, beautiful thoughts and hot tea.

I had just taken a large bite of meat and was reading my beautiful thought which said, "I have often regretted my speech, never my silence," when Sylvia threw up. I don't know whether she choked or was suddenly sick or had just read her beautiful thought, but she threw up all over her supper tray and down the side of the bed. It made me very sick. I quickly drank some tea and looked to see how Marie and Kimi were taking it. They weren't taking it any way. They were eating their supper as though it hadn't happened. I drank a little more of the tea.

Sylvia tapped with her spoon on the stand and eventually a nurse came in and cleaned her up. When she had finished, the nurse turned to me and said, "Eat your supper, Mrs. Bard. You must learn to ignore these things." She brought Sylvia another tray and some more tea and she ate her supper and so did I.

When the Charge Nurse and the doctor made their rounds, they came only to the doorway and said, "Everybody fine?" and so I put off asking the questions about tuberculosis until the next day. Half an hour after dinner we took our temperatures, mine was 98.6°, Marie's 102°, Sylvia's 101°, Kimi's 99°, and almost simultaneously the radio came on.

First there was a program of dinner music, then a play, then music, then a play. The radio flowed on until lights out at nine o'clock. The music was very nice but the plays and programs were very irritating because the volume was kept so low we could only hear occasional words. At seven o'clock we were given nourishment again, hot chocolate or cold milk. At seven-thirty the day staff went off duty and two evening nurses came on. Immediately there was a low distinct hum of talking from all over the hospital. It was a soft undercurrent noise like the hum of a refrigerator but it stood out in the absolute quiet.

We talked too. I asked Sylvia how she got tuberculosis. She said that she had had it since she was a child, that all her life had been lived in sanatoriums. She had been in Switzerland, New York, Arizona, Colorado, New Mexico and California. The medical director of the last sanatorium she had been in, one in Arizona, had given her up and sent her home to die. She said that, without any hope and only for her mother's sake, she had gone to see the Medical Director of The Pines. He had told her that his ways were hard but that he might save her.

I asked her if The Pines was like any of the other sanatoriums. She said, "No. In all the other sanatoriums they have the rules but only in The Pines do they enforce them. The Medical Director here knows tuberculosis and people with tuberculosis and he is going to cure them in spite of themselves." I asked her if being cold was part of the cure. She said that she didn't think so. That she wasn't cold.

I asked Marie and Kimi if they were cold. Marie said only part of the time, Kimi said that she was cold all of the time. She said, "I have instructed my family to bring heavy sock, many sweater and mitten." I made a mental note to tell my family to bring sock, sweater and mitten too. Also a bed lamp and a stand bag.

The stand bags, made of bright chintzes, were like shoe

bags with large pockets for writing paper, bedroom slippers and hand mirror and smaller ones for pens and pencils, combs and brushes and cosmetics. They were pinned to the towel bar on the stand by safety pins and their accessibility eliminated a lot of reaching.

At eight o'clock a nurse brought medicines. At eight-thirty we brushed our teeth with drinking water, spitting in our bedpans and Sylvia and Marie began to talk about bedsores. Sylvia told about bedsores in Europe, in New York, in California, in Colorado, in Arizona and New Mexico. Marie told about her grandmother's bedsores and her own. At nine o'clock the lights were switched out.

I pulled the clammy sheet up around my neck, stuck my feet timidly down into the icy regions at the foot of the bed and thought longingly of delightful hot climate diseases like leprosy, cholera and jungle rot.

→»VI«←

Anybody Can Have Tuberculosis

The next morning I was awake with my eyes open and feet braced when the lights blared and the washwater girls came crashing into the ward. To my astonishment, one of the washwater "girls" was a small, white-haired, very old woman.

I wanted to say, "But, you're too *old* to have tuberculosis." Instead I asked her how long she had been at the sanatorium. She said, "Almost a year. In fact it will be a year next Thursday." I said, "And I suppose you had been sick at home before you came out here?" She said, "My goodness no, I was never sick. Dad used to say, 'There's one thing about you, Nellie, you're never sick. You're thin as a picked chicken, but you're never sick.' I had a cough, of course, for years and years but we thought it was asthma. Dad used to say, 'Everything but me gives Nellie asthma.' When Dad passed over the doctor examined me and sent me out here. It was lucky for me in a way too because I missed Dad something awful. Dad used to say, 'Nellie, you look like the wind will blow you away but I'll bet you outlive me.' Everybody's just lovely to me out here. It's just like a real home to me." I thought grimly that if this was just like a real home to her she must have been raised in a reform school. She went on. "Dad used to say, 'Nellie loves people and people love Nellie.' "

81

It was easy to see why people loved Nellie because, in addition to loving people, she filled the wash basins clear full of hot water. I asked her hopefully if she was going to be on washwater duty every day. She said much as she liked people and washwater duty, it was a rule down at the Ambulant Hospital that all eight-hour patients should take turns on washwater duty. She wouldn't be on again until the next Sunday.

The other washwater girl, a large, boisterous young blonde, when admonished by Nellie for giving only the usual two cupfuls of washwater said, "My gosh, Nellie, you fill the basins clear up and we'll have to make another trip for hot water." Nellie said firmly, "Durdree Swanson, you act like you was never in Bedrest and tried to wash in a little bit of lukewarm water. Now go down to the bathroom and fill up another pitcher." Durdree said very unenthusiastically, "O.K., Nellie," and took the pitcher down to the bathroom.

When she had gone I said, "What did you say her name was?" I thought perhaps Durdree was some native Swedish name. But Nellie said, "Her name's Durdree, D-e-i-r-d-r-e. Her mother got it out of a book. Sounds funny don't it?"

Durdree had cheeks like camellias, deep blue eyes and ash blond hair. She was so pretty, so generously proportioned and so vital that I felt that The Pines should put one of her up in every ward to give the patients something to work toward. She was the last person in the world anyone would associate with tuberculosis. I said so. She laughed, showing many perfect white teeth and deep dimples, and said, "You wouldn't have said that if you'd seen me when I came in. I only weighed eighty-five pounds and I had been coughin' night and day for a year. Mama and the doc thought it was just a cold. Finally the school nurse sent me to The Pines Clinic." (She pronounced it "Clink," which considering its atmosphere wasn't too far off.)

Durdree was eighteen. She had been at The Pines for

two years and expected her discharge any day. She told us that her "boy friend" was in the Navy and that as soon as she got out of the sanatorium she and her "girl friend" were going to hitchhike to San Diego. I was quite certain that this would not come under the heading of "Accepted Forms of Occupational Therapy" but I was equally certain that Durdree would have no trouble getting a ride.

By breakfast time a very consumptive sun had begun to peer wanly out from under its hood of fog and we all said hopefully that there would probably be sunshine for visiting hours. I wondered sadly if anyone would come to see me. Kimi said, "I certainly hope my family received all my letter. My mother is so rattle-brained at times. Always writing poetry and forgetting my instruction." I asked what her instructions were. She said, "The instruction were about the heavy sock and sweater and mitten. But it would be just like my mother to forget all about the warm clothing and bring me one of her beautiful poem about the spring."

There was a terrific clatter in the hallway and two nurses pushed in a large pair of scales, for in addition to its being Sunday and a visiting day, this was also the last day of the month and weigh day. As each of us was helped out of bed and onto the scales, the room was tight with hope, for gaining weight signified at least a foothold on the climb to health. Losing weight meant a sliding backward and we could almost feel Sylvia's wild desperate attempts to grab something that would keep her from slipping farther down toward the yawning chasm, as with scared eyes and indrawn breath she watched the impersonal nurses adjust the weights and push the balance back, back, back. Sylvia had lost six pounds. Marie had lost three pounds, Kimi had gained five pounds and I weighed the same as I had at the clinic, which was twenty-three pounds underweight for my age and height, according to the chart.

For a time after the scales had gone the room was still

and heavy with despair. Even the sunshine seemed to have lost its promise and was watery and without warmth. Sylvia looked ahead at nothing and plucked nervously at the sheet. Marie twirled the knob of her stand drawer with one thin finger. Her cheeks were flushed, her eyes dark and angry. Kimi examined the palms of her hands. I watched the wind flitter the corner of the paper napkin on which my water glasses stood.

Then from Kimi's corner there was a small sound. I looked over and saw that she was crying and blotting her eyes with her bed jacket. I asked her what the trouble was and she said in a forlorn voice, "I am not happy to be the only one who has gained. It makes me feel like a beeg lonely hog."

At this point the Medical Director came in. He was alone without the usual retinue of house doctors and charge nurses, which was as surprising as being handed an aspirin without water to wash it down. He came to my bed. He said, "How do you feel," and I could tell by the way he asked and from the expression in his eyes that he already knew and cared nothing for my opinion. But I said anyway that I was cold.

This evoked a lengthy lecture, excerpts from which were: "It is better to be too cold than too warm. . . . Too much heat makes patients restless. . . . The nearer a comatose state tuberculosis patients can be kept the better their chances of recovery. . . . Hibernation like bears would be best. . . . Rest is the thing and only rest and more rest. Just lying in bed is not resting. . . . Resting is done with the mind as well as the body. . . . Tuberculosis is caused by the tubercule bacillus, a red, rod-shaped microorganism. . . . To date no medicine has been discovered which will kill this bacillus and not be too toxic for the patient. . . . The only way a patient can get rid of the bacillus is to wall it off in the lungs. This walling-off process is done by fibrosis which is more delicate than a spider's web and can be torn by the slightest activity. . . . The poisons sloughed off by the tubercular sores in the lungs make the tuberculosis patient nervous, make his heart pound, make resting difficult. . . . Rest is the answer. Just rest, rest and more rest. Tuberculosis can and does attack every organ in the body. . . . Drinking lots of water helps to wash the poisons out of the system and to prevent tuberculosis of the kidneys."

The Medical Director gave his talk to the room at large, then he turned to me and said, "You are a very sick young woman and you have much to learn." He went to Sylvia, poked at her for a few minutes and told her that she had tuberculosis of the intestines. He said Happy Birthday to Kimi and asked Marie how in hell she expected to get well if she didn't eat. She told him about her constipation and he said, "The trouble with American women is that they read too many advertisements and take too many laxatives." He left.

After he had gone Marie cried because she was constipated, Sylvia cried because she had diarrhea, Kimi cried because she was eighteen and I tried to gather my thoughts into a neat bundle, which I intended to tie up securely and label "out to lunch."

Trying to gather up my thoughts was as futile as trying to pick up spilled mercury. I had two big main depressing thoughts and each time I touched them they broke into many little morbid pieces. Number one was: Who will support the children if I die? And number two was: Will I be able to support the children if I get well?

The first one broke down into a lot of horrid little thoughts connected with my life insurance, the empty chair at the dinner table, the children's education, how long it would take me to die, what were the first symptoms, etc. The second one brought many cheering mental pictures of me in a faded wrapper peeling the last potato; me in a faded wrapper earning a meagre living by addressing envelopes at home; me in a faded wrapper making the children's winter coats out of an old blanket, their sweaters out of old bathing suits.

Just after nourishment the Charge Nurse moved Marie and Sylvia. As we kept our same beds, beside stands and chairs all the way through the Bedrest Hospital, moving the patients was simple. The Charge Nurse put their chairs on the foot of their beds and wheeled them to a new location. Another nurse came for their bedside stands and flowers. We asked this other nurse if she would move Kimi's bed up across from mine, where Sylvia's had been. She said suspiciously, "Did the Charge Nurse order it?" and Kimi said, "Would we ask you if she hadn't?" The nurse moved us grudgingly and when she had gone, Kimi said, "I hate to resort to trickery but sometime it is the only way I can get my wish."

Dinner was a very pleasant meal. Among other things, we had fricaseed chicken, dumplings, asparagus and ice cream with chocolate sauce. I tried some of Kimi's shoyu on my asparagus and chicken and liked it very much, though I thought it was gilding the lily to put it on the chicken.

After dinner Kimi put on a little lipstick, while I put on quantities of liquid suntan makeup, mascara and bright pink lipstick. It made me look like an old sick Madam but raised my spirits several notches. Kimi instructed me to "hold the lipstick, mirror and comb clutched in a sweaty palm under the cover, then when the nurse has made the last inspection and just before the alien step of visitor are heard you may quickly repair the ravage of sleep." I did as she told me and held my lipstick, comb and mirror in my sweaty palm but it was unnecessary because I didn't sleep and I lay so quietly that when I looked every pore was in place.

Kimi's family came on the stroke of two. Her father with an armload of yellow chrysanthemums as big as grapefruit, her mother with a poem but also the sock, sweater, mitten and other presents, and her brother, George, a tall handsome young Japanese, with some sweet and sour spareribs, which he ate himself because he thought Kimi was too fat.

My visitors were late and Kimi's dear little mother, thinking that I had no friends or judging from my appearance that they were all cheap transients, brought me half of the yellow chrysanthemums and arranged them beautifully in a square white vase. She had just put the vase on the stand and had said in her gentle voice, "for you," when Granite Eyes came in to fill the water glasses. She said, "Patients are not allowed to keep flowers on their stands," and clunked the vase to the floor.

Then she said, "Patients may not talk to other patients' visitors, Mrs. Bard. If you break the rules your visiting privileges will be taken away." As Kimi's mother spoke only a little English and apparently did not understand what the nurse was saying, she smiled and bowed to Granite Eyes and said, "Thank you very much, it is a lovely day." Kimi's brother, who had been watching, turned and spoke to Kimi and her father in Japanese. They all laughed. Granite Eyes stalked out of the room but her back looked self-conscious.

Just then Mother, Mary and Jim, Mary's husband, came in. Jim walked purposefully up to the bed and immediately handed me everything he had in the way of conversation. He said, "You look fine." The rest of the two hours he spent looking longingly out the window or examining me from different angles, as if I were a building site.

Mary brought me a huge bunch of butter yellow chrysanthemums with chartreuse centers. Mother brought a bed lamp and a stand bag (Mary had unearthed an old friend and old patient of The Pines who had told her I would need these) and a box of hot fresh cookies. They were so curious about everything in the institution and I was so curious about everything at home that the two hours were up almost at once. Just before they left Jim said, "Very little is known about tuberculosis. How is the food here?" I said it was wonderful and he said, "Well, that's something."

When Charlie came in to put up the beds he said, "Well, I seen your two friends down the hall. They're in a cubicle together but they don't look too good to me. I doubt if either of them two ever gets out of here. Of course, they might send 'em home to die, but they'll never get out any other way." Kimi said, "Charlie, I think you are in the wrong work. I think your occupational therapy time should be spent in the morgue." This, for some odd reason, sent him into paroxysms of laughter.

Sunday night after supper the store girl came around and took orders. The store girl was an ambulant patient but always a *very trusted* one as she took orders from the men too. This store girl's name was Velma Martin and she had, in addition to her trustworthiness, a purple plaid coat, steel-rimmed spectacles, a nasal voice and a habit of working her tongue around the inside of her mouth as if she were looking for hidden crumbs.

Velma said that the store carried toothpaste, soap, writing paper, magazines, candy, gum, pencils, ink, Coca-Cola, pop, fruit and cookies but that bedrest patients were not allowed to order any of the food. We could have gum, though, said Velma sending her tongue way back behind her right-hand twelve-year-old molar after some little particle of the forbidden food. I didn't need anything but Kimi ordered gum and soap, and then seeing that I hadn't bought anything said, "It would be my pleasure to lend you some money if you need it." I thanked her but refused.

After Velma came the nourishment cart bearing, in addition to the regular milk and cocoa, all the excess food brought patients by their visitors. The nurse offered us dry white cake, always referred to in our family as "choke cake," chocolate cake, cup cakes, cookies and candy. She said that any food we had been given that we couldn't eat by lights out

must be put on the cart.   I felt it was a sacrilege to put
mother's cookies on the cart with the dry cup cakes and the
choke cake and was wondering what to do with them when
the night nurse solved the problem by eating them all while
she talked to us.

She told us that her name was Katy Morris, she was
twenty-four years old and very interested in t.b. because her
brother had died of it.   Kimi said, "I suppose that most of
the patient here will eventually die."   Katy said, "Nonsense!
Most of the patients here will get well.   A few will die certainly, but most everyone who does what he is told and tries
to get well, gets well."

I told her that I was surprised to learn that an old woman
like Nellie could have tuberculosis.   Katy said that there were
several very old men downstairs and that all too often old
people who had had catarrh or a couth for years and years
were found to have had active communicable tuberculosis.
She said that in one room down the hall there was a woman
seventy-eight years old and little girl thirteen.

Just before she left Kimi said, "Just on the chance that I
may be one of the few who die, will you turn the radio up
just a leetle."   There was a radio control in our ward and
Katy, winking at me, turned it up until we could understand
all the words.

We spent the rest of the evening listening to the programs
and drinking water to wash the t.b. poisons out of our sys-
tems.   I thought that evening, and again and again in the
weeks to come, how fortunate I was to have gentle, intelligent, considerate, witty, beautiful Kimi for a roommate.

Being suddenly thrust with perfect strangers and forced
to live with them without any privacy at all for twenty-four-
hour period after twenty-four-hour period is as much a problem in adjustment as a planned marriage but without the
impetus of curiosity or the surcease of sex.

I like people but not all people.   I'm neither Christian

enough nor charitable enough to like anybody just because
he is alive and breathing. I want people to interest or amuse
me. I want them fascinating and witty or so dull as to be
different. I want them either intellectually stimulating or
wonderfully corny; perfectly charming or hundred per cent
stinker. I like my chosen companions to be distinguishable
from the undulating masses and I don't care how.

Like a wonderful woman I once knew who spoke beautiful
English and lived in her chicken house. She had hung up
gold velvet portieres in the middle of the chicken house to let
the chickens know that they were sharing their quarters and
while we drank our tea my friend bemoaned, in her beautiful
English, the sad plight of the educational system in America
and completely ignored the fat hens clucking and scratching
and bumping into the gold velvet portieres which swayed and
parted so that little brown feathers and small pieces of chaff
flitted between them and landed on our tea table.

Or like a one-time neighbor whose husband raised Mallard
ducks in their basement and she was so anxious to be grand
that she always referred to the duck raising as "my husband's business enterprise," which made it seem huge and
important like the gas works. Or another woman I enjoyed
immensely who was so obsessed with being refined that she
blinked her eyes and hesitated carefully before she trusted
herself to say anything at all and then produced gems such
as "Between you and I, Betty, Charlie don't like living so
neah the trolley line" and "He don't care for nuts but would
you and she wish for some?"

From my stay at The Pines I learned that a stiff test for
friendship is: "Would she be pleasant to have t.b. with?"
Unfortunately, too many people, when you try separating
them from their material possessions and any and all activity, turn out to be like cheap golf balls. You unwind and
unwind and unwind but you never get to the pure rubber
core because there isn't any. When I started unwinding

Kimi I found that under her beautiful covering she was mostly core. She said, "It is not character on my part, Betty, it is just that if you have to have tuberculosis it is easier to be Japanese."

Monday, immediately after rest hours, Kimi and I were handed a new problem in adjustment. Her name was Eileen Kelly and she was young and pretty with very long red hair and very long red fingernails. With disapproval radiating from her like heat, Granite Eyes wheeled Eileen in and helped her out of the wheelchair.

Eileen took off her robe, which was pale blue and leaned far from the required warm sensible bathrobe and heavily toward a peignoir. She had on sleeveless, backless, black satin pajamas and an anklet. Granite Eyes took her by the bare arm disdainfully as though she were holding her up in two fingers and disposing of her.

Eileen, not at all disturbed, leapt nimbly into the bed, but as she slid down between the icy sheets she let out a yell. "Jeeeeesus God, this bed's cold!" Like a shout in any empty church the yell bounced against the walls of the completely quiet Bedrest Hospital. At once the Charge Nurse was projected in the doorway. Eyes flashing, lips stretched tight with disapproval, she demanded an explanation of this very unorthodox noise. Granite Eyes said, rather inanely, we thought, "Miss Kelly's cold." The Charge Nurse said, "Miss Kelly, patients of The Pines do not shout."

She noticed a bare shoulder. Then turning back the covers, as though she were looking for maggots in a sack of flour, she revealed the rest of the bare and satin-clad Miss Kelly. Her nostrils swelled almost to the bursting point. She said to Granite Eyes, "Miss Murdock, go to the lockers and get a pair of outing flannel pajamas." She turned to Miss Kelly. "Did you read your list of requirements?" Miss Kelly said that she had. "Then," said the Charge Nurse, "why have you come here wearing *silk* [she breathed out heavily as she

said this loathesome word so that it came out "suh-hilk"]
pajamas and nail polish?" Miss Kelly said wisely, "I don't
know."

Just then Granite Eyes came puffing back with a very
ragged pair of blue and white flannel pajamas which, Kimi
pointed out to us later, had probably belonged to a patient
who had died. The Charge Nurse snatched the pajamas and
sent Granite Eyes back for oil of peppermint. Then she
removed Eileen from the black satin and stuffed her into the
outing flannel with purpose and dispatch; with sharp surgical scissors, which she carried in her pocket, she cut about
half an inch from the long pointed blood red fingernails;
removed the polish from the remaining stubs with oil of
peppermint; and informed Miss Kelly that the next morning
her hair would be cut to within one inch of the ear lobe.
Her stiff white uniform switched angrily through the door
and she was gone. Miss Kelly sat bolt upright in her bed,
a deadly sin, and stuck out her tongue at the retreating
Charge Nurse. Then she turned round hostile blue eyes on
Kimi and me and said, "Jesus, what a dame!"

She disdained to communicate further with us until suppertime when she picked up the beautiful thought from her tray
and read, " 'Intellect is invisible to the man who has none.'
Now what knothead thought that up?" she asked no one in
particular.

When the House Doctor and the Charge Nurse made
rounds a little later Eileen complained of the cold and asked
for a hot-water bottle. The Charge Nurse said quickly,
"Hot-water bottles are filled at eight-thirty in the morning
and at seven-fifteen in the evening." Eileen said, "I wasn't
here at eight-thirty this morning and I'm cold now." The
Charge Nurse said, "Your hot-water bottle will be filled at
seven-fifteen this evening."

It was unfortunate that on that of all evenings the hot-
water bottle filling should have been assigned to Miss Muel-

bach, who was so slow that even if she had put hot water in the bottles, which she never did, they would have been cold by the time she got them distributed. She threw mine on to the foot of my bed, dripping and cool. I looked over at Eileen. She said a very bad word and threw her hot-water bottle on the floor. It lit with a resounding clunk but, with Miss Muelbach on hot-water bottle duty there were so many resounding clunks up and down the ward, this one passed unnoticed.

Eileen waited for a few minutes, eyes on the door, then turned her face to the wall and bawled with loud slurping sobs. I felt desperately sorry for her. I knew how cold, unloved and unwanted she felt. I knew how hateful everyone at The Pines must seem but I couldn't think of anything to say that wouldn't sound like a beautiful thought or a quotation from the book of rules. Kimi solved the problem by saying, in her small sweet voice, "Eileen, all crying will do is to make your pillow and sheet wet and colder. When Katy, the evening nurse, comes on duty she will fill your hot-water bottle. Don't be sad, we are your friend and are in sympathy with you."

Kimi's speeches always sounded as though they should have been on parchment with a spray of cherry blossoms or a single iris painted across one corner. Eileen coughed hard without covering her mouth, in fact with her mouth wide open and aimed toward the hall, then she wiped her eyes on the sheet and turned over. She said to Kimi, "Why do they all have to be so goddamn mean?" Kimi said, "It would be wiser not to talk until the day staff goes off duty. In a few minute we can exchange confidence without fear of punishment."

When Katy came on duty she gave Eileen a fresh hot-water bottle, some hot milk and some advice. She said, "We're not trying to be mean to you, honey, it's just that we have a routine and a set of rules and we have to see that the patients conform." Kimi said, "What you say is true, Katy, but it is also true that an insensitive person often becomes overbearing when given unlimited authority." Katy said, "These nurses are mostly just young kids, right out of training. Lots of times when they act mean they are only trying to obey the rules."

I said, "I think that for the benefit of both the patients and the nurses, there should be a short adjustment period. Tossing a normal fun-loving human being into The Pines and expecting him to blend immediately in to the tuberculosis routine is as asinine as tossing a hot-blooded Spaniard into a snowbank in Norway and telling him to By God begin skiing and speaking Norwegian."

Katy said, "But in many cases there isn't time. By the time some patients had willingly adjusted themselves they would be dead." She was probably right but I thought I had a point too.

Subsequent exchange of confidences revealed that Eileen was twenty-one years old, an only child and an orphan. She had been brought up by her "Gramma," educated by the Catholic Sisters and employed, since the day she graduated from high school, by a very large motion picture theatre as an usherette. Eileen adored her job, loved all moving pictures, read nothing but movie magazines, and was an inexhaustible source of information about all movies and the private lives of the stars.

She started the very next morning bringing warmth and color to that cold, filmy period between washwater and breakfast by telling us the stories of movies she had seen. Her mind was as quick as a rocket and her memory was excellent but her method of telling and her vernacular made all the stories sound exactly the same. It was possible to distinguish between a tender delicate picture like *Good-bye, Mr. Chips* and a George Raft gangster picture only by the locale.

Eileen's antics were amusing to Kimi and me but they

were not curing her t.b. and they were definitely not resting. At first Kimi and I pointed this out to her. Her reaction was immediate and violent. She said, "These are my lungs and if I want to sing with them or talk with them or laugh with them or cough with them it's nobody's goddam business but mine, see."

After a while Kimi and I got so we didn't even flinch when Eileen crawled down to the foot of her bed, reached far above her head (absolutely forbidden) and turned the radio control up; or read movie magazines under the covers during rest hours; or wrote letters under the covers all day; or sat up in bed and polished her anklet with toothpowder; or sang songs; or talked constantly when the nurses weren't actually in the room.

Eileen had a severe cough, her various activities brought on many coughing spells and both her mother and father had died of tuberculosis, but Eileen was not at all concerned. She considered her tuberculosis merely a punishment inflicted on her by her "Gramma." She regarded The Pines as a reform school and the nurses as wardens.

When the barber (an ambulant patient interested in, or with past experience in, or with no experience and no interest in barbering) came to cut Eileen's hair, she decided suddenly that rather than have her hair cut she would go home. The barber, a long pale shy boy, fetched a nurse, the nurse fetched an assistant charge nurse and finally the assistant fetched the Charge Nurse.

The Charge Nurse sent the others away and said, "It is immaterial to me whether you go or stay, Miss Kelly, but I think that you are being very unfair to your wardmates. You say that having your hair cut will make you look like an ugly old hag yet Mrs. Bard and Miss Sanbo have both had their hair cut and I don't think they look like hags." Eileen looked at us and said, "Well, it didn't improve 'em any." Then she looked at us again and said grudgingly,

"Well, okay, but only to here." She measured a good three inches below her ear lobe and the Charge Nurse dumfounded us all by acquiescing.

The barber was called back. He came in red-faced and sweating and began in a most unprofessional and unsure way to hack off Eileen's lovely long hair. Eileen's frequent loud cries of "Ouch" and "Watch yourself, Buster" added nothing to his self-assurance nor did the fact that when he finished, her hair looked as if it had been cut with a very dull pair of pinking shears and one side was at least an inch shorter than the other, giving her an appearance of holding her head permanently on one side. Eileen looked in her hand mirror and said, "Well, Jesus God, will you look at that!" She turned to the barber shaking and blushing by the door and asked, "One arm shorter than the other, lover boy?" He beat a hasty retreat.

Eileen had one visitor each visiting day. On Sundays her grandmother, a belligerent little old Irish woman, came and fought with her for two hours. Busy with our own visitors, Kimi and I couldn't hear the quarrels, but Eileen told us about them afterwards. "Gramma's gone back to tradin' at Busby's Market. I don't know what's wrong with her head anyway. Busby's such a big cheat that he don't even try to hide the fact that he's layin' his whole arm on the scales when he's weighin' the meat but Gramma says it's closer and her bunions won't stand the extra block to the Super Market. Gramma said for me to quit tryin' to mind her business and to hurry and get well so I can go back to work." Or "Gramma found an old bill where I paid fifteen dollars for a pair of green shoes and, boy, did she hit the ceiling." Or "Gramma is still going to church with that dumb old Mrs. Wallady. Mrs. Wallady lives next door and she's stone-deaf and talks out loud in church and when she goes to confession you can hear her shoutin' her sins for three blocks. Gramma won't quit though. Says she feels sorry for Mrs. Wallady."

In spite of the quarreling, Gramma's visits seemed to exhilarate Eileen. Deciding such homely things as whether to shop at Busby's Market, or whether to go to church with dumb old Mrs. Wallady or how much she should pay for a pair of green shoes, pushed The Pines and its sputum cups and rules and bedpans, so far into the background as to make them invisible until well after Sunday supper.

On Thursdays, Jackie Fiske, Eileen's "boy friend" came to see her. Jackie had a small black mustache, high heels on his pointed black oxfords and long straight oily black hair that he wore folded one half over the other in the back. He was a musician and very unhealthy looking. He always brought Eileen flowers and sometimes a box of candy or a large stuffed animal that he had won on a punchboard but he never stayed more than fifteen minutes. "He don't like hospitals," Eileen explained, "and anyway he can't go more'n five minutes without a smoke. Jesus that fellah smokes a lot."

After his first visit Eileen asked Kimi and me if we didn't think that Jackie was "a wolfie-lookin' guy." We certainly did but we didn't say so. Eileen loved Jackie and intended to marry him some day but in the interim she showed an avid interest in any and all other males.

Within twenty-four hours after her admittance, she had learned that the Men's Bedrest Hospital was on the same floor as the dentist and that in order to go to the dentist a patient, no matter what his sex, had to be wheeled through the men's ward. She spent that evening planning on having her teeth pulled one by one.

The next morning, she sprayed herself heavily with My Sin and complained to the Charge Nurse of a toothache. She was sent to the dentist. When she came back she said that the dentist had nearly killed her, refusing to use novocain, but that it was worth the pain to have the Charge Nurse wheel her through the men's ward. She said, "The Old

Dame went so fast the tires screamed but I saw two real cute fellahs down near the dentist. I'm goin' to ask Charlie who they are."

Charlie, when asked, knew their names all right, one was Sandy and one was Arthur, but he didn't think that either of them would last six months. Eileen said that in that case she had better write them a note and cheer them up but Charlie said that sending notes between men and women was absolutely forbidden and he wouldn't deliver it, so Eileen gave Sandy and Arthur up temporarily and took to spraying herself heavily with Surrender just before the House Doctor's visits.

Thursday morning at breakfast a nurse informed me that Thursday was my assigned bath day and that right after temperatures and pulses I was to get ready. I was very happy both because Thursday was the best bath day of all, as it meant I would be very clean for one visiting day and reasonably clean for the other, and because I knew that the bathroom would be warm.

As I got out bath powder, clean pajamas and soap, I hummed a little tune under my breath and wondered which nurse I would get for the bath and how long she would let me stay in the tub. Frankly I was hopeful for Granite Eyes and her "all patients must be boiled."

My first disappointment was in drawing a scared little new nurse. My second blow was to learn that bedrest patients were not allowed tub baths. "Oh, well, at least the bathroom will be warm," I comforted myself, as visions of me soaking in a steaming tub faded into an accurate picture of me lying on a bed being hastily soaped and not rinsed by a bored nurse.

As two patients were bathed at one time, who your bath partner might be was an important contributing factor to the pleasantness or unpleasantness of the bath period. I was very fortunate in drawing for my first bath partner, a charming colored girl, Evalee Morris. Evalee was shy and quiet but when she spoke her voice was deep and as soft as melted chocolate.

After the nurses had deposited us, each on a bed, and covered us with our night blankets and told us to undress, they filled small tubs with hot water, put them on stools beside the beds and told us to wash our faces and necks, shave our armpits and legs, cut our toenails and perform any other little niceties we thought necessary. They warned us that this was to be accomplished in absolute silence, which was a good idea but didn't take into consideration our being human and female as well as tubercular.

The nurses left to change the beds and we turned on our sides and began to wash. Evalee looked at me occasionally shyly from behind her washcloth but I stared frankly at her. She had a flame-colored woolen scarf knotted around her head turban fashion, smoke-colored skin and a body so plump and firm and shiny it looked like white marble with black chiffon stretched tight over it.

Lying on her side languidly dipping her hands in the tub of water, against the background of the pale green bathroom walls, she looked like a poster advertising the Bahamas. I told her so and she laughed, showing white teeth and deep dimples, which only added to the illusion.

Evalee was twenty-seven years old, had graduated from the University of Washington in Home Economics, was married and had two children, a little girl three and a baby ten months. As her husband was a porter and away a great deal and her mother worked as a maid in a hotel, the Medical Director had allowed Evalee to put both children in the Children's Hospital. She said, "You should see the children out here. They play out of doors all day every day and they never wear anything but shoes, socks, shorts and hats. Billy and Rosanne haven't had a cold yet and they've been here five months."

She told me that her bed was on one of the big screened porches. She said that it was very cold out there but on clear days she could see the water and every day could hear the laughter and voices of the children when they took their walk.

She said that the woman in the next bed to hers threw up halfway through each meal and in order to finish before the woman threw up, all the porch patients had to choke down their food in double-quick time. One woman had complained to the Charge Nurse but she had said, "We must find happiness in little things."

I asked her if anyone could go out on the porch or if you were chosen by the Charge Nurse. She said that usually only very trustworthy patients were allowed on the porches because they didn't get quite as much supervision out there, but in her case she supposed that even if she had been noisy and boisterous they would have put her out there because she was colored.

"What difference would that make?" I asked, thinking of course it had something to do with colored people's resistance to cold. "Oh, it solves the roommate problem," said Evalee matter-of-factly. "Most white people would object to sharing a room with a colored person. Even on the porch where we are quite far apart, there have been complaints."

My bed bath turned out to be even more unsatisfactory than I had anticipated, for the little nurse was so new and so timid that she merely made stroking motions toward my body with the washcloth, not once getting up enough nerve to touch me. After she had not washed me she dabbed fearfully at me with a towel and I slapped on quantities of carnation bath powder and soaked my hair until I looked like a seal.

When I returned to bed, warm and cheerful, the Charge Nurse was waiting for me with a wheelchair and whisked me down the hall for a throat examination. The throat doctor, who was old and disagreeable, stuck a flashlight so far down my throat I thought he had dropped it. He asked me if I had been hoarse and I told him a little. He stuck the light down even further and said, "You've got bad tonsils." By that time he was so far past my tonsils it was like using a stomach pump to diagnose dandruff. I told him that I had had my tonsils taken out but he merely grunted and wrote on a chart and asked me if I wore glasses. I told him that I did when I read and he said, "Date of last eye examination?" I said, "A month ago." He wrote on the card, pushed me out of the way and jammed his light down into the next patient. As the Charge Nurse pushed me past the door of Sylvia's and Marie's cubicle I smiled and waved. They were both reading but looked up as we creaked past. They showed recognition with their eyes but dared not go further.

When Charlie came in to put up the beds for dinner he said that Evalee had said hello. He said, "There's one that won't be here long." I said, "You mean she's going to be discharged?" Charlie said, "I mean them niggers don't have no resistance to t.b." I said, "Don't be so depressing and don't call Evalee a nigger." Charlie said, "I've saw plenty of niggers die out here. They don't have no resistance to t.b."

Eileen said, "I won't take a bath with no nigger. Niggers stink." Charlie said, "You bet they do." I wanted to say, "Look who's talking," for Charlie's b.o. preceded him like a fanfare and followed him like an echo. Instead I said, "It's as ridiculous to say that all Negroes smell as it is to say that black cats are bad luck or if you shiver somebody's walking over your grave."

Eileen said, "I don't care what you say, niggers stink." Kimi said, "In Japan they think that white people smell."

Eileen was incredulous, "You mean that Japs smell different from white people?" Kimi said, "It is our opinion that we Japanese do not smell at all." The nurses came in then with the dinner trays.

Friday after rest hours another new patient was wheeled in. She was twenty-four years old, very thin, very blond and very Southern. Her name was Minna Harrison Walker. She had large, slightly prominent, pale blue eyes, white eyelashes and she blinked when she talked. When the nurse thrust her into bed and told her to keep warm with rules, she smiled up at her and said, "Ah declah, Miss Swenson, you ah the sweetest thing. Ah'm so lucky to be heah. Pore little ole me would have died if that nice doctah hadn't taken me in heah."

Eileen looked over at Kimi and me and held her nose. Miss Swenson was murmuring to Minna. Minna said, "Of course Ah don't want you to get in any trouble, you sweet lil ole thing, but Ah've got this awful pain in my tummy and Ah suah could use a hot-water bottle." She got it.

When the Charge Nurse made her rounds that evening Minna said, "You know that ole list didn't have a bed lamp on it and it's so dahk and lonely heah in the cohnah. Ah wrote mah Sweetie-Pie to bring me a bed lamp but it won't be heah until next visitin' day. Ah suah am lonely." The Charge Nurse brought her a bed lamp, which had probably belonged, Kimi gently reminded her, to some patient who had died. At that time Eileen didn't have a bed lamp either and she was furious. As the Charge Nurse finished attaching Minna's lamp, Eileen said, "Well, Jesus, honey, it's dark ovah heah too," but all she got was a cold look.

The next day it rained. Cold, wet, gray, chilling rain. It blew in the windows and under the covers and Kimi and Eileen and I were cold and miserable. Granite Eyes filled Minna's hot-water bottle twice. During rest hours Eileen read movie magazines under the covers, but Minna read the Bible and let herself be caught doing it.

It was a little new nurse who caught her or the punishment would have been more drastic. She rattled the pages just as the nurse came to the door and the nurse threw back the covers and there was little Minna clutching her Bible and looking up with big, scared, pale blue eyes. The nurse said, "Reading during rest hours is forbidden, Mrs. Walker. Any activity during rest hours is forbidden, Mrs. Walker. New patients may not read or write for one month, Mrs. Walker." Minna said, "Oh honey, Ah'm so sorry. The other girls were readin' so I thought it was all right. Oh, hush mah mouth, what have Ah said? Ah didn't mean to tell."

She looked over at us. Kimi was asleep. Eileen had slipped her movie magazine under her mattress. The new little nurse said, "Well, I won't report you this time but next time the Charge Nurse will hear about it." She rustled self-consciously out. Eileen reached down and got out her movie magazine again, then looked over at Minna and said, "Bitch." Minna had her eyes closed. The Bible was conspicuously placed on her bedside stand.

The staff at The Pines did not discuss tuberculosis with the patients. If you asked the doctors or nurses about your progress or lack of progress you got a noncommittal stare and no information. However, the Medical Director did issue printed pamphlets on tuberculosis, its cause and cure. These were in the form of Lessons and were mailed to the patients every few days.

My first lesson on tuberculosis began; "*Tuberculosis is contagious:* The germ is thrown off in spray or sputum from the nose and throat. Patients must ALWAYS cover the nose and mouth when sneezing and coughing. Handshaking and kissing are means of spreading the germ. Do not wipe the hands or face on the bedclothes. Do not swallow sputum.

It is dangerous! It may be the start of that complication known as intestinal tuberculosis. . . . The careless patient is not conscientious and lacks Character. If he will not learn he should be sent home."

I asked Kimi if she knew how she got tuberculosis. She said, "I don't know exactly but I think it was from the high mark. I went to American high school from eight to three-thirty and Japanese school from four to six. My father required me to get high mark in both school. I ended up with two diploma, two honor pin and tuberculosis." I asked her if anyone in her family had ever had t.b. She said, "No, but the Japanese as a race have no resistance to tuberculosis. When I had my tonsil removed and my throat did not heal my doctor suspected tuberculosis. I have a light case but with no resistance, who knows, I may die within the year."

She asked Eileen how she got t.b. Eileen said, "Well, it says here that it's contagious and handshaking and kissing are means of infection. I guess I got it from handshaking." She laughed. She said that, as both her mother and father had died of t.b., her gramma was forever telling her that she was going to get it. "I guess she's glad now," she said. Minna said, "Eileen Kelly, that's a horrid thing to say about youah pooah old grandmaw."

Eileen said, "A hell of a lot you know about it. You've never seen my gramma. And how did you get t.b., Little Eva? From some ole Yankee travelin' man?" Minna said, "Ah was nevah strong. Ah was a real sickly child, all big blue eyes and spindly legs. Mama said she nevah in the world expected to raise me." Eileen said two short bad words.

Minna ignored her and went on with her story. She said, "Ah used to have real bad attacks of pleurisy every wintah and the doctah used to give me light treatments. He nevah x-rayed mah lungs and the doctah at the t.b. clinic said Ah'd had t.b. for yeahs and yeahs. Ah'm real bad. Cavities in both lungs . . ." "And a big one in your head," Eileen finished rudely.

I told them about the man in my office and everyone was very incensed. Kimi said, "It is so hard to tell with men. They all seem to cough and spit so much." Then the nurses came for the supper trays and it was time for the House Doctor.

Eileen, from her large assortment of perfumes with atomizer tops, chose a heavy, musky scent and sprayed plenty of it on her hair and on her pillow, Minna used some violet toilet water and arranged her Bible within easy reach on the coverlet, but the new young doctor merely looked in the door and said, "Everybody fine?" and left. From behind him, the Charge Nurse winked and I almost fainted. After they had gone Minna said, "No wondah he didn't want to come in— it smells like a hoah house in heah." I thought what a pretty word whore was with a Southern accent.

On October fifth, Kimi had an x-ray and the next day was given fifteen minutes a day reading-and-writing time. The Charge Nurse came in before rest hours and said, "Miss Sanbo, you may read and write for fifteen minutes a day," and Kimi said, "Thank you very much, but I do not think I will have the time." Eileen said, "When can I have reading-and-writing time?" Minna said, "Oh, Ah thought you already had youah readin'-and-writin' time." There was a terrible silence and Minna covered her mouth and said, "Oh, hush mah mouth, what have Ah said?"

After supper the Charge Nurse took Eileen to her office for a little talk. She delivered her back in about a half hour, red-eyed and defiant. After the Charge Nurse had left, Minna said, "Ah declaah, honey, Ah didn't mean to tell. Ah really thought you did have readin'-and-writin' time." Eileen said wearily, "Oh, shut up!" Then she crawled to the foot of her bed and turned the radio very loud.

Minna had only one visitor but he came on the stroke of two each visiting day and stayed the full two hours. It was "Sweetie-Pie," her adoring husband. Sweetie-Pie was about fifty years old, bald, fat and doughy-faced, but he brought Minna flowers and candy and bath powder and fruit and bath salts and jewelry and perfume and bed jackets. She always referred to him as though he were a cross between Cary Grant and Noel Coward and said often, "Ah just don' know how I was lucky enough to get that big ole handsome husband of mine."

Once, right at first, Eileen had said, "You can stop right after the 'big old,'" and strangely enough Minna began to cry. She said that "she loved that big ole handsome man" and that he was her "Sweetie-Pie" and after that nobody said anything. After all if it made her happy to think dough-face was handsome, that was the important thing.

The day after she gave Kimi her reading-and-writing time, the Charge Nurse told her she could walk to the bathroom once a day. Kimi was ecstatic until after breakfast when she stood up to put on her robe. Then Minna said, "Oh, honey, youah so tall, youah just enohmous! I had no idea you were so big!"

Kimi, looking as though she had been slapped, said, "The Japanese are such little fellow, already I felt like Gulliver with the Lilliputian." I said, "But you're not very tall, Kimi." Kimi said, "Oh, yes, already five and one half feet and probably still growing." I said, "But I'm five feet seven," and Eileen said, "And I'm five feet five." Minna said, "And poah little me can't reach five feet with high heels. It's shuah lucky foh me that Sweetie-Pie says that good things come in small packages." Eileen said, "And I can get just as sick to my stummick on a little of your guff as I can on a whole lot." "And the bite of a little rattlesnake is just as deadly as the bite of a big one," Kimi said, moving slowly and regally out the door.

➤➤VII◀◀

Heavy, Heavy Hangs on Our Hands

THE FIRST TWO weeks at The Pines went whizzing by. Everything was new, everything was interesting, and I was sick. In spite of Eileen, Minna, washwater girls, store girls, Charlie, Bill, the store boy (who delivered the store girl's orders) and visitors, I rested and rested and rested and rested. And as the Medical Director had predicted, the resting grew easier, my pulse pulsed slower and I relaxed more as long quiet day succeeded long quiet day.

Exactly two weeks, to the day, after I entered the sanatorium I slept the whole night through and the next morning I didn't cough at all when I woke up. By ten o'clock my sense of well-being was so great it was almost choking me. I had energy, my brain was clear, I didn't ache any place, and I loved The Pines and everyone in The Pines. The depression and terrible sense of foreboding I had been wearing around my shoulders since the night I learned I had tuberculosis, had been mysteriously lifted off during the night and though it was a cold foggy morning and both the washwater and my hot-water bottle had been lukewarm, I brushed these off the day like a crumb off the bedclothes. I felt well!

At noon Miss Muelbach, whom Eileen had christened Gravy Face, brought the mail and threw it at us so that a letter from Mother went into my cup of tea. "Poor thing,"

I thought as an aura of sweetness and light flared up around
me, "probably tired." I smiled benignly at Miss Muelbach
and she glared stonily back at me. I started to wipe the tea
off Mother's letter but she said, "You know you're not supposed to read your mail until you've eaten your dinner."
"Oh, I'm not going to read it," I said so sweetly I was almost
singing. "I'm just wiping the tea off it." "Well, all right
then," said Gravy Face and stumped out of the room on her
gray hairy legs.

Mother's letters have always been a delight and she is such
an untiring and fluent letter writer that the family often refers
to her as "Scrib." In my letter writing I usually take some
small incident and by a process of lies and poor descriptions
build it up and up into something dull but very long. Mother
never bothers with such deceit. She merely sits down at her
desk and writes what is going on at the moment.

This letter told me that one of the dogs had run a thorn in
his foot. That a neighbor was just outside the window improving the shining hour by cutting the last living branch
from his wife's poor little prune tree. That she had just
baked an applesauce cake. That Anne was begging her to
find a school that did not include "rhythmetic" in its cur-
riculum. That large boys of sixteen and seventeen knocked
at the door constantly to ask if Joan could come and pitch
for their baseball teams. That Dede was making a coat and
with her usual hardheadedness was not taking any advice
from anyone. Mother wrote, "It is quite difficult for me to
sit quietly by, evening after evening, watching her try to
force the sleeves in upside down." That Alison was still sur-
rounded by "the locusts," as mother called her high school
friends, who descended on the house after school and ate
everything that wasn't metal or hadn't been baked in a kiln.
That Madge was just then playing the piano very beautifully
in spite of a bandage almost to the shoulder on her right arm.
Mother said that Madge hadn't yet revealed whether the

bandage denoted t.b. of the bone or that she was preparing to get off work, later in the week. That everyone missed me terribly but the children were becoming very well adjusted to my absence.

The whole letter was as much a part of Mother as though she had snipped off a piece of herself and sent it to me. I read it for the fourth time just before rest hours and that day, at last, I was able to think of home and the children without the slamming of a coffin lid as an off-stage noise. I spent the rest hours making plans for the future and they differed from any previously made because they were based on a premise of "when I get well" instead of "if I die." The rest hours still seemed two hundred hours long and I was still cold but there was some reason for it now. It was like bearing the pain to remove a sliver instead of bearing the pain just to bear pain.

When at last the nourishment cart came clanking down the hall, I didn't have my usual end-of-rest-hours nervous frustration. I felt relaxed and refreshed. As I was drinking my buttermilk, a nurse came in and brought me a large box of pale pink carnations, my favorite flower. The nurse took the box and returned with the carnations jammed into what appeared to be a large hunk of spleen. Closer observation showed it to be merely a pottery vase, shaped and colored to look like spleen. At least it had not impaired their smell and lying on my side close to the edge of the bed, in a direct line with the cold raw wind, was almost as satisfactory as burying my face in the carnations.

The room was very quiet. Eileen was writing a letter under the covers, Minna was sleeping and Kimi was using her fifteen minutes' reading-and-writing time to look at some movie magazines, generously delivered in person by Eileen early that morning. I smelled my flowers and listened to the faint scratch of Eileen's pen, the soft little swish as Kimi turned a page. Suddenly the Charge Nurse was in the room.

She was angry and her really beautiful blue eyes sparked. She said, "It has been reported to me by other patients that there is noise in this ward in the evening. Is that true, Mrs. Bard?" I said, "Why, er, uh, er . . . " Eileen said, "Who's the snitcher?"

The Charge Nurse turned and gave her a look like a dipper of ice water. She said, "I want to know if the report of noise in this room at night is true." Kimi said, "How many people have reported this noise?" The Charge Nurse said, "What difference would that make, Miss Sanbo?" Kimi said, "If many people have reported the noise it must be the radio because if the noise were sufficient for many people to hear, the nurse would also hear it and stop it. We occasionally exchange pleasantry in the evening but not for the ear of the whole ward." The Charge Nurse looked completely baffled. She said, "But this patient said," and we knew then that it was one particular patient, "that she could hear you laughing and talking." Not one of us said anything. The Charge Nurse said, "She said that she heard you very plainly, Mrs. Bard." I said, "But I haven't spoken out loud since I got here. How could she recognize my voice? All whispers sound alike you know." Eileen said, apparently to herself but in a very audible voice, "Dirty little snitcher." The Charge Nurse said, "You will hear more of this!"

I noticed that not once had her accusations included Minna. I also remembered that Minna had that morning gone with her for a throat examination. I could almost hear that "hush mah mouth, what have Ah said?" I looked over at her but she was feigning sleep with her white eyelashes lowered over her pale eyes. I was sure I hadn't talked any more than anyone in the hospital and certainly not one millionth as much as Eileen, but I was frightened. What if I should be sent home for breaking rules? Me, a grown woman. Whether or not I had broken the rules was unimportant, the important thing was the implication that I hadn't been intelligent enough to see what was being done for me.

Eileen said, "It seems goddamn funny to me that the Old Dame never once looked at Little Eva. It also seems god- damn funny that Little Eva was with the Old Dame this very morning. Hush mah mouth, what did you say, you dirty little snitcher?" Minna kept her eyes closed but her lids twitched noticeably. Kimi said in a voice as gentle as breath, "In Japan, I believe it is customary to pour boiling oil over the tongue and down the throat of a betrayer." Minna turned her face to the wall.

When Charlie came in to put up the beds, Eileen told him what had happened. He said, "There's one in every ward. I don't see why they do it unless it's because they like to keep things stirred up." I said, "But I didn't do anything wrong." He said, "Oh, you won't convince the Charge Nurse of that, because she's convinced that everybody's wrong and she just loves a chanct to point it out to them. Right or wrong, you'll probably get a letter from the Medical Director."

My beautiful sense of well-being was gone and in its place was such a feeling of dread and depression that it shriveled my stomach and tied my intestines in knots. When the House Doctor made rounds and asked how I felt, I told him I felt as if I'd swallowed an outboard motor. He laughed, punched me in the stomach and ordered a sedative. The Charge Nurse compressed her lips and wrote it down.

After pulses she came for me in a wheelchair. She took me down to the examination room and told me that there was no room in the hospital for ungrateful patients who did not obey the rules. I told her that I had not broken any rule. She said that the patient who reported me had said that she could not rest in the evening because I made so much noise. I said that that was obviously ridiculous and for her to ask the night nurse. She said that she was going to take the mat- ter up with the Medical Director and I said that I didn't see what she had to take up. She didn't answer, merely swelled her nostrils and wheeled me back to bed.

When Katy brought my sedative, I told her the whole childish incident. She said, "You know that's one thing that's wrong with this place. They forget how important peace of mind is in resting. Oh, well, the worst you'll get will be a letter from the Medical Director, so drink this and have a good sleep." After lights out and just before we went to sleep, Kimi said, "I forgot to tell you that Indians used to stake an informer to the ground, then press on his eye socket and pop out his eyeball like a grape."

The next day I got my letter. It was a quotation: " 'Suppose it were perfectly certain that the life and fortune of every one of us would, one day or other, depend upon his winning or losing a game of chess. . . . Yet it is a very plain and elementary truth that the life, the fortune and the happiness of every one of us, and more or less, of those who are connected with us, do depend upon our knowing something of the rules of a game infinitely more difficult and complicated than chess. It is a game which has been played for untold ages, every man and woman of us being one of the two players in a game of his or her own. The chess-board is the world; the pieces are the phenomena of the universe; the rules of the game are what we call the laws of Nature. The player on the other side is hidden from us. We know that his play is always fair, just, and patient. But we also know, to our cost, *that he never overlooks a mistake,* or makes the smallest allowance for ignorance. To the man who plays well, the highest stakes are paid, with that sort of overflowing generosity with which the strong shows delight in strength. *Anyone who plays ill is checkmated—without haste, but without remorse.'* " The letter was signed by the Medical Director.

That night my stomach was in knots again and the House

Doctor ordered another sedative. When Katy brought the sedative, she read the letter and passed it to Eileen and Kimi. Eileen read it and said, "I only play checkers myself." Kimi said, "I cannot believe in the omnipotence of one who never overlooks a mistake, particularly since I have been taught that 'to err is human, to forgive divine.'" Katy said, "And a grudge will soon rot the pocket you carry it in. What do you say we wipe the slate clean and start tomorrow off fresh?"

I was glad to, Minna was pitifully eager, Kimi agreed but Eileen said, "You don't remove a skunk's smell by paintin' out his stripe." Katy said, "Come on, honey, for the sake of the cure, let's have peace." Eileen said, "The first time you get a knife in your back it's the other fella's fault. The second time it's your fault. Little Eva's had her knife in my back about three times. From now on she's strictly poison." Katy winked at Kimi and me and left. Eileen crawled down to the foot of the bed and turned the radio so that it was clear and loud.

The next day was a visiting day and Sunday and bright with sunshine so the incident was forgotten and the ward was peaceful until Velma, the store girl, came after supper to take our orders. She said, as she pulled her mouth over to one side and massaged her upper gums with her tongue, "I heard through the grapevine that the Charge Nurse caught all you kids out of bed playing checkers." This seemed to put the proper light on the whole silly episode and for a time, at least, we all harmonized and did not need sedatives.

My great sense of well-being returned but this time it was accompanied by a terrible restlessness and irritability. I felt perfectly well and it drove me insane to lie there hour after hour, day after day, doing nothing. Absolutely nothing. Kimi was restless also and had unwittingly extended her reading time from fifteen minutes to about twelve hours, but as she was not allowed to read books, only magazines and papers, even this palled after a time. Eileen, always tremendously active, and always cheerful, suddenly became quiet and surly. Minna slept.

She slept so soundly at night she had to be awakened by the washwater girls every morning. She had to be awakened by the nurses at breakfast time. She had to be awakened for nourishment, for dinner, for supper. It was certainly a harmless enough activity and highly recommended by the staff, but it became a major irritation to me.

Every single morning, seven days a week, when the washwater girls had finally roused her, she yawned and stretched and rubbed her thick white eyelids and said, "Oh, my, Ah'm so sleeeeeeeeeeepy." Right after she had washed, she snuggled down again saying, "Uhm, mmmm, uhmmmmmm, Ah'm sleeeeeeepy," and I wanted to scream. Every time I looked at her she was asleep, lying on her back, her pale pink mouth, moist and partly open, her white eyelids pulled down and rounded over the slightly bulging, pale blue eyes. I longed to shout and shoot a gun off just above her head. Her sleeping was as unnatural and nauseating to me as watching someone eat or drink themselves into a stupor. She was apparently about as complicated emotionally as a bowl of mashed potatoes. Quite naturally, she was the favorite of the Charge Nurse because by comparison she made anyone who wasn't under ether seem like a lighted stick of dynamite, and caring for her required the same amount of initiative and thought as stuffing dirty clothes into a Bendix. At mealtimes watching her emerge from her cocoon, blink her heavy white fringed eyelids over her pale eyes, and raise her pale head, was like watching a sluggish white worm poke its head out of an apple.

Except for meals, Minna came to life and evinced enthusiasm only when she talked about tuberculosis. Minna loved tuberculosis and enjoyed discussing each small repulsive detail of her illness. She had none of the new patient's optimism about getting out of The Pines in less than a year and she counted on being on complete bedrest for three years and, with possible and probable relapses and good luck, maybe five.

She read her lessons avidly and discussed her symptoms with anyone who would listen. She probed the nurses, flower girls (ambulant patients with six hours' up, who came to the Bedrest Hospital twice a week to fix the flowers), washwater girls, cleanup men, store girl, store boy and Charlie, for gruesome details of operations, hemorrhages and deaths. In Charlie, of course, she found a bottomless pit of bad news and depressing rumors.

So far, no one in our ward had had any treatment other than rest and Eileen certainly hadn't had much of that, but we all seemed to be progressing favorably. I didn't cough at all, now; Kimi never had; Eileen coughed only in the morning and when she talked and laughed, and Minna only when she exerted herself unduly, discussing rumors or case histories. We all had voracious appetites and took any and all food that was offered and as much as they would give us. Our letters home were always pleas for more food, and on visiting days our ward looked like a delicatessen.

Then one day without warning, Minna was wheelchaired away during rest hours and given pneumothorax. We had heard of pneumothorax, always referred to as "gas," from the ambulant patients but we weren't sure what it was and we thought it was only for the very sick.

When Minna came back she told us that the Medical Director had explained to her that pneumothorax was to a tubercular lung what a splint was to a broken leg. That it was the introduction of clean air into the pleural cavity, which in turn forced the lung to collapse through its own elasticity. It was like forcing air between the covering and the bladder of a football so that the bladder couldn't expand.

She said that the Medical Director had told her that she was very lucky to be able to take artificial pneumothorax as it could not be given to many patients due to adhesions (places where the lung had grown to the pleura).

She said that while she lay on an operating table on her back with her right arm over her head, the doctor painted a small area under her right breast with mercurochrome, injected novocain and then forced a hollow needle, about as large as a big darning needle but much longer, in between the lung and the pleura. After it was in, he attached it to a contraption that forced the air in. She said it hadn't hurt a bit and showed us the small bandaged place.

Then she told us that she didn't want to alarm us unduly, but it was her impression from her lengthy and illuminating talk with the Medical Director, that patients who weren't taking any form of treatment were so far gone that the institution didn't dare risk it. With this cheering remark she closed her eyes and went to sleep.

By bedtime that night, however, she had changed her mind about who were the lucky ones, for Charlie had told her about spontaneous collapses. A spontaneous collapse, according to Charlie, was almost always fatal and happened very frequently. Minna said, "He told me that some patients' lungs ah just full of holes, mine probably ah, and when pressuh is put on the lung through pneumothorax, the lung collapses like an old tiah with a blowout. Charlie says that patients are dyin' like flies around heah with these spontaneous collapses."

A tuberculosis sanatorium, like a boarding school, is rife with gossip and rumors. But the gossips and rumors at The Pines, instead of being about cheerful things like boys and parties, were always about poor little patients who were mistreated by the staff. The doctors out of pure cussedness were always forcing too much air into the patients' lungs so that they collapsed, ripping out all their ribs for the joy of it, putting them on enteric diets for meanness, ignoring vital symptoms so they could watch them suffer, and giving them medicines which did no good.

We heard about poor old patients who had so many night sweats that there were puddles around their beds, yet the nurses wouldn't even bring them clean pajamas or sheets. Just left them to drown in their own juice. We heard about ambulant patients who were kept on janitor duty while spouting blood from every pore. We heard about mothers and daughters in the same ward but not allowed to speak to each other so that they died of a broken heart. We heard of patients without teeth who were given nothing but tough steak to eat.

The rumors were all based on a little bit of truth but turned out like the whispering game we used to play as children where we sat in a circle and the starter whispered something to the person next to him and that person whispered it to the one next to him until it had gone all around the circle. The last one said out loud what had been whispered to him and the starter told what he had originally said and "Mary's dress is pretty" would go around the circle and come out as "Garry's lips are spitty," or "Charlie's scalp is gritty," or "Harriet has a kitty."

I asked Katy Morris about some of the rumors and she told me that the janitor supposedly forced to janitor while hemorrhaging was actually a very lazy patient who always had some excuse for not getting his supervised exercise. His hemorrhage was in reality a very slight nosebleed caused by blowing his nose too hard. The mother and daughter, who were separated and died of broken hearts, was actually a case of a very stupid mother and a very sick daughter. When they were in a room together the mother talked to her daughter constantly and gave her all kinds of forbidden food.

When they were separated they sulked and complained. They both died eventually of advanced tuberculosis and lack of cooperation.

Katy said that she knew of only two spontaneous collapse cases and that in both instances the patient was so far gone, it was a case of trying anything to save them. She said that, as far as surgery went, there were patients who were not ready for it, begging for surgery; and patients who were ready for it fighting against it. She said that the only reason that patients were put on an enteric diet was because they had t.b. of the intestines, because any fool knew that it was easier to feed everybody the same thing at the same time.

She said that she knew that old man without any teeth and that he was an old devil and in addition to not wearing his teeth, which he refused to do out of arbitrariness, he wouldn't take any of his medicines because he was curing his t.b. by correspondence course. He belonged to some sort of New Thought group and they sent him his instructions every day in the mail. The Medical Director didn't send him home because home was with his daughter and five small children.

Katy said, "There's nothing as dumb as people with t.b. You tell them, 'Now if you do this you'll get well but if you do this you'll die,' and they always try to do the thing that will kill them." She looked over at Eileen, who was lying on her side, her red hair fanned out on the pillow, her deep blue bachelor-button eyes round and bright with interest. Under the covers she had her writing paper, her fountain pen and five movie magazines. Kimi said, "Katy, if the nurses were all like you, it would be much pleasanter for the patient." Katy said, "Kimi, if the patients were all like you it would be much pleasanter for the nurses."

Minna was given pneumothorax every other day and her lungs didn't burst or blow up and she continued to sleep twenty-three hours out of the twenty-four, but when poor old Sweetie-Pie came bouncing in on visiting day, wreathed in smiles and loaded with packages, she entertained him for two hours with her operation, her suffering and the horrible things that had happened to other patients and that might and probably would happen to her. We watched him droop and sag like a melting snowman.

After he had gone, Minna sat up and ate every crumb of her supper including two helpings of the main dish. Kimi looked over at her, wearing a new pink angora bed jacket and happily eating soup, while the mournful steps of the deflated Sweetie-Pie dragged along the corridor, then said softly, "With what a vast feeling of relief he will close the lid on your coffin." I choked on my soup and Eileen shouted with glee. Minna said only, "Next week he's bringin' me a pink hood to match this jacket."

⤜⤜VIII⤛⤛

I'm Cold and So Is the Attitude of the Staff

The Pines was a very cold place and that included the attitude of the staff as well as the temperature of the rooms. We patients wore woolen socks, as many as three pairs at a time, outing flannel pajamas, two, three and four sweaters, bed jackets, mittens, woolen hoods and scarves until we looked like bundles of old clothes but we were all cold all of the time.

From the first of October on, it rained and rained and rained and rained. When it wasn't raining it misted and fogged, and everything, including our hair and the bedclothes, was damp and clammy. There was heat in the building we knew, because we heard the radiators clank and hiss in the early mornings, but with every window opened wide and all the partitions beginning a foot off the floor, it was as useless to try and heat that place with radiators as to heat the tundra with lighted matches. The cold made us irritable and snappish and ice cold bedpans slipped under the covers at stated intervals did nothing to alleviate the tension.

We were the living proof that colds do not come from draughts, chills, or continual dampness and that the human body will not grow mold. Most of the patients froze passively but I was not a good sport about the cold because I couldn't see any reason for it. The hospital had thousands and thousands of gallons of boiling water which they could put in our hot-water bottles. They had cupboards loaded with nice thick warm blankets which they could put on our beds.

I complained, begged, cajoled, whined, even bawled and at last my efforts were rewarded with a large wrinkly brown *paper* blanket. The Charge Nurse brought the paper blanket herself with an air of "I don't know what you'll want next in the way of pampering." She handled it as carefully as though it were made of llama hair and charged with electricity. As this paper blanket signified that I had won the battle, I couldn't go any further with my fight without appearing like a victor who shoots all the captives, so I shut up.

The paper blanket rustled and crackled cheerfully but actually made me colder because it was so stiff that it let in draughts and kept my own blankets from clinging to me. How I envied the lucky patient in the private room who, Charlie reported, was burning up with fever.

The food, at first cool in the morning and evening, but hot at noon, was finally as winter progressed, all cold. The food was brought from the kitchens via the tunnels and supposedly served from steam tables but judging from the sanatorium's idea of steam, they were more likely lukewarm tables. Anyway, even if they had been steam tables and everything had started out boiling hot, wheeling it up and down those icy windswept corridors a few times produced the same result as setting it down in the Arctic Circle and having a hundred Eskimos blow on it.

I didn't mind so much the food's being cold because it was always well chosen, well seasoned and well cooked, but being luke-warm did nothing for the coffee, which even when hot, tasted as if it had been made out of burnt toast crumbs boiled well with ground-up rubber bands.

Lesson III began, "You are occupying a bed badly needed for someone else. The cure of tuberculosis is very, very expensive. . . . All the nurses are graduate nurses and they are being trained, while at The Pines, to give the best of nursing care to the bed patient, to teach the tuberculous patient the many things he should know about control of infection, rest and exercise, and self-control. . . . Patients must be grateful to the nurses, the doctors, and to the Sanatorium." The lesson ended, "IF YOU THINK RIGHT, YOU WILL ACT RIGHT."

Eileen read her lesson and said, "All this guff about being grateful all the time. Be grateful to the nurses—be grateful to the doctors—be grateful to the sanatorium. It's a good idea but why run it into the ground?" It was unfortunate that Miss Muelbach should have come in just then.

Miss Muelbach's thick, gray, hairy legs looked as if they had been driven into her shoes and when she walked she stamped and the stands and tables jumped around like tiddlywinks. Her skin was oily and swarthy. She was also big and strong and when she made beds with one of the smaller, weaker nurses, the covers would be tucked in four feet on her side and wouldn't reach the edge on the weak nurse's side.

When we entered The Pines the Charge Nurse instructed us never to pick up anything from the floor. If we dropped something we were to wait for a nurse, as it was part of her work to retrieve things from the floor, she told us. This came under the heading of an Ideal State or Utopian Dream, for few of the nurses would ever pick up anything for the patients and the Misses Muelbach and Murdock never.

This day Muelbach stamped over and opened the windows as wide as they would go. It was raining hard and the wind was blowing and immediately there were pools under the windows and spitty gusts on Kimi and me. We asked her please to close the two outside windows as the Charge Nurse had done in the morning, but she said, "Rule of the Sanatorium is that all windows must be open at all times." She stamped out and our water glasses danced around on the stands. Eileen said, "See what I mean? Asking us to be grateful for that is just running things into the ground."

Minna said, "I think this place would be much pleasantah if they would use ouah names. That Mrs. Walkeh stuff all the time is right depressin'." Eileen said, "Oh, that's because the joint's free. You never get nothing for free with a smile. You should see how snooty they were to Gramma down at the Relief Office. They Mrs. Kelly'd her from one end of the dump to the other and then wouldn't give her her false teeth for three months. That's why I hate soup so much. We had nothing but soup for the whole three months. 'Jesus, Gramma, *I* got *my* teeth,' I used to tell her but soup's all we got."

Kimi said, "I think they use the Miss so much because they do not want to become too fond of the patient when so many of them die." I said, "It is because of the discipline. They have to be impersonal in order to enforce the discipline and the discipline is what makes us get well." Eileen said, "But they run things into the ground out here. There was an old dame down at the dentist's who's been in this joint seven years. Seven years and they're still callin' her *Miss* Ryan. Jesus, how long does it take to get acquainted?"

Adjusting to complete impersonality was difficult, not only for the patients, but for the new nurses who felt sorry for the patients and were afraid of the charge nurses. New nurses were at first sweet and friendly in a frightened sort of way but after a week or so under the training of the Charge Nurse, they changed and became cool, impersonal, and very efficient like the Charge Nurse and her assistants.

Eileen always referred to the Charge Nurse as "The Old Dame," but this was not an accurate description of her as she was neither old nor a dame. She was probably thirty, tall, slender, beautiful, cool, controlled and fanatical in her devotion to duty. Under her supervision the Women's Bedrest Hospital clicked off its hours and days like a card punch machine. She knew every pore of every patient and if they were open and why. She was the perfect nurse, the vision in every hospital superintendent's dream.

She slipped up and down the halls without a sound and prevented the patients from, or caught them in the act of, laughing, talking, reaching, sitting up, looking out the window, reading, or writing when they were not supposed to, or exceeding their reading-and-writing time when they were supposed to, talking to the ambulant patients, coughing, curling hair, not eating "the egg," or reading mail on an empty stomach.

The only time I ever knew her to fail was in the case of Eileen. She slipped down to our ward fifty times a day but never caught Eileen reading, writing, sitting up, laughing, talking, turning up the radio, putting on makeup, curling her hair, fixing her nails or talking to anyone who would listen or answer.

Miss Murdock, Miss Muelbach, a Mrs. Macklevenny who was tall and disagreeable and always seemed to be smelling something putrid, a Miss Garnet, who was thick and white with very short legs and a low behind that banged against the backs of her legs when she walked, and a Miss Whiting who was very young but kept her lips folded in like a buttonhole, may have had their innate sympathy and kindness worn thin by the complete ungratefulness and foolhardiness of the patients, but to me it seemed more likely that they had obtained their vocational training kicking cripples and hitting small children. I spent nine months at The Pines longing for the day when *they* had t.b. and *I* was the nurse.

Once during my first week, I asked Kimi how she could lie in her bed so entirely immobile hour after hour. She said in her gentle way, "It is not difficult. In my mind, I am torturing the nurses." She only meant Granite Eyes, Gravy Face, Mrs. Macklevenny and Miss Garnet, of course. The rest of the nurses were unfriendly but not unkind. A few were darlings.

The darlings were Miss Hatfield; Katy Morris, of course; Ann Robinson, who came to The Pines the same day I did, was tall, dark, beautiful and gentle and after nursing us for seven months, contracted miliary tuberculosis and died in two months; and Molly Hastings, an English nurse, who had been at The Pines for two years but was still sweet and friendly to the patients and had a wonderful sense of humor.

Molly told us some of the trials of being a nurse at The Pines. She said that the discipline was not limited to the patients as the nurses were not allowed to smoke on the premises, had to be in every night by ten-thirty, were required to attend school three nights a week and were under twenty-four-hour surveillance to be sure that they obeyed these rules and many others, including no indulgence in SEX, thoughts of SEX, actions which might eventually lead up to SEX, discussions of SEX or literature concerned with SEX. She said that with the exception of the charge nurses, the nurses weren't allowed to speak to the doctors, which made it rather difficult as she and one of the staff doctors were engaged. She said, "If it weren't for Larry I wouldn't stay ten minutes in this nunnery."

Molly told us that only unattractive nurses were sent to the men's hospital because of SEX. We asked her if many of the nurses married patients and she said that many of them did. "And after all," she said, "what could be better? A sick man and a nurse to look after him the rest of his life." "You mean the men patients marry those ugly nurses?" Kimi asked horrified. "Sure," Molly said. "Anything looks good to you if you're sick enough." "A fellah'd have to be unconscious before he'd want Gravy Face," Eileen said. "Oh, she had a young man," Molly told us. "He worked in x-ray but he died before they got married." "Probably poisoned himself," Eileen said bitterly. "Jesus, imagine having t.b. and her too!"

⇛IX⇚

Kimi

WHEN I HAD been at The Pines almost three weeks, I realized that though Minna and Eileen and I seemed to be improving, Kimi was gradually disintegrating, hour by hour, joint by joint. She looked well, on the surface at least, with cheeks as plump and ruddy as winter pears, thick shiny hair and clear bright eyes, and her appetite was excellent. But for over a week, every morning and every evening when the Charge Nurse or House Doctor made their rounds, Kimi reported some slight ailment.

Sometimes it was a pain in the joint of her little finger, sometimes a little headache, "some prickle" in the leg, "small thumping in the heart." But always something. This morning it had been a "little stiffness in the large toe" and a dramatic closing of the eyes in pain when the Charge Nurse manipulated the toe.

I was worried, for I had heard gruesome sanatorium stories of the always fatal miliary tuberculosis that attacked every part of the body. At dinnertime, like a fool, I asked Charlie if he knew anything about miliary tuberculosis. He clicked his false teeth with pleasure over the really bad news he was about to impart and told me of seeing the chest x-rays of a patient who had died of miliary tuberculosis. "Lungs was so full of holes they looked like strainers," he said, "and the fellah in x-ray told me that there wasn't a part of that poor girl's body that wasn't just riddled with germs. Just riddled!"

During rest hours I stared at the cold green walls and saw Kimi's plump brown body riddled with germs, her lungs like strainers. By suppertime my depression was so great I couldn't stand it any longer. In a voice loaded with tenderness and concern, I asked Kimi if she thought her tuberculosis had suddenly become virulent and was causing all the little extra aches and pains. Slowly taking a large bite of pudding before answering, Kimi said, "Oh, no, Betty, it is not the tuberculosis. It is the lesson. Every lesson tells me they need my bed for someone else so I am making sure they know I also need it."

The lessons on tuberculosis were informative and helpful. They explained to us why we felt as we did, what tuberculosis was and what the cure was, but they also pointed out with irritating frequency that we were only there on sufferance.

"If you cannot do these things, go home at once and let us have the room for someone who will be of value" (Lesson I). "The obligation, then, upon you is the greater, for you are occupying a bed badly needed for someone else" (Lesson II). "Your conduct throughout your stay should show that you are grateful to the nurses, to the doctors" (Lesson III). "The careless patient is not conscientious and lacks Character, is a danger and is of no value to the Community. If he will not learn he should be sent home" (Lesson IV). "A patient who does not rest properly is not conscientious, and a patient who is not conscientious in following treatment should not be allowed to occupy a bed that is badly needed by someone who has not yet had a chance to make good" (Lesson VII). "The patient who does not take kindly to instruction and who does not set a good example to other patients, is occupying a bed that could be used to better advantage for some more deserving person" (Lesson XI). "Do not argue, and if you cannot obey the rules do not stay here and kick about them, but go home" (Lesson XXI).

The meat in Lesson V was: If you had a broken leg you wouldn't dance on it nor walk on it but would have a plaster cast or splints on it so that you couldn't use it even if you were foolish enough to try. If you had a sore on a joint or a knuckle, you would know that constant bending would break the sore open and prevent its healing quickly. When you have tuberculosis you have broken lungs with sores on them and the less you use them the quicker they will heal. How can you rest your lungs? By breathing less often and less deeply. A person resting quietly in bed, breathes two times less each minute than a person sitting up and of course much less than a person walking. Deep breathing, hurried breathing and excitement, cause both lungs and heart to work faster and to wash out more poisons from the tuberculous sore. This is what gives you that tired feeling, rapid pulse, fever, etc. Rest is the answer. Rest, rest and more rest.

The lesson ended with, "The cure of tuberculosis is not medicine but a new regime of living, not only during the sanatorium period, but for years and years, maybe for a lifetime afterwards."

Kimi finished reading her lesson, tossed it to the foot of her bed and said, "If that 'new regime of living' means cabbage for the rest of my life I would prefer death." Cabbage is a vegetable rich in vitamin C, easy to grow in this moist cool climate, procurable in winter and sure to produce indigestion in bed patients. We had it every day in some form. I didn't mind because I was fond of cabbage and had come to accept indigestion, along with continual cold and perpetual hunger, as accouterments of tuberculosis. But Kimi loathed cabbage, yet was so certain that leaving it uneaten on her tray meant that she would be sent home to die, that she ate it all every day, with tears in her eyes and moaning, "Cabbage are hahrrible medicine."

Other hahrrible medicine to Kimi were the once-a-week baths and once-a-month shampoos. The bathing and shampoo schedules, as was everything at The Pines, were established to keep the patient clean with the least possible amount of rest disturbance, for even such small things as a bed bath or a shampoo could and did increase the pulse and temperature of a sick patient. "But do they not realize that germ flourish on feelth?" Kimi asked angrily, as she dipped her small brown feet into her wash basin.

On bath days she began her preparations early. First she got out all the necessary equipment, then with her hair pinned into a hard black knot on top of her head, a towel around her shoulders, and looking just like a Japanese wrestler, she would sit crosslegged on her bed, manicuring her toenails. She seemed to have no bones in her legs for she would pick up a foot, turn it over and examine the sole with as much ease as though it weren't attached to her. Kimi's bath partner was a Japanese girl but when she returned from the bath, gleaming and beet red, and we asked about her, Kimi said, "She is a girl of no character," and refused to discuss her.

Eileen's bath partner was the very sick girl who had to be taken to and from the bathroom on a bed. Eileen had said, "Jesus, honey, wouldn't you know I'd draw some dame about to croak, for a bath partner? 'And how are you today?' I says to her. 'Ugh,' she says, looking at the ceiling. 'How long you been here?' I asks as I washed my face in the icewater old Granite Eyes had given me. 'Ugh,' she says, closin' her eyes. 'And an ugh to you and many of them,' I says. I didn't even learn the dame's name."

"Her name is Mrs. Fox," Kimi said. "She is very sick but they are trying to save her."

"What for?" Eileen asked.

"What are they trying to save any of us for?" Kimi wanted to know. "We will never be well and strong again."

"We may not be very strong," Eileen said, "but we manage to say something besides 'ugh.' That dame belongs on an Indian Reservation."

I asked Kimi where she had gleaned her information about our never being well and strong again. She said that she had heard it from other patients who had left The Pines apparently cured and had come back within the year, desperately sick.

I asked the nurse, Molly, about this and she told us that the patients who had breakdowns and came back were usually foolish patients who stopped taking pneumothorax, didn't report to the clinic, kept late hours, and didn't take care of themselves generally. She said that she knew hundreds of arrested t.b. cases who were married, had children, were working and living absolutely normal lives and were in much better health than most of the people who had never had t.b. and consequently didn't know how to take care of themselves.

Minna said, "If Ah eveh get out of heah, Ah'll neveh be well again Ah know. Ah don't know why Ah had to be so little and weak—everyone else in mah family is big and strong." Eileen said, "Oh, on every apple tree there's always one little wizened-up rotten one."

On October nineteenth, Kimi and I were moved. Just after rest hours the Charge Nurse suddenly materialized in our room and without a word put my chair on the foot of the bed and wheeled me up the hall into a cubicle on the east side of the building. I was pleased, for the last week had been very tedious and any change was welcome. I said to the Charge Nurse, "Oh, I'm glad you moved me today." She said only, "I have put you near the office where I can give you more supervision." Then, "I'm putting Miss Sanbo in with you, if you don't mind." Mind! I was delighted. She said, "Some people would object to sharing a room with an Oriental." I said that I would prefer it, so she went to get Kimi.

Our new little room was just large enough for our two beds, placed with the heads to the windows and tight against each wall, our bedside stands and chairs. By stretching only a little we could pass things to each other. The walls were the same mildewed green but there wasn't much of them for the front of the tiny room was mostly doorway, the back was all windows and the walls, like screens, began a foot off the floor and were only about six feet high. They were apparently made out of some kind of light plywood, for I could hear the woman in the next room breathing. She rattled faintly when she breathed, like an Indian basket Mother used to have that had a hollow bottom filled with little dry seeds.

It was strange to have anyone so close to you. When she took a drink of water I swallowed. When she turned the pages of a magazine it was as though I had turned them. "How cozy this is," I thought and made motions to Kimi to show her how close the woman was. Kimi made motions back to show me that she also had an unseen, unknown person half an inch away and we smiled at each other delightedly.

Our delight was short lived, however, for at suppertime my close companion, the Rattling Breather, coughed, gagged, cleared her throat, snuffled, snorted and spit all through supper. She was so close to me that sometimes involuntarily I covered my mouth when she coughed. It was horrible. Like having a Siamese twin. But one with far-gone tuberculosis and no sense of delicacy. I was making signs of disgust and nausea to Kimi when the woman across the hall from us threw up.

Having been taught since early childhood that no matter how sick I was I could control myself until I got to the bathroom, I couldn't get used to the complete abandon with which people at The Pines threw up. I did notice a preponderance of throwing up at suppertime and wondered if the beautiful thoughts had anything to do with it. That evening it had

been: "Little things affect little minds." "You don't say,"
I said angrily as I took a bite of scalloped potato and the
woman in the next bed prepared to clean out her entire
respiratory system.

Across the hall from us, in a room exactly like ours, were
two patients. One was small and yellow and whispered
constantly in spite of a large SILENCE sign pinned to the head
of her bed. The other, dark and buxom, had thrown up. I
noticed that the small, sallow one ate her supper while the
nurse swabbed off the other one. I also tried to put mind
over matter but I couldn't. I drank some tea and pushed
the tray away. Kimi did the same. She said, "I seem to
find vomiting stranger more repulsive than vomiting dear
friend like Sylvia."

When the Charge Nurse made rounds she said, "But you
haven't eaten your supper, either of you. Was the moving
too much for you?" She intimated that if it was she would
move us right back again. I motioned to the woman next
to me, who was just getting to work on her right bronchopulmonary lymph node. Kimi said, "The woman across the
hall was sick just as I began to eat." The Charge Nurse
said, "Oh, but we can't let little things like that bother us.
We have to learn to ignore them. Now eat!" Her voice was
gentle but she twisted our arms with her eyes.

I found that cold scalloped potatoes are even harder to eat
to the accompaniment of spitting than warm ones, so after
that I ate everything quickly and while it was warm. We
were nearer the kitchen now and the food was a little warmer.
The Charge Nurse was right, of course. My repulsive Siamese twin continued to clean out her nasal passages at mealtimes and the woman across the hall threw up at least every
other day, but after the first night Kimi and I didn't miss a
meal. Little things didn't bother us.

By lights out that night, Kimi and I had learned: We
could not see out the windows ever from our new room be-

cause of the location of the beds and the heavy windshields
over the heads of the beds, but that at mealtimes we could
see, through the windows on the opposite side of the hall,
the waters of the Sound and some madroña trees, the huge
sleeping porch and the children's hospital; it was much colder
and draughtier in the cubicles; we were much more closely
watched by the Charge Nurse; we missed Eileen and we
could not hear the radio because the patient nearest the
switch was an inspirational patient who would not turn it up.
The music swelled and fell with the wind, like parade music,
and the plays were like listening to a conversation in the next
booth in a restaurant: " . . . the axe . . . Joe . . . help! . . .
he said he couldn't help it . . . I have the head. . . ."

That night Katy brought us a long impassioned note from
Eileen. It said in part, "I have bawled ever since you kids
left. We have two new patients. An old dame who coughs
all the time and a skinny little dame with a Silence sign on
her bed. Minna's Southern accent has gotten so thick since
the new patients came that she sounds like they dug her out
of the Mississippi yesterday. Jesus, honey, how I hate that
dame! . . . After supper the Old Dame wheeled me down to
her office for another little talk. 'Miss Kelly you must not
read. Miss Kelly you must not talk. Miss Kelly you must
rest.' She nags me just like my Gramma used to. How I'd
like to get out of this dump! Minna says now that she thinks
it will take her 'lil ole lungie wungies about seven yeahs to
heal. . . .' I told her she'd better heal a little quicker or
some day ole Sweetie-Pie would look under another board
and find himself another wife. Jesus, did she burn!"

Kimi said, "Poor little Eileen, she doesn't understand tuberculosis at all. She will die, I fear." I said sharply, "Kimi,
don't be so depressing," but I knew she was right.

With the move, my bath day had been changed to Monday,
which meant that my bath would be hurried and scant, as
the nurses were overworked and impatient on Monday, and

I would be dirty for both visiting days. It was raining, a violent splattery rain and I thought longingly of hot tub baths and scalding showers, as I got out my clammy bath towel and damp lumpy bath powder.

Kimi lay in her bed with her eyes closed and two long sticks extending from each nostril. That morning her complaints had been "prickle in the nostril and a small pain in the head." She had told me confidently that she would soon get aspirin and a large pitcher of fruit juice, the sanatorium treatment for colds. Instead, the new young doctor had returned and stuck silver nitrate swabs in each of her nostrils. He had winked at the Charge Nurse and instructed Kimi to leave the swabs in her nose for at least half an hour. She looked like an enraged Burmese dancer.

A wheelchair creaked past. I looked up expectantly but it was only another throat-light patient. Kimi and I had learned from Kate that the Silence signs were not punishment, as we had thought, but meant that these patients had laryngeal tuberculosis and probably ulcerated vocal chords. They were given Alpine Light treatments in their throats every morning. The light room was a small room directly across from the Charge Nurse's office and Kimi told me that in addition to its use for throat light, it was used as the last gasping place for the dying patients. She said, "If they take you in there, Betty, be sure you have made your will."

In spite of Kimi's gloomy talk, no one had died during the time I had been at The Pines. There was Margaretta, a beautiful Negro girl in one of the private rooms, who took throat light, and every time she went by Kimi said, "This will probably be her last trip," and even Katy admitted that her case was hopeless, but so far she had held her own.

That morning Margaretta had waved at us as she went by and even though she was thin, I had thought she looked cheerful and very much alive. Not at all like Camille or "poor little Beth." I had remarked on it and Kimi had said,

"Those bright eye and that rosy cheek are not health—it is the disease."

The rain splatted on. My bed was as cold and damp as an empty house. Gravy Face had filled our morning hot-water bottles and had thrown them at us, cool and dripping. There is nothing as cold as a cold, metal hot-water bottle. I kicked mine petulantly down between the end of the bed and the mattress. Kimi said, "I am thinking that from now on I will be very well." A wheelchair careened into our cubicle and Gravy Face said, "Patients are not allowed to talk, Miss Sanbo." To me, "Hurry up, you, I've got four more baths to do this morning."

She stuffed me into my robe and slippers and off we went, banging from wall to wall, crashing into a trusting little new nurse so hard we almost snapped her legs off at the ankles, and slamming through the bathroom door. She rammed the wheelchair into the bed and I climbed thankfully out and began to undress. While I undressed, Gravy Face filled my little tub with tepid water, then went thundering off down the hall to change the sheets on my bed.

My new bath partner was a gray-faced girl with toothpick legs and no voice. Her name was Beryl Hanford and she was very sick and on absolute silence, but she talked incessantly. While we washed our faces, Beryl told me in a hoarse whisper, that her name was Beryl; that she had t.b. of the throat, lungs, stomach, intestines and kidneys; that she thought The Pines stank; that she thought the food at The Pines stank; that she thought the nurses at The Pines stank; that she thought the doctors at The Pines stank; that the eggs at The Pines stank. She said, "I never eat nothing but what Chet brings me from home. Yesterday he brought me a whole roasted chicken and twelve chocolate eclairs [she called them "eeeclears"] and that's all I'm gonna eat until next Thursday."

I asked her how she managed to keep food in her stand as

it was absolutely forbidden. She said, "Oh, I wrap it all up in my clean pajamas." I asked her how she got t.b., although I really didn't care, and thought she deserved it. She said, "I was workin' in a candy factory dippin' chocolates and one day I had a hemorrhage." I asked her if she had had a cough. She said, "Oh, God, yes, for years and years. I never thought nothing of it." I thought something of it. I thought of all those chocolates she had dipped and sprayed with germs.

Beryl was so stupid, so uncooperative and so ungrateful that in comparison Gravy Face seemed like an angel of mercy as she knocked me around, finally forcing me into clean pajamas while I was so wet and soapy that when I climbed back into bed I pulled and snapped as if I had been dipped in glue. I told Kimi about Beryl. She said, "Oh, I know that one. I have been to x-ray with her several time. She is ogly and ignorant and she will die very soon. With t.b. of the throat she will probably choke to death," she finished pleasantly.

The next day Kimi had her first shampoo. Our hair was supposed to be shampooed once a month but if there were many new patients and the nurses were busy we sometimes had to wait six weeks. A shampoo at The Pines had absolutely nothing in common with a beauty parlor shampoo, with its setting of waves, pin curls and hair styling. A shampoo at The Pines meant a good scrubbing with green soap, a slight rinse and a thorough drying with the hot forceful blower. What you did with your hair afterwards was your problem.

Kimi, red-faced and furious, jerked the comb through her thick black hair. "It is like a whisk broom. Only the blowtorch would curl it now." She put on a woolen hood and saved the sugar from her supper tray. That night after lights out she mixed up a solution of sugar and water in her water glass, wet strands of hair in it and rolled them up on curlers. The next morning she had to chip the curlers off and she said combing her hair was "like raking weed." To make it worse, the effect was not a soft curl as Kimi had anticipated but more like black uncoiled springs distributed over her head. As it was very obvious that she had done something to her hair other than a simple combing or brushing, Kimi had to wear her hood all that day.

It was one of those days with the rain thrown at us at intervals like some giant sprinkling clothes and by night our pillows and all of us that was outside the covers was damp. Very damp. Kimi went to remove her hood, before going to sleep, and found that it was stuck to her hair. She ripped it off angrily and left little blue wool tufts on the springy curls. She brushed and combed vigorously, but the wool stuck and her hair merely straightened out in gluey hunks.

I suggested that she confess to the Charge Nurse and maybe get another shampoo. Kimi said, "Nevair. They would throw me out to die. I am the object lesson these patient have needed for a long time." I told her I was sure that a patient had to do something much more serious than dipping his hair in sugar and water in order to be evicted from The Pines but Kimi said, "Yes, but you are not sure and I cannot afford to be the test case."

For one month she suffered with the sticky hair, peeling her head off the pillow in the morning and peeling her hood off her hair at night. Then she had another shampoo and came back from the bathroom, red-faced, and furious, with her hair exploding from her head. As she forced the comb through it she looked at me with flashing black eyes and said, "I am contemplating the sugar again."

On October twentieth, I had my first x-ray and my first trip through the tunnels of The Pines. The x-ray laboratory was underground somewhere between the Administration Building and the Bedrest Hospital. To get there I was taken in a wheelchair via elevator to the basement of the Bedrest

Hospital, then wheeled rapidly down hills and around curves in a lighted cement tunnel, until we came to a door labeled X-RAY.

The patient to be x-rayed had to strip to the waist no matter what his sex and stand in the large x-ray room and assume different poses, while the technician and the two assistants took the x-rays.

At first I was horribly embarrassed as I stood with hands on hips, but no tops to my pajamas, bending right and left and raising the right and then the left arm. I soon got used to it, however. At The Pines nobody cared about any part of your body but your lungs. Kimi said that when they first x-rayed her they laid her on a marble slab and x-rayed her in one-inch strips. She said, "It was like a hahrrible nightmare with those alien male eye and alien male patient putting chalk mark on my naked back. Now I am like a native of Bali and feel fully dressed with only a skirt."

On October twenty-eighth, a wild and stormy Sunday morning, the Charge Nurse came into our cubicle and said, "Mrs. Bard, you have been here one month today. The doctor says that you may read and write for fifteen minutes a day and you may walk to the bathroom once a day." She smiled and said, "I have brought you the Sunday papers. Do not exceed the time."

A few minutes ago our little room had been cold and depressing with the wind howling through the windows, the rain splatting on the sills, the green walls dank and confining. Now, with my first assurance that I was getting well and the delightful prospect of walking to the bathroom, the whole picture changed. I turned on my bed lamp and snapped open the funny papers. How cozy everything seemed.

I looked over at Kimi busily writing a letter, at the two women across the hall reading the Sunday papers, at the brisk efficient nurses whisking past the door. From the diet kitchens came the cheery clatter of trays being emptied, dishes being stacked. The elevator doors clanged, there was the pleasant male rumble of a doctor's voice and the creak of a wheelchair. A sharp puff of wind and a dash of rain sent me further under the covers but I didn't mind. I read the papers and thought what a pleasant place The Pines was to be in on a stormy Sunday morning.

Like everything else, walking to the bathroom was governed by rules. A patient enjoying this privilege put on her robe and slippers right after breakfast and sat on the edge of her bed until the patient across the hall, or whoever she was to follow, had returned from the bathroom. Then very slowly, and looking neither to right nor left, she walked to the bathroom.

In the bathroom, patients were not supposed to speak but of course did. On my first trip I was assisted by a nurse. She happened to be friendly and told me who each patient was on the west side of the corridor. When we passed the four-bed ward Eileen waved lustily, even though the Charge Nurse was in there making rounds.

In the bathroom that first morning I met a small brown-haired girl named Myra, who told me that she had been at The Pines on complete bedrest for three years, that she had cavities the size of teacups in both lungs, that she was taking bilateral pneumothorax, that she had been married just six months when she got sick, that she hated all the food at The Pines and was hoping for a "thoro." (The nurse explained that this was a thoracoplasty operation in which a small section of all the ribs on one side was removed—thus making that side very much smaller and effecting a permanent collapse of the lung.)

Myra asked Kimi and me if we were taking any kind of treatment or had had any operations. We said no and she said that was too bad but that sometimes cases were so far gone they didn't dare try anything. Kimi said angrily, "A patient who was that far gone would not be walking to the bathroom." Myra said, "Oh, they try to make the last months pleasant for bad cases." She left then, taking her large cavities and her black outlook with her.

Sylvia was also in the bathroom. She said that she had had a phrenic operation and didn't cough at all now. We asked her what a phrenic operation was and she said that it meant crushing the nerve that controlled the diaphragm so that the diaphragm pressed up against the lower part of the lung and caused a partial collapse. She was hoarse and breathless. She said that her stomach pains were much better since she had been put on an enteric diet. She was sweet and cheerful but painfully, horribly thin and it made Kimi and me ashamed of our fat faces and well-filled bathrobes. Sylvia said that Marie still had a temperature and so hadn't been given the bathroom privilege.

In the bathroom also were the little girl of thirteen and the old woman of seventy-eight. The old woman said, "Nothing sets with me but tea. Everything else repeats on me and gives me gas." She pronounced it "gazz." The little girl had round scarlet cheeks and said nothing. The old lady said, "I've got so much gazz on my stummick I can't sleep. The Charge Nurse don't do nothing about it. She don't care because she's up and around, not laying in bed with pains."

The little girl giggled behind her hand, then coughed. Her cough was deep and resonant and didn't sound like a child's cough at all. It left her shaking and leaning against the bed. I recognized the cough. It was the one we used to hear from the four-bed ward. The old lady said, "Just listen to that. They don't do a thing for that poor child. Just stick her in a bed and leave her to die." The little girl looked at Kimi and smiled. She didn't speak.

On the way back from the bathroom, Eileen was waiting for us. She was kneeling at the foot of her bed leaning out into the hall. As we went by she hissed, "Only four more days and I get moved and walk to the bathroom. Jesus, honey, you should hear Hush-mah-mouth now. She goes on about her symptoms all day long. I wish they'd put her on silence." Kimi and I waved and smiled and walked as slowly as we could. Minna waved too and said, "Ah wish Ah was big and strong like you two. Kimi, you'ah fat as a pig." Eileen said, "Here we go again. 'You'ah so big! You'ah so enorhmous! You'ah so fat! Ah'm so little! Ah'm so tiny! Ah'm such a goddamn little stinker!' " Minna said something but we were past the door and couldn't hear her.

In the room next to the four-bed ward were the little red-cheeked girl, who waved to us, and old Gazz-on-Her-Stum-mick who didn't. The name on the little girl's bed was Evangeline Constable. Next to them in a single room was a Miss Sigrid Hansen, a pretty blonde who stared at us unsmilingly as we went by. In the next double room were a red-haired girl with her eyes closed, her name plate covered by her robe, and a Mrs. Melville, who had on a yellow turban and large earrings and looked like an old Gypsy. Then came two little Japanese girls and judging by Kimi's averted head and narrowed eyes, they hadn't a shred of character between them.

Then I slowed my steps for I was coming to the cubicle next to ours, the home of Rattling Breather, and I wanted a good look at her. She was much younger than she sounded. Apparently in her early twenties. She had pale blond hair, small brown eyes, pongee-colored skin and was crocheting something large and orchid. She waved and smiled at us, showing a friendly spirit and far-apart little brown teeth. The name on her bed was Mrs. Helen Cranston. Her roommate was also young but dark and plump. Her name was Miss Charmine White. She was crocheting something large and black. "A shroud, perhaps," Kimi said softly to me as she smiled at Charmine.

In addition to being weighed once each month, our progress was checked by a blood sedimentation, urinalysis, x-ray, and sputum test. As the rest in bed made almost everyone gain weight and stop coughing, only by laboratory test and x-rays could the Medical Director determine each patient's progress or lack of progress.

Of this progress we were told nothing. The only way we could tell whether we were getting well or dying was by the privileges we were granted. If we were progressing satisfactorily at the end of one month we were given the bathroom privilege and fifteen minutes a day reading-and-writing time. At the end of two months, if we continued to progress our reading-and-writing time was increased to half an hour, we were allowed to read books and were given ten minutes a day occupational therapy time. At the end of three months we were given a chest examination, along with the other tests, and if all was still well we were given three hours' time up, one hour occupational therapy time and could go to the movies (if chosen by the Charge Nurse).

The time up began with sitting up in bed. Fifteen minutes the first day, twenty minutes the second day and increasing five minutes a day until the patient reached half an hour; then fifteen minutes a day in the morning and fifteen minutes in the evening, increased five minutes a day until an hour was reached. Then the patient was taken to the porch to sit in a reclining chair morning and evening and the time was increased ten minutes a day until the three hours was reached. At that time, if the progress was still good, the patient was sent to the Ambulant Hospital.

Lesson VI had stated: "There is no advantage in gaining weight rapidly as it only throws extra work on the sick lung. You should gain in weight slowly and gradually, keeping pace with improvements in your lung, until you have reached the weight that is normal for your height and age. Therefore, do not stuff. *Do not be a pig.*"

Kimi was hurt and thought the lesson had been directed at her for she had gained five pounds. I had gained three and Eileen wrote us a violent note telling us that there was now no point in her getting out of The Pines as she had gained twelve pounds and wouldn't fit any of her usherette uniforms. Kimi wrote back, "You should complain. Already a giant among my own people, I now face a life of lonely spinsterhood."

I had been at The Pines a month and it was Sunday and a visiting day. On the stroke of two I opened my eyes and there were Anne and Joan and Mother. Anne and Joan had on new dark blue coats and their own shining faces and were beautiful.

Anne said, her eyes filling with tears, "I would like to kiss you." Joan said, "I can do a figure eight on my roller skates." Anne said, "The nurse said that we couldn't even touch your bed." Joan said, "I can do a figure eight on my roller skates."

I said, "Don't you think this is a beautiful hospital, girls?" Anne said, "It smells!" Then added tactfully, "Like medicine. When can you come home, Mommy?" Joan said, "When you come home you can see me do a figure eight on my roller skates." Kimi's family came in then and the children were fascinated and had to be turned around and faced in my direction.

I asked about school and Anne told me about what "a terrible cheater Charlie Thomas is but the teacher loves him so much she lets him cheat—even helps him," which sounded unlikely. Joan asked, "What is cheating?" I said, "Oh, asking other people to help you with your work, copying off other children's papers, looking in the book during tests." Joan said, "Oh, I do those things all the time. Everybody does. Only I get so mad at Marilyn because when I copy her arithmetic paper she has all the answers wrong. I did two figure eights on my roller skates yesterday." Anne said,

"Oh stop talking about those old figure eights." Joan said, "Well, Grandmother told us not to talk about being Japanese." Then the Charge Nurse came and the ten minutes were up. The children threw me kisses and went away with the nurse, taking my heart with them.

After supper, in that most depressing and lonely time of day, early evening, the radio seemed possessed and concentrated on tunes lie "Sonny Boy," "My Buddy" and "Boy of Mine," all played on the organ. Our little room was morbidly quiet and sorrow was heaped in my corner like dirty snow.

I was staring at the ceiling and going over a little scene in which Anne went from door to door in patched shoes taking orders for greasy doughnuts that I baked at home and Joan skated in the street to show me how she could do a figure eight on her roller skates and was hit by a truck, when Kimi said, " I would rather have beautiful children I could see but once a month than ogly little monster I could see all the time."

Kimi's mother and father and brother came every visiting day, crowned with happiness and sagging with presents. New robes, sweaters, bed jackets, ribbons for Kimi's hair, bath powder, toilet water, Japanese Sembi (a wonderful little shiny brown cracker, that tasted like a mixture of pretzels and peanuts), fried chicken in shoyu sauce, fruit, candy, apples and magazines. Although they always spoke in Japanese and I could not understand what they said, I detected a slight note of imperiousness in Kimi's attitude toward her family.

That day she had lain back on her pillows, a pale yellow bed jacket tied close under her chin, a yellow satin ribbon holding back her thick dark hair, a great mass of white chrysanthemums by her bed, looking like a very beautiful Oriental princess directing her slaves. I asked her about this. She said, "Sometime they bring me the gift with little fuss. Sometime I have to twist their arm a little."

Kimi was twelve years younger than I, but rooming with her taught me that intellectually we were equals, emotionally she was my superior. I was her superior in experience only. She said that this was not true. That it was just that she was Japanese and used to obeying without question. She said that as a first step in teaching me to emulate the Japanese, she would teach me the language.

She worked hard at this but eight months later, when I left The Pines, all I could say in Japanese were Good-morning, Good-night, How are you today and She is not my friend. I taught Kimi French and when she left The Pines she was reading *Sans Famille* and *La Tulipe Noire*, but her conversations with me were limited to "L'oiseau est sur l'arbre," or "Où est le crayon?"

⇒⇒X⇐⇐

A Smile or a Scar

LESSON IX EXPLAINED the most common surgical methods used at The Pines to arrest tuberculosis. These were:

Artificial Pneumothorax—compression of the affected lung by the introduction of gas or filtered air into the pleural cavity (between the chest wall and the lung). Refills of air were first given every other day, then twice a week, once a week, once every two weeks, once a month, finally every four to six weeks. Pneumothorax was to be continued for a period of from two to four or more years.

Bilateral Pneumothorax—compression of both lungs by pneumothorax. Actually only a portion of both lungs was collapsed and patients taking bilateral pneumothorax, though short of breath, could lead moderately active lives.

Intrapleural Pneumolysis—cauterizing of adhesions between the chest wall and the lung. Such adhesions prevented a satisfactory collapse of the lung.

Thoracoplasty—removal of the ribs on one side of the thorax to accomplish a permanent collapse of the affected (diseased) part of that lung. This type of surgery was necessary when pleural adhesions prevented successful pneumothorax. The mortality rate in thoracoplastic surgery was so low as to be almost nonexistent.

Phrenicotomy—division or crushing of the phrenic nerve

146

on one side causing elevation of the corresponding diaphragm, thus compressing the lower part of the lung on that side.

Extrapleural Pneumothorax—stripping the pleura from the chest wall (extrapleural pneumolysis) to form a pocket for pneumothorax or the use of oil (oleothorax). This operation, not altogether successful, is now seldom used, and was referred to by the patients as a "stripping," and tactlessly explained by one of the nurses as "being similar to the operation performed by the butcher in making a pocket for stuffing in a roast." Extrapleural pneumothorax was used when the involvement was not sufficient to warrant thoracoplasty but too many adhesions were present for intrapleural pneumolysis.

A successful collapse of the lung, whether it was accomplished by pneumothorax, thoracoplasty, phrenicectomy or stripping, favored rest for the infected part of the lung and facilitated healing of the disease. Collapsed lungs, being immobile, naturally healed more rapidly than working lungs, even though the working was kept at a minimum by complete bedrest. As the Medical Director had explained, collapsing a lung was like putting a splint on a broken leg.

Other forms of surgery now in use and new since my time include:

Pneumonectomy—removal of the entire affected lung.

Lobectomy—removal of an infected lobe of the lung.

When we were discussing the lesson on surgery, we were informed by Charlie, the store girl, or some other bad news distributor, that people with pulmonary tuberculosis could not take ether. At the time, as I remember, I made inquiry as to what anaesthesia was used in place of ether and was given the impression that the doctors merely knocked the patients down and ripped out their lungs, or adhesions or ribs, without benefit of anything stronger than an aspirin.

As The Pines commanded the services of the finest doctors in the city I knew that this was ridiculous so I asked the

Charge Nurse about anaesthesia. She said that for pneumothorax and phrenicectomy and intrapleuralpneumolysis in-
jections of novocain were given; that a few patients were
allergic to novocain and took pneumothorax without anaesthesia which no doubt accounted for the no-anaesthesia-for-
anything rumor; that for major surgery such as thoracoplasty or "stripping," sodium pentothal and gas were used.

She said that thoracic surgery was a very wonderful accomplishment and without it many former patients now
maintaining good health and living normal useful lives, would
be dead.

The maxim on our supper trays that night was: "You are
not dressed for work until you wear a smile." "Or a scar,"
Kimi added.

On October thirtieth, a month and two days after I had
entered The Pines, a nurse appeared in our doorway at the
beginning of rest hours and ordered me to get ready for a
ride in a wheelchair. I asked her where I was going but she
said only, "Shhhhh!" and left. There was probably some
excellent reason for it, but the practise of coming for patients
in wheelchairs and not telling them where they were going,
or what was to be done to them, always seemed cruel and
senseless to me. A wheelchair brought to your bed could
mean the dentist, surgery, light treatments, examinations,
x-ray, fluoroscope, the movies, a lecture, dismissal, moving
to another hospital, a death in the family, any number of
things, generally unpleasant but never as unpleasant as the
not knowing, the speeding down corridors with racing pulse
and rocks in your stomach.

I knew that a wheelchair during rest hours usually meant
the treatment room. The treatment room for me! My
hands quivered like springs as I tried to tie my robe. I sat
weakly on the edge of the bed and phrases from the lesson
on surgery swooped around my head in a horrifying circle
like bats. "Phrenicectomy, thoracoplasty, bilateral pneumo-

thorax, collapse of both lungs." My heart pounded and my hands grew wet and clammy as I waited.

Kimi tried to comfort me. Her cheeks scarlet with excitement and apprehension, she said, "At least you know that anaesthetic have been discovered and whatever they do to you will be painless." I said, "Yes, but just the fact that they are going to do something to me must mean that I'm not getting well. Remember the lesson: 'There are cases that do not improve with rest, fresh air, and good food.'" We could hear the creak of the approaching wheelchair. Kimi said, "Breathe deeply quickly with both lung. It may be for the last time."

The nurse came in, I fumbled my way into the wheelchair like a trembly old lady, we rolled down the hall past the Charge Nurse's office, through large, double swinging doors and into the treatment room, where I was delivered wheelchair and all to the treatment room nurse, a Miss Welsh. Miss Welsh looked cheerful and proved both understanding and kind for she told me at once that I was to have artificial pneumothorax. She said, "For heaven's sake stop looking so scared, there's nothing to it."

The treatment room, a very large old-fashioned operating room, was divided into sections by white sheets hung on rods. Miss Welsh whispered that all new patients were started on pneumothorax by the Medical Director, that he was behind the curtains and was very irritable when operating. Indicating by rolled up eyes and a finger on her closed lips that I was to be absolutely quiet, or else, she disappeared behind the curtain.

The treatment room had windows to the ceiling, pure white walls and strong overhead lights and I sat in my wheelchair, absolutely quiet but blinking and squinting in the strong light and feeling like a mole that had suddenly burrowed out into the sunshine.

There were two other patients waiting. One was the

blonde with the gold tooth, who had brought washwater on my first morning at the sanatorium. She wore the same maroon sweater and was tatting something shrimp pink. She smiled but said nothing.

The other patient was a young man with thick straight dark hair, very sunken brown eyes and feverish red cheeks. His navy blue flannel robe had a blob of egg on the lapel and I could tell that he was a very new patient because his fingers were still brown with cigarette stains. He showed not a glimmer of interest in me, the blonde or his surroundings, but stared morbidly at a large black framed motto which read, "It's good to have money and the things money can buy —but it's good, too, to check up once in a while and make sure that you have some of the things money can't buy." "Like tuberculosis," I thought bitterly.

I was getting very sick of mottos and maxims and beautiful thoughts and as the minutes slogged by and there was no human sound from behind the white curtains, only occasional metallic clicks or the gushing sound of a faucet, I grew more and more apprehensive. "What were they doing behind there? Had something gone wrong? Why didn't somebody say something!"

I moved my wheelchair back a little but this only brought me face to face with another motto, "Worry, the interest paid by those who borrow trouble." I felt just like Eileen and wanted to shout rudely, "What knothead thought that up?" Just then the curtains parted and out came Little Miss Teacup Cavities of my first trip to the bathroom. She said goodbye to the Medical Director and Miss Welsh and was retrieved by a nurse from our ward who curtly took possession of my wheelchair.

Miss Welsh indicated that the feverish boy was next and that I was to sit down on a bench beside Gold Tooth. I was so scared I was practically in a coma. Pneumothorax! Collapse of the lung! I was sure that I would suffocate. I remembered with disconcerting vividness the time, when I was twelve years old, I had tried to crawl between the crossed supports of a diving platform and had become firmly wedged. I drew air into my lungs in great gulps as I recalled the horrible smothering sensation and the long breathless terrible minutes it took Cleve to free me.

I derived small comfort from the fact that everyone had told me that there was no sensation, no pain, to pneumothorax. Hadn't everyone told me that having a baby was just like a little case of indigestion? Indigestion maybe, but the kind you'd get from swallowing a cement mixer. I could now see the wall that had been behind me and it framed another motto. "Let thy speech be better than silence or be silent." Obviously somebody's mother had been scared by Bartlett's *Quotations*. I resolved to burn my copy the minute I got home.

The thin blonde began to cough, first, however, neatly laying down her tatting shuttle and covering her mouth with a paper handkerchief. When she had finished she put the used handkerchief into an envelope of heavy waxed paper, put the envelope into her sweater pocket, then picked up her shuttle again. I could feel a cough bubbling in my chest. I swallowed hard and concentrated on "a cough can be controlled," for in my hysteria I had forgotten my waxed paper envelope and clean paper handkerchiefs. It was very warm in the treatment room and as I controlled my cough I could feel my face turning a dark unhealthy red. A nurse opened the outside door and looked in at us. Apparently neither the blonde nor I was what she wanted, for after looking at my red face suspiciously for a minute or two, she shut the door again.

I grew fascinated with the blonde's tatting shuttle. It darted in and out of the shrimp pink like a dragonfly in a hollyhock. The pink thing was square and lacy and seemed to be some kind of a yoke. I had seen many such yokes displayed at county fairs and could easily picture it completed, its virulent color clutching the top of a too-short white cotton petticoat, cut on the bias and sucked in at the knees.

Miss Welsh finally emerged again from behind the white curtains and motioned to me. My heart gave a wild leap of fear but I got up and marched resolutely over to her. Whatever it was, I was willing to face it, to get it over. She helped me off with my robe and the tops of my pajamas and up onto an operating table. She told me to lie on my back with my left arm above my head, then painted the entire upper left half of me with mercurochrome.

The Medical Director was washing his hands over in the corner, his back to us. When he had finished washing the nurse handed him a pair of rubber gloves, which he put on without speaking. Then he poked me experimentally in the ribs, looked at my x-rays, examined my case history and said, "Yell if you want to but don't flinch!"

I felt the prick of the hypodermic needle, just under my left breast, then an odd sensation as though he were trying to push me off the table, then a crunchy feeling and a stab of pain. "There now," the Medical Director said, as he attached the end of what looked like a steel knitting needle to a small rubber hose connected to two gallon fruit jars partially filled with a clear amber fluid. The nurse put one jar higher than the other and I waited frantically for my breathing to stop and suffocation to start. There was no sensation of any kind for a few minutes then I had a pulling, tight feeling up around my neck and shoulder. The doctor said, "I guess that's enough for today," took the needle out, slapped a bandage on me and I got down from the table, dizzy with relief.

Climbing back into bed, I had a terrific, overwhelming desire for a cigarette. A cup of hot coffee and a cigarette. Laughing so that she would know it was just a little joke, I told the nurse but she looked disapproving and brought me two aspirin and some lukewarm water.

By suppertime I had sharp knifelike pains in my chest and had spit up a little blood. I excitedly reported these symptoms to the Charge Nurse and she immediately put my bed down flat and said that I was not to walk to the bathroom and was to eat all my meals lying down for three days. She then explained calmly that the pains were adhesions tearing loose, the blood was probably from my nose, that I was most fortunate to be able to take pneumothorax. She said the only reason I hadn't had pneumothorax as soon as I entered was because of the shadow on my right lung. She said that this shadow had cleared and I was a very lucky young woman.

Lying on my back, spilling tea and little slimy pieces of canned pear down my neck, it was difficult for me to see eye to eye with the Charge Nurse, especially as I had felt perfectly well without a single pain of any kind before I got so terribly lucky and was given pneumothorax. The maxim on my tray was: "I would rather be able to appreciate some things I cannot have than to have things I cannot appreciate."

From then on until I left The Pines, like all the great clan of "gas" patients, I was given a jigger of "gas medicine," a brackish-tasting liquid, before every meal.

For three days and nights, each time I moved I had severe tearing pains in my left lung. I took aspirin and tried to concentrate on feeling fortunate but succeeded only in feeling very tubercular.

Friday morning, just after temperatures and pulses, a strange man stopped at our door, read my name from a list he was holding, told me to put on my robe and slippers, helped me into a wheelchair and started toward the elevators. "Now what?" I asked myself, my fear-addled brain trying to recall the various forms of surgery used if pneumothorax was not successful.

When the elevator door had clanged shut, the man said,

"Ever been to fluoroscope before?" I said no, and he said, "You'll like it. You can talk and you'll see people from all over the hospital." My sigh of relief almost collapsed my other lung.

Before we had rounded the second bend of the tunnel leading to x-ray, we heard what sounded like the chirping and twittering of thousands of nesting birds. "Fluoroscope patients," the x-ray man explained. The noise was almost deafening as we rounded the last bend and came on about eighty patients, both men and women, but carefully sorted according to sex, sitting on benches along the walls of the tunnel and waiting to be fluoroscoped.

The x-ray man pushed my wheelchair to the door of the laboratory and callously left me facing the benches and the eighty strangers, who immediately stopped talking and unabashedly looked me over. Feeling like a pimply blind date and very conscious of my gray lips and uncombed hair, I lowered my eyes and examined the fingernails on my shaking left hand.

When the talking at last began again, I was sure much of it was about me but I was able to raise my eyes and observe. Most of the patients were young, in their teens and early twenties, and appeared robust and very healthy. The female patients from the Ambulant Hospital wore makeup and hair curled and arranged in slightly out-of-date fashions. The degree of out-of-dateness varied with the length of time the patient had been at The Pines and what had been in vogue when she entered. Most of the women were doing some form of fancywork and knitting needles, tatting shuttles, crochet hooks and embroidery needles flicked and darted as they talked.

The men just sat. This made them appear sadder and sicker than the women. All the patients were dressed in bathrobes or housecoats. The women's were floor length and bright colored. Coral, turquoise, pale green, bright red, electric blue, lavender, yellow, and of course magenta. The men's robes were short and drab. Dusty dark blue, maroon, earthy brown and gray. The men were combed and clean shaven and actually as fat, pink cheeked and bright eyed as the women, but they didn't make the same effort to look healthy and happy. They sat in dejected attitudes looking as unemployed and beaten as possible, and coughing and spitting constantly. It made me wonder if any occupational therapy other than spitting was provided for male bedrest patients.

From past experience with sick males, I knew that no form of occupational therapy, including how to make your own diamonds, would get a very enthusiastic reception, as a man's natural reaction to illness of any kind seems to be to see how big a stinker he can be and how much resistance he can muster against all forms of treatment. However, even the novelty of being a stinker must wear off after the first year, and it seemed to me that there should be something for those large idle hands to do. Something to bring a smile to those sad dejected faces, to lessen the tedium of the tuberculosis.

I was wondering what that something could be, when the door of the x-ray lab opened and Miss Welsh winked at me, jerked my wheelchair into pitch darkness, took off my robe and the tops to my pajamas and put a sheet around my shoulders. When my eyes had become accustomed to the dark, I saw that there were several doctors sitting facing the fluoroscope with their backs to me.

A door to the right of the fluoroscope opened and a girl came in, closing the door quickly behind her. She sat down in front of the fluoroscope, slipping the sheet from her shoulders as she did so. There was a buzzing noise and I could see her ribs and lungs. They looked just fine to me but the technician ran his finger over the plate on her right lung and the doctors grunted unintelligible things to each other. They told her to raise and lower her arm.

When she left it was my turn. The technician asked me my name, the House Doctor found my card, the technician ran his finger over the plate on my left side, I was told to raise and lower my arm, the doctors grunted unintelligible things to each other and it was over. Miss Welsh pushed me out into the hall again and over to the bench on the women's side, where they crowded over to make room for me.

The woman next to me was embroidering "When you come to the end of a perfect day" in bright orange yarn on a maroon velvet pillow. Just behind the word "come" she had already embroidered half of a large orange with spikes protruding from it. This puzzled me a good deal until she turned the pillow around and I realized that the prickly half-orange represented a sun setting behind a maroon horizon.

The Perfect Day woman was talking to a girl, who had a big heap of loose curls on top of her head and winked every time she spoke. She was crocheting something in ecru string. Perfect Day said, "I was talking to Bill, Thursday, and he said that the Charge Nurse wouldn't send Mervin to the dentist because he was going to die anyhow and the Institution don't want to waste their materials fixin' his teeth." Heap O'Curls winked and said, "And I've heard that the poor kids in the four-bed ward up in Bedrest are starving and the Charge Nurse just laughs when they ask for seconds." Perfect Day said, "It's a wonder to me that anybody gets out of here alive."

The girl on my other side was making a rag doll. It was supposed to be one of those long-legged French bed dolls but there had evidently been no pattern for the girl had made the body as long and thin as the legs and arms. The result looked like a squid. A tough delinquent squid with its face all pulled down on one side and bright orange hair exploding from its peaked head. The girl was attaching an arm and as she sewed she told her neighbor on the other side about a hemorrhage she had had at dinner before coming to The

Pines. "A cup full of blood!" she finished triumphantly and I wondered where and how she had measured it.

All the conversations were about operations, hemorrhages, ambulant patients who were to be sent back to Bedrest and bedrest patients who were to come to the Ambulant Hospital. I said to Perfect Day, "My, everyone certainly looks healthy!" She said, squinting as she threaded more orange yarn into her needle, "Don't let it fool you, honey, those red cheeks are t.b. flushes and only show germ activity."

Rag Doll leaned across me and said, "Hazel, I had a chest exam yesterday and if it's o.k. I'll get six hours and my clothes. Mama said she'd buy me a whole new outfit." Perfect Day said, "God, honey, I'm prayin' for you but I wouldn't count on it. Henry Welter had a chest exam last week and they sent him back to Bedrest this morning." The Rag Doll girl said, "Really! Oh, the poor kid!" They both sewed in silence for a minute or two in honor of poor Henry's memory.

A very attractive blue-eyed, dark-haired girl motioned to me. As she was sitting about ten people down the bench from me, in order to talk to her I had to lean forward. This almost got me Perfect Day's needle in my eyeball, so the dark girl moved up next to me. She said, "My name's Sheila Flannigan and my brother Red went to college with your sister Mary." I said, "Why I remember Red, but how did you know I was out here?" She said, "Molly Hastings told me." Sheila also told me that she had been at The Pines three months, had time up and was at the opposite end of Bedrest in a room with a former schoolmate of my sister Alison. I began to think that my sister Mary was right and that "practically everybody has tuberculosis."

Catching my eye over the Perfect Day pillow, Sheila said, "That, my dear, is occupational therapy. 'There's a little bit of the artist in each of us,'" she said, quoting someone in a high squeaky voice. Looking at the maroon pillow I thought,

"But what a tiny little speck in some people," and then the x-ray man came for me with the wheelchair.

As I climbed into bed, I realized with surprise that the unaccustomed noise and confusion had been tiring and it was nice to return to the peace of our cold little cubicle. Kimi wanted to hear about everything and during the turmoil of returning patients to their beds, I managed to tell her most of what had happened. When I finished she said plaintively, "You know, Betty, it seems to me that the institution is making a greater effort to save you than to save me." I laughed, which immediately drew a disapproving nurse to the doorway, for fluoroscope was over and the ward was again so quiet that a whisper sounded like a steam jet in full release.

On November twelfth, Kimi and I had a long bitter letter from Eileen. She had been moved into a room by herself. She said that she had thought that rooming with Minna was as low as you could get. Her exact words were, "Jesus, honey, it was like livin' under a stone with a grub but now I'm still under the stone but all alone." She said that the reason for the move was: "Gramma brought old Mrs. Walladay out with her last Sunday and Mrs. Walladay yelled so loud the nurses told her three times to be quiet and finally the Old Dame came down and raised hell and Gramma said, 'Ain't you ashamed, a big strong woman like you makin' fun of a pore old deaf lady!' Jesus, kids, I almost choked." So apparently had the Charge Nurse for she moved Eileen by herself. I felt very sorry for Eileen but didn't realize the extent of my sympathy until I was moved by myself on November fifteenth.

It all happened so quickly I didn't even have a chance to say good-bye to Kimi. I opened my eyes after rest hours and the next I knew I was in a cubicle by myself at the opposite end of the building. A few minutes later Kimi was wheeled past my door and a pathetic note from her that night informed me that she had been put in a room with the Japanese girl with no character. She said, "If not speaking will heal my lung I should be out of here within the week." The note ended, "Why did the Charge Nurse separate us? How could she perform such an act of cruelty?"

That's what I wanted to know so I asked her. She said, "It is better for the patients to move every so often. To adjust to different personalities. It is better for you to be by yourself." I loathed being by myself. It was dull and depressing and I found it impossible to adjust to my own personality.

My new little room was very comfortable with a window opening on a huge porch beside the bed, a radiator within easy reach, so that I could thaw out my feet occasionally in the early morning, and a delightful view of the Children's Hospital, the waters of the Sound and many trees. It was the first time since entering the hospital that I had been able to look out of a window and I found watching the writhing trees, the angry gray water and the driving rain very exhilarating for a day or two. Then I began to miss Kimi. I missed her gentle voice, her understanding and her acid tongue. Being alone made the whole day seem like the rest hours and I soon lost my feeling of high spirits and exuberant good health, and spent much of my time longing for the children and thinking about death.

There were six or seven beds on the porch and the patients in these beds were very quiet, almost immobile. It was undoubtedly because of the cold that they lay so very still under covers pulled high and tucked in, only their faces showing above the white spreads but to my morbid eye they seemed very sick, probably dying. At night when I lay wide awake, cold, lonely and sad, the beds looked like rows of white biers, and the patients' faces gleamed greenish white and dead in the pale reflected lights from the Administration Building.

Before coming to The Pines, death, if I thought of it at all, which was seldom, was something swift, awe inspiring, cataclysmic, dramatic and grand. Death was a lightning bolt, a flood, a fire, a hurricane, a train wreck, an airplane crash, a pistol shot, a leap from a high bridge.

When I had told this to Kimi one evening she had said, "Oh, that is not at all my idea of Death. To me Death is a lecherous, sly, deranged old man. His beard is sparse and stained. His eye are coarse lidded, red rimmed, furtive and evil. His loose red lip are slimy and drooling. He pants with anticipation. His partially opened mouth shows brown shaggy thread of tooth. He shuffles up and down the corridor at night, his malodorous, black robe dragging behind him."

I was horrified and told Kimi that she was morbid. She had said, "I cannot help it. Each time Margaretta or any other very sick patient passes our door I fancy I see Death's evil face peering around the corner. I think I see his black robe swirl through the doorway ahead of the wheelchair. I can see him hovering like a great bat over the emergency ward, the light room, the private room. I can hear him shuffling up and down the corridor at night." (He must have done his shuffling in the very early evening for Kimi closed her eyes on the stroke of nine-thirty and did not open them again until the washwater was delivered.)

Now that I was alone and had long sleepless hours to think, to listen and to observe, I thought Kimi's idea of death much more realistic than mine and I too began to see his evil peering face, to hear him shuffling up and down the corridors in the night. I'd awaken when the night nurse made rounds at about one or half past, and when the friendly yellow eye of her flashlight had darted off the ceiling and the soft pad of her retreating footsteps had been absorbed by the dark, I'd lie waiting. Stiff with dread. Then it would start. From far down the hall a cough—dry and rattling like seed pods in the wind. Then another nearer—gurgling and strangling and leaving the cougher gasping for breath. Then from across the hall a harsh deep cough with a strange metallic ring. Then the girl in the private room, the girl with skin the color of old snow, the girl with arms and legs like knobby sticks, whose voice was gone, would begin to gasp dreadfully. Involuntarily I'd try to help her until my tongue felt swollen, my throat ached, my lungs seemed crushed. "Hurry, hurry," I wanted to scream, because over it all I could hear the slow, sure shuffle of Death. Up and down the halls he went, never hurrying, knowing that we'd wait for him.

One morning the Charge Nurse said, "The night nurse reports that you do not sleep well, Mrs. Bard. Is something troubling you?" I said no, not any one thing. She said, "What kind of thoughts do you have before going to sleep?" I said with mistaken honesty, "I long for my children and I think about death." She said with horror, "Death! Why Mrs. Bard, how awful!" Then quickly recovering and jerking herself down so that not a speck of revealing human being showed, she said, "We do not allow patients of The Pines to think about death, or other unpleasant things. You must have pleasant cheerful thoughts." I said, "But I can't have cheerful thoughts when I'm by myself. I hate to be alone." She said, "It is better for you to be alone. You must have cheerful thoughts or I will report you to the Medical Director." I wrote to Kimi that night and told her that the institution was now controlling my thoughts. She replied, "If only they could. I look at my roommate and think of murder twenty-four hour a day."

From then on, while by myself, I spent the days trying to line up cheerful thoughts to mull over during the night. As I lay quietly assembling cheer, the two women in the next cubicle compared ailments. One of them had a liver that was crowding her tonsils; the other a uterus hanging by a thread. One had an ingrown toenail; the other a loose crown on her tooth. One of them belched and the other had pains because she didn't. One's sinus was so clogged she could not get any breath, the other had an empty tunnel from one ear to the other through which cold air whooshed, giving her ear-aches and other discomforts. One had fluid on her lung which had to be aspirated, the other was taking pneumothorax. They were each sure they were being given the wrong treatment and the wrong medicines.

One of the women had a sweet motherly voice and talked about her organs as though they were little friends. "Old Mr. Gall Bladder acting up this morning," she would say right after breakfast, or "All my little intestines are crowded today, I don't think they liked the salad we had last night." I could picture Old Mr. Gall Bladder pounding on her liver with his cane and all her little intestines with bibs on crowded around the table not liking the salad.

The other woman's insides were all little machines that didn't function. She was sure that if the Charge Nurse would only give her something to stir up her bile, the bile would start the wheels in her liver, the wheels in her liver would start the pistons in her stomach, the pistons in her stomach would generate enough juice to run her intestines, which would in gratitude wind around her uterus and keep it from dropping on the floor.

The thing that amazed me was how either of the women had ever gotten tuberculosis, because according to their conversation, for years and years before coming to The Pines, they had spent every day but Sunday in various doctors' offices and had grown so familiar with all germs that they should have recognized the tubercle bacilli and swatted them like gnats.

I was surprised the first time I saw Friendly Organs' visitors. I had thought of course that like her they would be dreary operation talkers and symptom discussers. But they weren't. They were hard bright women with lustreless dyed black hair, black sealskin coats, bright pink rouge, felt hats with vizors like policemen's hats, and big patent-leather purses. Their talk, loud and cheerful and punctuated with claps of laughter, was entirely about poker parties, drinking beer and people named Chet, Murphy and Vera. When they left, the air around Friendly Organs swirled with the musky scent of tuberoses and gardenias and the air around me swirled with pictures of the visitors at home in their one-room downtown apartments, drinking beer, opening cans of beans and being pinched on the behind by Chet or Murphy.

On the days when the poker players didn't visit Friendly Organs, a small man dressed all in black came and stood stiffly, like an exclamation point, at the foot of her bed for the two hours. I guessed that he was her husband but could not picture him fitting in with Chet, Vera and Murphy.

The woman with the Little Machine intestines had a husband and son who came every visiting day. They were as pale as oysters, dressed alike in brown belted overcoats, tan fedora hats, and yellow pigskin gloves, and looked like burglars. I was amazed therefore, on a day when my visitors were late and there was a sudden little block of quiet, to hear the older burglar say in a gentle, tender voice, "What did you have for dinner today, Sarah, honey?" Sarah said, "They had cabbage again and I'm all bloated up." Son said, "Gosh, Ma, you know you can't eat cabbage. It always talks back to you." The older burglar said, "Have they done anything for your sinus, honey?" Honey lowered her chin on her chest, belched, patted her stomach, looked at her husband accusingly and said, "See! Cabbage! It's just poison to me."

Every morning the Friendly Organs woman would tell the Charge Nurse that she needed a "good cleaning out," or something for her ingrown toenail. The Little Machine woman would ask for something to stimulate her "nasal drip." When the Charge Nurse came to me she dared me to complain about anything and I didn't dare. I was cold and lonely and hated tuberculosis but I had cheerful thoughts, By God. "And how are you this evening?" the Charge Nurse would ask, her eyes steely and forbidding. "Just splendid," I'd answer dutifully reciting my catechism. "Simply splendid."

⇒XI⇐

Deck the Halls with Old Crepe Paper!
Tra, La, La, La, La, Lala, La, La!

I HAVE ALWAYS liked any special day, be it Mother's Day, Groundhog Day or Bastille Day and the big full-bodied holidays like Christmas, Thanksgiving and Easter fill me so full of feeling and spirit that I can get tears in my eyes just looking at a fruitcake.

Lying in bed at The Pines day after day, week after week, month after month, engaged in pursuits such as listening to the split, splat, splat of the rain hitting the gutter outside my window or waiting my turn to have my lung collapsed, should have increased this feeling for holidays about a billionfold. It didn't. The days were all so exactly alike and followed each other with such monotonous regularity that I lost all interest in holidays as such.

I knew them only as "gas" day, bath day, fluoroscope day, visiting day, supply day or store day. It was in part infiltration into sanatorium life, divorce from normal living. It was also in part the childish self-centered attitude of an invalid. What I was doing, how I felt, what was to happen to me became more and more important to me as time went on.

At first when my visitors told me of happenings in the outside world I was vitally interested and relived each incident vividly with the telling. Then gradually, insidiously, like night mist rising from the swamps, my invalidism obscured

164

the real world from me and when the family told me tales of happenings at home, I found them interesting but without strength, like talk about people long dead. The only real things were connected with the sanatorium. The only real people, the other patients, the doctors, the nurses.

At home Thanksgiving had always been a delightful occasion even when we were being thankful for meatloaf shaped like a turkey. We thought about Thanksgiving, planned for Thanksgiving and talked of Thanksgiving for weeks beforehand, but the evening before the actual day was the best time of all. Then the house seethed with children and dogs, with friends and cooks, and with delightful smells of baking pies, turkey stuffing and coffee. Every time the doorbell rang we put on another pot of coffee and washed the cups and by the time we went to bed we were so nervous and flighty that when accidentally bumped or brushed against, we buzzed and lit up like pin-ball machines. Thanksgiving morning usually found us all quite nasty and with too many things planned for the oven, but even the fighting was fun. Warm, family fun.

At The Pines I awoke the morning before Thanksgiving to darkness and drumming rain and thought only, "Shampoo, today. I wonder which nurse I'll get." In the bathroom after breakfast, I overheard Sheila telling Kimi that we were having turkey and coffee without saltpeter for Thanksgiving dinner. "Thanksgiving?" I said. "When is it anyway?" "Tomorrow," Kimi said with obvious disgust. "Surely you have not forgotten how, with tear streaming from your motherly eye, you begged the Charge Nurse to let Anne and Joan come four day early so that you could see them on Thanksgiving." I remembered then and was lightheaded with joy at the prospect of seeing my darling Anne and Joan, but I had no feeling about Thanksgiving until after supper that night.

The ward was very quiet. The radio had been turned off and the smooth surface of the evening stillness was broken

only by the faraway clatter of the nurses washing nourishment cups and the dreary slip, slop of the rain. I tried to
read but kept losing my place and reading the same paragraph over and over again.

Every magazine story seemed to be about a girl who was
nauseatingly little, nauseatingly thin and said "Jeepers." As
I was only interested in stories about large plump women
with tuberculosis, and had always nourished an overwhelming desire to kick in the groin anybody, no matter how tiny,
who said "Jeepers," I threw the magazine to the foot of the
bed and turned off my bed light. "Pulitt, pulatt, pulitt,
pulatt," said the irritating rain on the roof of the porch.
There was no other sound from anywhere.

I lay and thought about the quiet until it finally dawned
on me that this was the night before Thanksgiving, that
everyone was thinking about home, that the air was so thick
with longing, so crowded with memories that it was difficult
to breathe. Someone across the hall, pushed aside the heavy
curtain of remembering to draw a long shuddering breath.
There was a sigh from the room next door.

I too sighed as I thought of candlelight and the dear faces
of the family around the dinner table; of the delicious
Thanksgiving morning smells of cranberries, freshly chopped
parsley and boiling giblets; of the time Dede made the gravy
thickening out of powdered sugar; of how invariably at
the last minute somebody in the family unearthed a big
bore who of course had no friends, no other place to go for
Thanksgiving.

I remembered the year we had sat at the dinner table for
four hours listening to a deservedly lonely man from Mary's
office recall every bridge hand he had held since 1908; the
old Alaskan friend Cleve had produced who sharpened his
knife on his tongue and spit tobacco juice at the fireplace;
the girl from my office who ate four helpings of everything
and then ran around the table so that we could all see how

full she was, how her stomach rang like a drum. "Oh, thanks
for the memories . . . dada, dada, da, da. . . ."

Thanksgiving Day dawned cold and rainy and for dinner
we had cold turkey, cold mashed potatoes and gravy, cold
peas, cold squash, cold fruit salad, cold coffee, which tasted
the same with or without saltpeter, and cold pie. Our trays
were set with little baskets of candies and the nurses were
very pleasant, even closing the windows before dinner in
honor of the day. The Pines had certainly done their share
in trying to make the holiday a success but in spite of good
intentions, I ate little and without relish. I longed for meatloaf shaped like a turkey and my warm loving family.

On the stroke of two, my dear unselfish, faithful mother
brought Anne and Joan, with new raincoats, shining eyes and
fresh damp curls. They were all in determinedly high holiday spirits and I thought what a trial it must have been for
Mother to have to leave her family, her warm house and open
fire, to come miles and miles in the rain by bus to that chilly
cheerless hospital; to sit in a draught and listen to me complain. It was hard on Anne and Joan too, who, though they
loved the ride on the bus and looked forward to each visit
with me, had to spend one hour and fifty minutes in the
dreary fireless reception room.

I asked them how they would pass the time while waiting
for Mother, and Anne said, "I brought along the *Mexican
Twins* and I'm going to read to Joan." Joan said, "She said
she was going to read to me whether I wanted her to or not."
Then Anne presented, in an intensely dramatic fashion, a
play they were rehearsing at school. She took all the parts,
throwing herself into each with such fervor and abandon that
at the finish there was applause from some of the nearby
cubicles.

Joan had brought out a book of interesting facts and at
each pause in Anne's recital she produced an interesting fact.
Anne: "No, no, you wicked queen, you'll never marry the

Prince!" (Pause for character change.) Joan: "Betty, did you happen to know that the earthworm has a life span of seven years?"

By December I had been moved across the hall to a two-bed cubicle, I had one hour reading-time, I was taking pneumothorax but once a week and I was colder than I had ever been before. Our bedpans and water glasses froze solid each night and we wore woolen mittens and woolen hoods even at mealtimes. My new roommate, Eleanor Merton, was an inspirational patient and on silence, which was as near as you could get to being by yourself with someone four feet away from you twenty-four hours a day.

In the cubicle next to me, with her bed separated from mine only by the thin plywood partition, was a woman who smelled like a skunk and coughed like a barking dog—"haha, haw haw, haw, haugh haugh, hawwwwww, huh!"—day and night. She was never told that "patients can control their coughs—a cough can be controlled," which made me think that either she was dying or owned a half-interest in the institution.

Eleanor explained in her kindly way that the Barking Dog could not help the cough, that she had had an unsuccessful stripping operation. This explained the cough but not the pungent skunk smell that arose and spread like smoke from a bonfire each time she moved.

Also by December first I knew the entire Bedrest Hospital routine by heart and could tell exactly what was going to happen every minute of every day. This made the time move with glacial slowness, made me even more restless and crotchety. Things which I had grown to accept as part of being institutionalized suddenly became unbearable and, I regret to state, I began to complain constantly about everything, finally even developing small vague aches and pains which I eagerly reported, morning and evening, to the long-suffering Charge Nurse, who gave me meaning looks and aspirin.

Of course the major irritation of all was my roommate, who was so damned happy all the time, so well adjusted. She loved the institution and the institution loved her. She loved all the nurses and all the nurses loved her. She loved all the other patients and all the other patients, but one, loved her. That one used to lie awake in the long dark cold winter nights and listen hopefully for her breathing to stop.

One night the maxim on my supper tray was: "Dare we face the question of just how much of the darkness around us is of our own making?" The Official-in-Charge-of-Beautiful-Thoughts was not only Miss Bartlett of Bartlett's *Quotations*, she was psychic.

On December twelfth Kimi was given a chest examination and three hours' time up; Sheila was moved to the Ambulant Hospital and Eileen had a hemorrhage. Molly Hastings brought me the news and she was grave about Eileen. She said that for weeks they had suspected Eileen of shaking down her thermometer, of not reporting her cough, that the hemorrhage had been severe and was a bad sign. She also said that Eileen was not like herself, that she was sullen and quiet and seemed to have lost all her spirit.

I said passionately, "It's because she's alone. It's horrible to be alone. Look what it's done to me." Molly said, "But you're not alone now," and she smiled at Eleanor who looked inspirational and smiled back. I said, "Why don't they move Eileen in with me, I know I could make her want to get well." Molly was very unenthusiastic. She said, "Neither of you would get well and you'd probably both be thrown out. In tuberculosis it's each man for himself."

Each man for himself or not, I wrote Eileen a long and probably unconvincing letter, telling her about Kimi's time up and how much fun it would be when we were all at the

Ambulant Hospital. I didn't get an answer from Eileen, who was not allowed to write, but I had a note from Minna that should have been bordered in black. Minna said that her pneumothorax was not successful, as she knew it would not be, that she was scheduled for a thoracoplasty operation, but she had little hope of its success as she was so tiny and delicate and the doctors were so incompetent. Then she told me about Eileen's hemorrhage. She said, "I knew it would happen some day. Eileen won't take care of herself, won't obey the nurses. They've got her down now with sandbags and ice packs on her chest, but I suppose this is the end."

I also had a note from Kimi. She wrote, "I have had my chest examined and have been granted three hour time up, but I feel no joy with Eileen so sick and the grim raper [I gathered that she meant reaper] so near. The only bright spot in a succession of long dark cold days is the removal of my former roommate to the porch and the moving of Pixie Josclyn in here with me. Pixie is small and young, like Eileen in disposition and with the long red nail. She was a dancer in a nightclub and eats like a mouse for fear of losing her figure. One pea, a crumb of bread, an eyedropper of tea and she is filled to bursting, while I, like a giant steam shovel sit across from her and demolish mountains of food. I also have occupational therapy time . . . one half an hour a day. The occupational therapy teacher is forcing me to crochet. She says it will release tension. I have made a chain eleven feet long. It is knotty with released tension and dirty with sweat which I find releases more readily than tension. 'What will be the use of this chain,' I ask the O.T. teacher but she evades answering and helps Pixie with an enormous Bertha collar she is tatting. When I ask Pixie what she will do with the collar as Bertha collar have not been in style since about 1923, she says she cares nothing for the usefulness, she merely follows the pattern. When I pointed out that by filling in the large center hole she could change it to a tablecloth, she said for me to release my tension and she would release hers."

That night, after confused dreams involving hospitals and mice and Death wearing a big, Bertha collar, I awoke in the cold, early night to the dark stillness of the ward. I always hated The Pines at night. It was so much a hospital where anything might happen, anyone might die. My pajamas and three sweaters were in a lumpy uncomfortable mass under my ribs, so moving slowly and carefully I tried to straighten them out. The paper blanket immediately reacted like some vindictive living thing and snapped and crackled like a newly lit fire.

The Barking Dog began to cough, her coughs bursting from her like balls from a Roman candle. She coughed twenty-two times, then drank water and put the glass back on the stand with a clink. The woman across from her coughed, drank water and coughed again. Then all was quiet. Everyone was asleep with faint buzzing snores sounding faintly at intervals. My right leg grew lumpy with a cramp and I had to turn over quickly. When I moved, the paper blanket exploded with noise, waking the Barking Dog who began to cough, which disturbed her roommate who aroused the woman across the hall. Finally everyone seemed to be awake and there were coughs up and down the halls like a relay race. A grim terrible race with Death holding the stakes. I thought of Eileen cold and alone with sandbags on her chest. Sylvia had said that hemorrhages were very frightening. That the blood was bright red and foamy.

Someone was tapping on her stand. It was the way to summon a nurse but never used, especially at night, except in an emergency. The tapping went on, clink, clink, clink, clink. The nurse didn't come. I could hear her in the office telephoning. The elevator door clanged shut. The tapping went on, clink, clink, clink. It seemed to come from down the hall where the private rooms were. Eleanor said in a whisper, "Something's happened. I hear a doctor."

I grew panicky and thought of course that Eileen was worse. The tapping on the stand grew louder, more insistent. Everyone was awake now. There was a low hum of voices, the carrying sibilance of whispering. The elevator door clanged again. The tapping on the stand was now demanding, bang, bang, bang! No one heeded.

Morning came at last, dark and wild with wind and rain lashing and clawing at the windows. The ward was oppressively quiet. The day staff came on duty, cheerful and brisk, bringing breakfast. I gulped two cups of warm comforting coffee but I couldn't shake off the horror of the night before. I felt as though I'd been in a dark filthy cellar and must and cobwebs still clung to me.

As I walked down the hall to the bathroom I thought I detected an ominous undercurrent. There was a furtiveness to the whispering. In the bathroom I learned, from one of the older patients, that a girl in emergency had died during the night. I had never seen the girl, didn't even know her name but it was my first death. My slowly built up confidence and assurance of recovery were kicked from under me. I shivered uncontrollably. My windows had framed a magnificent expanse of sunlit sky, mountains and ocean, but when I looked out I saw only the hideous leering face of a Peeping Tom.

On Sunday, December eighteenth, Mother, Mary and Dede came loaded with food and enthusiasm. I immediately skimmed the cream from their visit by telling them of the woman who died, of my preoccupation with death. Dede said, "For you to be worrying about death seems to me as asinine as someone who is tone deaf worrying about losing his voice." I said coldly that I didn't get the allusion. She said, "My God, haven't you looked in the mirror lately?

You're so big and healthy you're frightening." We all laughed and I cheered up a trifle.

Then I told them about Eileen's hemorrhage. Mother asked if the sandbags were a punishment and I explained that they were to keep her lung compressed. My sister Mary said, "You knew from the very first that Eileen was resisting every effort to cure her t.b. The only reason the Medical Director is keeping her here is because tuberculosis is contagious. Now for heaven's sake close the door of that vault and cheer up, Christmas is coming and so is another spring!"

The maxim on our trays that night was: "Mental sunshine makes the mind grow, and perpetual happiness makes human nature a flower garden in bloom." According to the maxim I was just wondering where to put my garden; Eleanor was about five acres in full bloom.

On her rounds after supper the Charge Nurse informed us that we would draw names and exchange small Christmas presents, that we were not allowed any kind of a Christmas tree, not even imitation ones, as it made too much work for the nurses. She said that the institution would decorate the wards. She also said that any presents sent by us to the outside world would first have to go through fumigation.

Having seen the results of fumigation on my sweaters and pajamas I realized that this limited my gift selection to objects of stone but I didn't care, Christmas was in the air at last and I borrowed Eleanor's two-year-old Sears Roebuck Catalogue and spent a happy evening roaming from plows to perfume. I slept all night that night and never again became obsessed with death.

The next afternoon two nurses fulfilled the Charge Nurse's prediction and decorated the wards. I had counted on cedar boughs and pine cones and waited breathlessly for their spicy scent to vie with the lysol for domination of the ward. What I got were limp festoons of red and green crepe paper (obviously well fumigated) and red cardboard bells, hung slightly askew in each doorway. In my new happiness, I didn't care, it was something and it spelled Christmas.

The nurses began delivering packages twice a day. Eleanor got one or more with each delivery. The nurses put them under her bed, where they rested within my vision, opulent and exciting and attesting to the fact that good sports had hundreds of friends. I knew that I would have to depend on relatives, people who had to like me because of blood, for anything I got.

I don't know whether it was due to Jesus' influence or just plain holiday spirit but as Christmas drew nearer and nearer the nurses let their austerity slip down a little, showing small areas of well-rounded warmth and friendliness. Eleanor too became more friendly, even offering to lend me her copy of *Science and Health*.

The day before Christmas it began to snow. The flakes were big and wet and thudded straight to the ground, where they surprisingly did not melt but soon coated the lawns, the trees and the buildings of The Pines in a most Christmas cardy way.

Christmas Eve my brother Cleve, calmly ignoring every rule of the sanatorium, suddenly loomed in my doorway large and handsome, smelling deliciously of cigarettes and out of doors and bearing a huge carton overflowing with presents from the family. The evening nurses arranged our presents in exciting heaps on the foot of our beds but instructed us not to open them until morning.

Except for large wrinkly packages, bearing thousands of Christmas seals, which were easily identified as being from Anne and Joan and brought quick tears and a large lump to my throat, it was like Christmas Eve in boarding school. We drank hot chocolate, talked and laughed furtively and listened to the clear sweet voices of carolers coming up the drive.

There were several groups of carolers and they wandered around the grounds stopping by the porches and under the windows and singing all the lovely familiar Christmas songs. "Hark! the Herald Angels Sing," "Joy to the World," "Silent Night," "Adeste Fideles," "Wind Through the Olive Trees," "We Three Kings of Orient Are," "O Little Town of Bethlehem," "Once in Royal David's City," "Oh, Holy Night," and "Away in a Manger." They were apparently volunteers from church groups or good-hearted local people, for their voices were untrained and discorded occasionally in a homely, friendly way.

As they moved around the grounds the songs came to us now loud, now faint like songs from a campfire or over still water on a summer evening. When they sang under the windows of our ward, the melody was interwoven with sounds of deep sorrow, weeping and long broken sighs, for some of the patients were spending the second, third, even sixth Christmas away from home and a few knew they would never be home for Christmas.

But in spite of wet snow and thick dark the carolers sang with spirit and vigor, and "Joy to the World" came streaming joyously in every open window and soon drowned out the sighs and strangled sobbing. When the carolers left, the ward was perfectly still, frosted with peace and good will.

⇒»XII«⇐

Occupational Therapy

THREE MONTHS WAS the gestation period at The Pines. We were conceived at the Administration Building, confirmed by a staff doctor, approved by a Charge Nurse and for the next three months existed as embryos carefully fed and cared for by the Mother Hospital, alive but not living. At the end of three months we emerged and were individuals to engage in occupational therapy, attend the movies, read books and, if strong enough, have time up.

My gestation period ended December twenty-eighth and this date was more important to me than Christmas. I made a large red mark in my journal and worried constantly for fear the staff would not remember that this was The Day, would not arrange for me to have a chest examination, the preliminary for all activity.

On the morning of the twenty-eighth, when the Charge Nurse made rounds after breakfast, I looked at her expectantly. She said nothing. When the nurse came to take pulses, I asked her if I was scheduled for a chest examination. She said nothing. Finally in desperation I asked Eleanor if she thought I would have a chest exam. She said, "The rule is that you *can* have occupational therapy time and time up *after* three months. That means a chest examination *any* time after three months. It could be today—could be six months from now."

176

I knew that she was probably right but I wanted to hit her hard with something big. Just because she was always so right, so above my childish enthusiasms and pettiness. When I said anything disagreeable about any of the nurses, which I did often, Eleanor always looked directly at me and said, "Oh?" with a rising inflection. This invariably made me want to do some asinine thing like shouting that the nurses were all prostitutes and I could prove it. Eleanor's complete and perfect adjustment to The Pines' routine made my maladjustment eight million times more noticeable and reduced me to a mental level of "my dad's a policeman and he'll get you."

In addition to irritating me, Eleanor had a deft way of deflating me, of skimming the joy from me. One visiting day, as I put on makeup she said, "I think that after a woman has reached a certain age she shouldn't try to improve on nature." I should have looked at her pale yellow face, pale yellow eyes, pale yellow hair and pale yellow teeth, and considered the source. Instead, I blushed, felt seventy years old and like an old toss-her-head-try-to-be-young, and told her a big lie about how I really just hated to wear makeup but I did it to cheer up Mother, who used to be on the stage.

In spite of Eleanor's intimation that I might have to wait anywhere from a week to several years for a chest examination, all morning long I jumped each time a wheelchair went by and was rigidly hopeful up until rest hours. After rest hours I knew there was no hope and so I tried to be like Eleanor and adjust myself to the fact that I might be at The Pines for the rest of my life. "At least I will go through the menopause under medical supervision," I was just telling myself with a gallant smile, when a nurse came for me with a wheelchair and I was given a chest examination. A thorough chest examination by one of the staff doctors who, when he finished, told me that I could have one hour of occupational therapy time and three hours' time up.

I was almost hysterical with joy and wanted to hurry back and say, "Yah, yah, yah!" to Eleanor. Instead I told her of my good luck quietly, taking into consideration the fact that she had been on complete bedrest for two years. She didn't even look up from her knitting. She finished up a row, carefully changed her needles and said, "Sounds to me like they were strengthening you for surgery."

The next morning I took my first time up—fifteen minutes sitting up in bed—and was visited by the occupational therapy teacher, an ambulant patient named Coranell Planter. Coranell gave me a white card on which I was to mark down my occupational therapy time. She said, "You got an hour, see? So if you crochet from nine-fifteen to nine-thirty, put it down. If you embroidry from two to two-thirty, put that down." I said, "If I embroider from two to two-thirty I'd better pack my bags because those are rest hours." She said, "God, Betty, you're a boot! Now what do you wanta do, knit, crochet, tat, embroidry? Name your own poison, kiddo!"

She unpacked her O.T. bag and covered my spread with samples. A round pillow made of variegated green yarn tied in knots and clipped so that it looked like a sea of old parsley stems; a crocheted woolen afghan done in wavy stripes of eye-putting-out turquoise and throat-gripping magenta; a gray hand-knit man's slipover sleeveless sweater with enormous armholes, big pouch pockets and a v-neck so small that a tennis ball couldn't have been wrenched through it; crocheted doilies, tablecloths, tidies, and runners all in deep ecru cotton; a lovely lacy white, very large tatted collar; many crocheted purses; two crocheted neckties, one maroon cotton, one black silk; crocheted pot holders in the shape of pots, kettles, cups and pigs; a white string knitted lettuce bag; natural string-colored woven belts; a khaki-colored crocheted shopping bag with Kelly green braided handles; and a bunch of straggly ill-formed entrail-colored yarn flowers, "to wear on your coat," Coranell explained, holding them experimentally against her maroon tweed coat where they drooped palely.

It looked like a collection rooted from some lonely spinster's bureau drawers and made me want to cry, for I had thought that occupational therapy meant useful work. Something I could learn to do well while in bed that would support Anne and Joan and me after I left The Pines and while I was not strong enough for my regular job. If I learned to make every single thing displayed on my bed, the only thing it could possibly do for me would be to turn me into a watery-eyed old lady running my own Gifte Shoppe in the front room of my small cabbage-smelling house in a poor part of town.

I asked Coranell what the men did for occupational therapy, hoping that they were offered something that I could do too, that was just a little more useful and slightly more up-to-date than yarn pillows or tatted Bertha collars. Coranell said, "Oh, the fellas do the same kinda work as the girls except that most of the fellas don't do none. They think that knitting is sissified, they won't learn to crochet, they say that those braided belts are useless and of course they won't embroidry. Some of them do a little leatherwork, one or two knit but most of them just lay."

It was a most depressing picture and I made a silent vow that when I got out of The Pines I would start a world-wide movement to improve occupational therapy among the bedridden. I didn't keep the vow, unfortunately, and apparently no one else has felt the urge, for the other day I asked a woman, whose young unhappy husband is in a tuberculosis sanatorium, about occupational therapy and I got the same old story. She said that in her husband's ward, a few knit, one crochets, one or two do leatherwork, two or three make little lapel pins out of x-ray film. The rest just "lay."

Coranell told me not to be in a hurry choosing what I wanted to do, that I had all the time in the world, haha, and that she would be back the next day. So saying, she gathered up all the ugly examples of therapeutic occupation, stuffed them in her voluminous canvas O.T. bag and left. I lay in bed and fumed. I wouldn't make any of those useless things. A white string knitted lettuce bag, indeed! I had never liked fancywork. I saw no earthly use for it and I wasn't going to change. I would do something useful with my occupational therapy time. I would make brilliant satirical line drawings of the patients and nurses and I would make brilliant satirical notes for a book. I'd show them!

After supper the Charge Nurse congratulated me on my time up and asked me what I was going to do for occupational therapy. I said that I thought I'd sketch and write a book. I tried to sound very well trained and bursting with talent. The Charge Nurse, not in the least impressed, said, "Drawing [she spoke of it as though it were coloring in a book with crayons] and writing notes are all right for fun but you must do something useful with your hands. Something to release your nervous tension, like knitting or crocheting." I said, "I thought occupational therapy was training for some kind of work." She said, "Not while on bedrest. Bedrest is supposed to be bedrest and occupational therapy is only to relieve tension."

The next morning I told Coranell rather resentfully that I guessed that I'd learn to tat. Cheerfully ignoring my unenthusiastic attitude, she said, "Well, that's fine. I'll lend you a shuttle and some thread until you can have some brought from home. Now this here's the way to hold the thread, see? And this here's the way to hold the shuttle, see?"

Coranell was patient and kind and apparently used to people like me. She was enthusiastic over even the slightest progress on my part and never cross with my clumsiness. When she left she said, "You know, Betty, it don't really matter whether you crochet, knit or tat, or whether you make a tablecloth or just a simple chain, the important thing is that you're doing something besides layin' in bed."

So I tatted and like Kimi learned that sweat is easier to release than tension and that it made no difference what I did, I was doing something besides "layin' " in bed. Tatting, no matter how proficient I became, would never give the children piano lessons, but it made listening to the radio, time up, in fact, life in general more pleasant, and proved to me again that the staff at The Pines always knew what they were-doing.

When my time up, which was increased five minutes a day, had reached one hour, I was wheeled to the porch morning and evening to join the other time-uppers. Bundled in everything we owned and wrapped in our night blankets, we sat in reclining chairs and during the morning light, manipulated our crochet hooks, tatting shuttles or knitting needles with our frozen fingers. The evenings were dark so we just sat and shivered.

There were five of us. Kimi, me, the Friendly Organs woman, a former nurse and a small, dauntless woman who was trying time up for the fifth time that year. Each morning, after our time up, a nurse recorded our temperature and pulse and if there was any increase in either, the time up privilege was taken away and we were put back on bedrest. Mrs. Harmon, the small, dauntless woman, said that she could not get past two hours without running a temperature but at least they didn't take her O.T. time away from her. She was crocheting a lace tablecloth and her bet was that it would be big enough for forty people by the time she got to three hours.

The former nurse, Helen Smith, was making one of the yarn pillows but had chosen shades of tan yarn so that she was creating a sea of dead grass instead of the parsley stems. Friendly Organs knitted socks. She knitted rapidly and perfectly and never looked at her work except when turning the heel. As she knitted she told us about the operation removing her ovarian tumor; about the operation removing a cyst from her wrist; about the operation removing a bunion from her big toe; about the operation to drain her sinus; about the exploratory operation she hoped to have as soon as her t.b. was a little better. The combination of her low, motherly voice and her memory for detail made each of her trips to surgery sound like a "Through the Andes with My Own Llama" travelogue.

On stormy mornings when the wind swooped rudely through the porch, slammed rain against the screens, dashed noisily through the trees and pounded rain on the roof, we experienced difficulty in keeping up with Friendly Organs. One morning we lost her just as she was being given a shot of morphine, heard nothing of the trip to surgery, the six cans of ether, the specialists called in, or the two blood transfusions. In fact, we didn't pick up the thread of the story until she was back in her hospital bed being fed through the veins. Listening to her long dull stories and gently soothing voice was as lulling as hearing the *Congressional Record* read aloud, as therapeutic as our handiwork.

Mother was, of course, delighted over my time up and occupational therapy. She brought me a tatting shuttle, several large balls of white thread and a thick book of instructions. According to this book, you could tat anything and there were alluring pictures of filmy collars and cuffs, lacy edgings, place mats like snowflakes, children's clothes, even bedspreads and tablecloths. I read the fine print and worked hard but for a long time I was able to produce only many small therapeutic pustules of grayish white thread.

I showed this work to Kimi. She said, "It's hahrrible, what is it?" I said, "It's tatting. I'm going to make a collar." She said, mournfully pulling yards and yards of dirty crocheted chain from her bathrobe pocket, "Is this all that lies ahead of us, Betty?" Because her family had always bemoaned the fact that Kimi was interested only in intellectual pursuits, that she cared nothing for domesticity, she insisted that I make a sketch of her crocheting. "Don't waste time on the face," she warned me. "Concentrate on the crocheting."

Having never seen Kimi engaged in any form of occupational therapy other than the simple crocheted chain, I was suspicious when she produced, from time to time, exquisite, finished products of embroidery, cross-stitching, knitting and crocheting. I asked her about this one evening as we sat coldly in our chairs watching the great red double-barred cross on the top of the Administration Building flash on and off and turn our faces, our swaddled forms and the misty spray of rain forced through the screens by the wind, now red, now white like reflections from a fire.

Kimi said, "Everything at this hospital reminds me of tuberculosis. Look how the red light turns the raindrop to little drop of blood, like a small hemorrhage." I said, "Stop hedging, Kimi."

She said, "Well, I used to have my mother buy the material and bring them to me. Now I have her buy the material and bring me the finished product because after all, as I am well adjusted and she is not, she should be the one to engage in occupational therapy."

➤➤XIII◀◀

My Operation

On January sixth the Charge Nurse invited me to The Pines moving picture show, but she handed me the invitation so thickly encased in rules it was like being given a present of one smelt wrapped in the New York Sunday *Times*.

She said in part, "You are on the list to go to the movie tonight, Mrs. Bard. You may wear makeup, if you wish, but you may not talk or laugh. You are to be ready by seven o'clock, in your robe and slippers, with your pillow and night blanket. You will be called for by a *male* [she said male in a low throbbing voice as though it were some dangerous new sex] ambulant patient but you are not to speak to or to laugh with your escort. Your temperature and pulse will be taken as soon as you return to bed and if your temperature or your pulse has increased you will not be allowed to go to the next moving picture show." I thanked her, promised not to speak or to pulsate and she left.

When she had gone I dug down under the thick depressing wrappings and found that my little present was still there, I was going to the movie! I was going to leave my bed and spend a perfectly delightful evening losing myself in the lives of people who had nothing to do with tuberculosis. I hoped that the picture would be either a musical extravaganza in technicolor or a gangster picture with lots of shooting and screaming tires, but I didn't really care if it turned out to be

184

a travelogue or something starring Rin Tin Tin, it was a movie and I was going to it and it would be my first strong step toward normal living.

After supper I was so excited my heart pounded like a jungle drum and my hands were as fluttery and unmanageable as freshly caught sole, but I smeared on lipstick, wet my hair with drinking water and thought, "This is living!"

Eleanor, who was also going to the movie, remained, of course, as unruffled as a turnip. She knitted methodically and unemotionally until one minute before seven, then she put her knitting down temporarily while she made her first and only gesture toward the evening by pulling her pale hair behind her large transparent ears, anchoring it firmly with black bobby pins, and getting out and putting on rimless spectacles. When she had finished she didn't even look in her mirror but returned immediately to the knitting, and not until we heard the first clang of the elevator doors, the creak of wheelchairs and unfamiliar deep voices reading off names from slips of paper distributed by the office, did she get slowly out of bed, slowly put on her tan bathrobe and tan leather slippers and slowly wrap her night blanket around her bed pillow.

I had been dressed, twitching on the edge of my bed, for half an hour so of course she was called for first. Her escort, large, handsome and cheerful, stopped at the door, smiled at both of us but read Eleanor's name from his little slip of paper. I was glad that she didn't believe in makeup and was happy to note that she fluttered coyly as she climbed into the wheelchair. When she was ready she turned and gave the handsome stranger one of her most inspirational smiles. She had intended to be alluring I was sure but the effect of her smooth pale head, the spectacles, the large myopic eyes, the waxy ears, the tan body, the gargoyle smile and the clutched woolen blanket, was so exactly like an eager brown moth about to eat lunch that the man flinched perceptibly and I almost laughed out loud. As they creaked off down the hall I could picture Eleanor flying out of the wheelchair in one of the dark tunnels, flittering along the walls and finally flinging herself drunkenly against the lighted windows of the auditorium.

When I finally heard my name being read in a high uncertain voice at the doorway of the wrong room, I knew that Eleanor had had the evening's luck. My escort had nothing in common with Eleanor's. He was not handsome, he was not cheerful and he wasn't a man. He was about seventeen years old, approximately six feet six inches tall, two inches thick, greenish and so shy that I was afraid that speaking to him would have the same disastrous melting effect as putting salt on a snail.

Resignedly I took my night blanket and pillow, climbed into the wheelchair, signaled that I was ready and away we went, silently and swiftly like a cold draught, in and out of elevators, through long dark tunnels, up and down ramps, in and out of buildings and there wasn't a word between us. The Charge Nurse would have been so proud of me. When we reached the auditorium my escort kicked open the swinging doors, tipped me out like a sack of coal and melted back into the dark tunnel before I could turn and give him one of my inspirational smiles.

Feeling like a package that has been left on the wrong porch, I clutched my night blanket and pillow and looked around. The auditorium was brightly lighted, rather small and rapidly filling to capacity. There were beds with the backs propped up along both sides and in the back of the hall, ordinary seats in the middle. I was wondering where I was to sit when an unsmiling strange nurse gripped my arm, steered me along the wall on the left side, helped me up onto a front bed beside Eleanor, stuffed my pillow behind my head, covered me with my blanket and told me not to talk.

All around me were robust, healthy looking people, finding chairs or climbing up onto the beds, but there was no noise. Not a sound. These were young Americans gathered together for an evening's entertainment but there was no laughing or talking or calling. Not even one excited little squeal. The room was perfectly quiet except for the occasional scrape of a chair on the cement floor, the soft pad of bedroom-slippered feet, an infrequent self-conscious click of high heels. It was like a movie without a sound track.

As always at The Pines, the sexes were carefully sorted. The men all on one side, the women all on the other, the space between carefully patrolled by gimlet-eyed nurses with powerful flashlights to make sure that the sexes didn't mingle in the dark.

I found that sitting on a bed with a pillow behind my head was the most comfortable way ever devised for seeing a motion picture but I thought the picture itself rather a tactless choice for the joyous entertainment of patients in a tuberculosis sanatorium. It was Greta Garbo in *Camille*.

Just to show me that in tuberculosis there is no sure thing, that all the paths of the tuberculous lead over quicksand, Monday morning, three days after I had gone to the movie and taken that first firm step toward normal living, I was informed that I was to go to surgery the following Thursday. My pneumothorax doctor, no longer the Medical Director but one of the regular staff, told me very casually after my pneumothorax that I was to "have some bands cut," an intrapleural pneumolysis, to be exact. He explained that small adhesions between the lung and the pleura, caused by fluid or an infection at some earlier time, often tore loose as mine had at first, but big strong adhesions required surgery. He said that I had one or two large adhesions and until they were cut I could not have a proper collapse of the lung.

I spent the morning of January tenth in x-ray, posing with one arm above my head, one hand on my hip, both hands on hips, both arms above my head, and the evening listening to Eleanor tell of recent deaths at The Pines. As she had never before talked to me in the evening, I knew that she was only talking about death because I was going to have surgery, but I listened anyway in fascinated horror.

She said that when patients, usually unsuccessful surgery cases, were going to die they got violent diarrhea and nausea, grew thinner and thinner, weaker and weaker, and were finally visited by the Medical Director and told to put their affairs in order because they were going to die. She said that when death was pretty certain the patients were moved to the emergency ward. When absolutely certain and not far off, they were put in the light room.

She said that Beryl Hanford, the chocolate dipper, would die; both the girls in my old single cubicle would die; Margaretta, the beautiful Negro girl wouldn't last two more weeks; the little thirteen year old would die; the girl in emergency who had hot packs on her stomach after every meal would die; the Barking Dog, Eileen Kelly, several of the ambulant patients and more than half of the Men's Bedrest Hospital would die. I asked her how she knew and she said mysteriously that she could tell. She knew the signs. She said that in the sanatorium magazine there were lists of incoming and outgoing patients and deaths were merely listed as outgoing.

She said that more men than women died at The Pines because of a distressing tendency on the part of wives to divorce their poor sick husbands and thus remove their incentive for getting well. I asked her if men didn't also divorce their sick wives but she said no, that men never divorced their wives, no matter how long the wives were at The Pines. I was amazed at this demonstration of "the faithful old male," especially as my experience with men in the business world had led me to believe that many men forgot all about their wives when away from them for very short periods, like all day at the office. Eleanor concluded that all some women seemed to want out of life was to paint their faces and go to nightclubs. It was with difficulty that I refrained from saying, "I'll say, kid!"

At eight o'clock, an evening nurse delivered a note from Eileen Kelly. Ordinarily I would have grabbed it and ripped it open for Eileen's letters, no matter what her condition, were always amusing, always made me laugh. But this evening Eleanor and her morbid predictions had me stuffed so far down in my crypt that I could not summon the courage to open and read what I was sure was Eileen's farewell letter. I put it on my stand unopened and continued to look out into the dusky hallway and think about my operation.

Just before lights out Katy stopped at our door and said, "Isn't it fine about Eileen?" I said, "What about her?" She said, "Didn't you get her letter?" I said, "Yes, but I didn't read it." She waited while I opened the letter and read that Eileen was much better, that she had been given half an hour of occupational therapy time and expected time up very soon. Katy said, "You see what being a good girl does for you?" and left. I said to Eleanor, "Well, there's one that won't die." She said, without looking up from her knitting, "I wouldn't bank on it if I were you."

The next afternoon Eleanor was moved, thank God, but her discussions of death, like the smell of flowers after a funeral, lingered behind her and when I was visited by the Salvation Army and handed a religious tract by a sad-faced old lady with stiff black hairs on her chin, I trembled with fear, forgot that the Salvation Army often came to The Pines, and thought the hairy old lady had been sent by the office in lieu of the Medical Director, to prepare me for death.

After supper my apprehension was increased by extensive preparations for surgery and a large sleeping potion. If the operation was going to be the simple little thing I had been led to believe, why the enema, why the shaving clear to the waist back and front, why drugs? Did it portend something more serious or was it merely a surgeon's caprice, like shaving the head and giving an enema before piercing the ears?

The next morning at seven-thirty, like a picador toward a bull, Miss Muelbach came charging at me with a hypodermic needle. "I'm allergic to morphine," I said mildly but she already had the needle in and was bearing down on the plunger, so I didn't pursue the matter further. Instead I put on the sterilized white stockings, white cap and white gown she handed me and when she had gone I looked in the mirrors. My reflected all-white image was so much like a young weevil emerging from a sack of flour that I expected to see a flour manufacturer's label embossed in blue on the bedspread.

I decided to put on some mascara. This was strictly against the rules but I thought the situation warranted it. After all if I died I didn't want my body sprayed with Black Leaf 40 and dumped on some compost heap. After I had put on plenty of mascara I looked again and found that I now looked like a weevil who hadn't slept. I was contemplating the removal of the mascara when two strange nurses wheeled in a stretcher, transferred me to it with one jerk of the sheet, and wheeled me rapidly to the surgery on the top floor of the Administration Building.

Because of my allergy the morphine, instead of dulling my senses, had made me very bright, alert and nervous. Very conscious of every sound, every smell, each new face. The surgery was high and very light with shiny white-tiled walls. Waiting for me were two doctors looking like wrinkled Ku Kluxers in their surgical caps and gowns, and three surgical nurses wound and bound in white. One of these identified herself as an operation artist, and a friend of my sister Mary.

I was transferred from the stretcher to the operating table and turned on my right side with both arms over my head. Then after a great deal of scrubbing and painting on my back and chest, novocain was injected in my left side under the arm and in my back in the vicinity of my shoulderblade.

The doctor who usually gave me pneumothorax explained what they had done, were doing or intended to do. "We are now making a hole under your arm. In this incision we will put a little light so that the surgeon can see what he is cutting from the incision he has made in your back." The operation artist, who was peering in the holes and drawing what she saw, also made comments. "Your lung is the prettiest shade of blue," or "You should see the neat job the doctor is doing."

As soon as they were ready to cut, the lights would go off and a blue light would go on. Then the surgeon would say, "Ought two," and a nurse would repeat, "Ought two" as she handed him the instruments and checked them in after he had used them.

It was very hot in the surgery and I was extremely nervous. Before long little rivulets of perspiration began running off my forehead and down into the mascara on my eyelashes. The mascara ran into my eyes and stung fiercely. Tears streamed down my cheeks. I tried to tell the nurse stationed at my head to wipe my eyes but every time I spoke the doctor told me to shut up as they were cutting my lung and talking apparently moved it.

The nurse finally noticed my tears and thinking that I was crying from pain or fear or both, hurriedly held spirits of ammonia under my nose which made my eyes water more and released more mascara.

After what seemed like years the doctor explained that they had anaesthetized for two adhesions but had found four and were going to have to cut them anyway. I was to be brave, he said, and was not to flinch. I was very brave and didn't flinch but only because the slight burning from snipping the unanaesthetized adhesions was nothing compared to the torture I had already endured from the mascara.

At eleven-thirty I was wheeled back to the Bedrest Hospital and put, in spite of loud protestations on my part, into the light room, reserved, according to Eleanor for the surediers. At two o'clock Mother and Mary brought me an armload of spring flowers and I blanched when I saw them for I had forgotten that it was a visiting day and thought they had been sent for.

By four-thirty I had been moved back to my own room and only by a slight soreness under my arm and in my back and by my very red-rimmed eyes could I tell that I had spent the morning in surgery. I had been instructed to eat lying down for a few days but Charlie came to see me anyway. He gripped my right hand and said, "When Kimi told me you'd went to surgery I said to myself, 'Say good-bye to a good kid, Charlie.' " I said, "Why Charlie, there wasn't anything to it. I feel perfectly wonderful." He said, "You better wait until the next few days are over. There's many a slip 'twixt the cup and the lip."

My first slip came about seven-thirty when I noticed a peculiar scrunchy feeling in my left wrist. When I doubled my fist or flexed my fingers it felt like crumpling tissue paper. I asked the evening nurse about it and she looked frightened and immediately produced the House Doctor who gave me a sedative. In the morning the scrunchy feeling was gone. I asked the Charge Nurse what it was but she only smiled and asked me who had given me my hypodermic the morning before.

At noon Charlie, who acted very surprised that I had pulled through the night, asked me how I felt. I told him about the tissue paper in my wrist. He said, "Air in your veins. That's the way they kill rabbits at the laboratory. Shoot air in the veins and stop the heart. That bubble of air you got in your veins might get to your heart anytime now. It'll stop just like that." He snapped his fingers.

"Well, you won't know what hit you that's sure," he concluded comfortingly.

Two days after my operation I was given a new roommate. A girl named Katherine Harte, who had curly black hair, large green eyes, dimples and empyema. Kate was twenty-five years old, had been in The Pines for two years, had eaten almost nothing for two weeks, had to have her bed propped up day and night, and was ready to die. She told me that she felt as if she were floating about six inches above her bed and that she saw everything through a thick gray mist. She said when the nurses talked to her they appeared and disappeared in the mist and if they were scolding her she could close her eyes and float away from them at will.

The next day after Kate moved in was a visiting day. As I put on makeup after dinner, Kate advised me that she had told her family to stay home because she intended to spend the visiting hours with her eyes closed floating in the gray mist. I didn't say anything. I felt guilty because I was so well and she was so sick and because I knew that Mother, Mary and Madge were coming to see me and my visiting hours were bound to be a delight.

At two o'clock Kate didn't open her eyes. She lay waxily in her white bed looking as if she had been drawn on the pillowcase, her lashes and brows bold black strokes, her hair a black smudge. Even when Mary, Mother and Madge came in and cheerfully unloaded an armload of forsythia, two books by Humphrey Pakington and a large box of oatmeal cookies on my stomach and while Mother told me about the children, the happenings at home, at school and in the garden, Kate lay as still as death, her eyes closed, apparently floating in her mist.

Then Mary told about entertaining a doctor from Boston who was so reserved, so Eastern and so disapproving of the informal West that after two days of him she had become so self-conscious about being Western that every time she walked she could hear her spurs jangle and when she spoke she had to check herself to keep from whirling her lariat around her head and calling him Pardner. Mary's stories were always funny but even if they hadn't been she was so warm and vivid herself that just having her in the cold rain-swept little room was as comforting as a bonfire.

Before Mary finished the story the Charge Nurse stopped at the door and warned Kate and me about laughing. Surprised at the inclusion of Kate, I looked over at her. Her green eyes were open and she was wiping away tears of laughter. I introduced her to the family. Madge said, "My God, you're beautiful! Why do you have to sit up like that?" Kate, carefully watching the door for nurses, explained that she had empyema, an infection of the pleural cavity, and added casually that she was dying. Madge brushed the dying aside as unimportant. What she wanted were the symptoms of this empyema, the details of how Kate had gotten tuberculosis, what her first signs had been.

I explained that if she wanted to talk to Kate she had better move over by her bed and pretend that she was her visitor. Madge moved with alacrity and Kate told her how, when working as a secretary for a large oil company, she had had a cough for over a year, had been very thin, had fainted one day at work and remained unconscious for over an hour, and had been sent by the plant nurse to The Pines Clinic.

The Medical Director had been very depressing and had told her that both her lungs were badly infected and that he had little hope of saving her. Even so neither Kate nor her mother was able to realize the seriousness of her illness and saw no reason why she should go to a sanatorium, why she couldn't get well at home. The Medical Director told them that it wouldn't work, but they tried it anyway for three months. At the end of that time, Kate's mother was worn

out from trying to care for her, Kate was worn out from trying to save her mother and from entertaining visitors who
came at any hour of the day or night, and her x-rays showed
no improvement.

Kate entered The Pines. At first she took pneumothorax
and got along very well, even going to the Ambulant Hospital in six months. Then she got empyema, became very
ill and was sent back to Bedrest. She had to have her pleural
cavity washed out with a chlorine solution every week and
she had had a stripping operation. She showed us the scar,
which was scimitar-shaped and extended across her thin back
from the right shoulder to below the right arm. She said
that she guessed she was dying but she didn't care.

Mary said, "Nonsense, you're not dying. Millions of people have empyema—common as measles," which was entirely
untrue of course but seemed to cheer Kate, who told Mary
about the floating and the gray mist. Mary said, "Malnutri-
tion, very usual symptom. Your stomach has probably
shrunk to the size of a crabapple. Here, eat a few of these
cookies."

Being married to a doctor, Mary felt that she knew more
about medicine than the American Medical Association but
the only people she was allowed to treat were her family, who
knew that no matter what their symptoms, she would diagnose them as being indicative of whatever disease she happened to remember from the latest medical journal. When
Dede was cutting her wisdom teeth Mary told her she had
every symptom of a rare South American virus disease, and
when Alison broke her leg skiing, Mary, who had just heard
about psychosomatic medicine, told Mother that Alison could
wear a cast if she wanted to but the whole thing was purely
a manifestation of her psyche.

She had apparently abandoned the psyche for little crabapple stomachs and empyema as common as measles, but it

made no difference what it was because it cheered up Kate, influenced her to eat several cookies and all of her supper, and evidently changed her attitude toward dying for she never mentioned it again.

It was probably the natural progression of the disease but it might have been, as Kate insists it was, the effect of my cheering visitors that made her temperature begin to go down the very next day, made her start to get well and was responsible for our both being given three hours' time up on the twenty-first of February.

⇶XIV⇷

Ambulant Hospital

MARCH TWENTY-FOURTH was a spring day. A nice regulation spring day patterned after a picture in a Second Reader. The sunshine was direct and warm and gave the straight pale green poplar trees and the small well-stuffed white clouds neat black outlines against the flat blue sky. Over all were pleasant usual spring noises. An airplane busily humming through the serene atmosphere, a boat whistling conscientiously as it threaded its careful way through the little islands of the Sound, a rooster crowing, the rhythmic ringing of a distant hammer, the whirring of a lawn mower, the hurried click of hedge clippers.

It was a day to hang out clean white clothes, to dig in the garden, to try out new roller skates, to put up a swing, but Kate and I had to be satisfied with lounging in lounge chairs on the porch, doing fancywork and taking our time up. We had reached our full three hours the evening before and we felt like eager fledglings teetering on the edge of the nest waiting for the push that would make us try our wings. From now on anything might happen, the Ambulant Hospital, a tub bath, a trip to the beauty parlor, work in the occupational therapy shop, six hours' time up—anything. All we had to do was to sit quietly and wait.

The friendly sun drew sparks from my laborious tatting shuttle, making it seem quick and agile. It picked up Kate's darting crochet hook and turned it into a tiny winking light. It even warmed and thawed the five porch patients so that they came up out of their white coverings like brave crocuses above the snow.

I said to Kate, "Isn't it much harder to be on bedrest in the summer?" She said, "Oh, my yes. You get hot and restless and itchy and irritable. It seems like a month between baths and like a year between shampoos and all the awful hospital smells cling to you until you gradually lose every vestige of appetite. It isn't so bad on the porches, which is why those poor things over there suffered out here through the winter—it gives them squatters' rights for the summer."

I said, "Why then do people go to hot places like Arizona to cure tuberculosis?" Kate said, "I suppose it is because people have heard that exposure to sunlight will kill the tubercle bacillus and they think that if they lie in the sun long enough the rays will penetrate to their lungs and kill the germs in them. According to the Medical Director, exposure to the sunlight is very dangerous for pulmonary tuberculosis, except under medical supervision. He warns us against sunbaths, even sitting in the sun without a hat, says it increases our temperatures and pulse and I suppose sends the germs whirling through our blood stream."

I said, "But what about people who live in hot climates? I should think they'd have to take the cure in a hot climate in order to determine their resistance to normal activity in a hot climate." Kate said, "The way I understand it, pulmonary tuberculosis is caused by tubercle bacilli in the lungs and to date the only way found to render these tubercle bacilli inactive is to wall them off in the lungs with fibrosis. The fibrosis forms quickest when the lung is at rest. If your lung was put at rest with pneumothorax or other surgery I shouldn't think it would matter whether you were in Alaska or South America, but if you had to depend on bedrest to build your fibrosis then I should think that a year-round cool climate at sea level would be the most pleasant."

"Why sea level?" I asked.

"Because," Kate said, "mountain air is thinner, requires the lungs to work harder for their oxygen, and is also exhilarating—which makes it more difficult to rest."

"But what if you lived in the mountains and intended living in the mountains after you were well? Wouldn't it be better to take the cure in the mountains?"

Kate said, "Wouldn't it be easier to try out a broken leg on the level? After you had proved that the break was all healed and the leg was strong then you could climb all the mountains you wanted."

"You know," I said, "much as I hate to look on the bright side of things, I'm glad that I was poor when I got tuberculosis; otherwise I might have rocketed off to the desert or the top of some mountain, and I'd be dead now, instead of sitting here on the porch avoiding the sun, making this great big ugly tatted collar and wondering where a large fat slightly tubercular lady could get a job."

Kate said, "Much as I hate to look on the bright side of things too, I am glad I was poor when I got t.b. because I know that, if I was rich and paying fifty or sixty dollars a week in some private sanatorium, I would never let the nurses boss me around as much as they do, and have done, here, and I wouldn't have this big dirty ugly lace tablecloth for my hope chest."

"And as long as we're counting our blessings," I said, "isn't it lucky that when we got our tuberculosis we happened to be living in a part of the country that is under water eighty percent of the year? No danger from too much sun up here, but watch out for mildew."

"Speaking of mildew," Kate said, "the Charge Nurse down at the Ambulant Hospital acts as though this hospital were built right on the Equator and if she knew where to get sun helmets she'd make them a required article of clothing. She makes all the patients cover their heads, even on the grayest days, when they walk to the store."

"How far away is the store?" I asked, thinking in terms of miles.

"About half a block," Kate said, "but the Ambulant Charge Nurse thinks The Pines is the whole world and that the sun sends its rays directly on to the patients like a person directing a flashlight beam."

The sun now had one or two of its beams aimed at my back, which made me feel like a frozen roast just slipped into a hot oven. I knew I should get up and move but I was hypnotized by the delicious warmth. I leaned back and closed my eyes and let the dangerous sunshine flow over me like warm oil. I was jerked from my lassitude by the Charge Nurse's voice. It quivered with horror as she said, "Mrs. Bard, you're sitting in the *sun!*" I said, "I'm sorry, I must have dozed. I'll move right away." She said, "No need to move, you and Miss Harte are to go for chest examinations." Chest examination! That meant the Ambulant Hospital! I wanted to shout with joy but I tried very hard not to register anything other than blind obedience. I looked at Kate. She winked and held up two crossed fingers. The Charge Nurse said, "You may walk to the examination room," and left the porch.

I had gained twenty pounds in the five months I had been at The Pines and I felt like a tank as I lumbered uncertainly up the long hallway, on legs unsteady with disuse and excitement. Once I stumbled and , when I grabbed at a cubicle was for support, it gave way under my tremendous impact and wavered indecisively over the head of a sleeping patient. Kate, ten pounds fatter than she had been a month ago but still as slender as a nutpick, laughed at my joust with the walls. Before we had passed the last cubicle in our ward we could hear the whispers, "They're going to the Ambulant

Hospital. They've got six hours' time up. They're going for chest exams." News about us traveled faster than we did.

When we reached the examination room the Charge Nurse was waiting for us. She sent me in first. The doctor examined my chest and lungs very thoroughly but said nothing. When I came out my face was hot with excitement and I was afraid the Charge Nurse would think I had the dreaded t.b. flush. Before Kate went in she said in a tense little voice, "Pray for me hard." Her eyes were wide with fear, the pupils dilated to cover the whole iris.

While Kate was examined I shuffled slowly back to my bed, now in a four-bed ward at the opposite end of the building from the entering ward. My wardmates, besides Kate, were Mrs. Harmon, the small, dauntless woman of my first attempt at time up, and Lizzie Merritt, a former nurse. As Lizzie had been on bedrest for two years and had no hope of time up for at least another year, and Mrs. Harmon had just lost her time up for the sixth time that year, I was not eager to share the news about Kate's and my chest examinations.

When I came to the door of our ward I was glad to see that Lizzie was asleep and Mrs. Harmon was gone. I climbed into bed and for once the icy sheets felt soothing to my excited, flushed body. I looked in the mirror and my face, as I had feared, was a mottled tomato red. I put my cold, damp washcloth over it and closed my eyes. My heart was pounding boom, boom, boom, and my unused muscles twitched convulsively like a dying chicken, so of course the Charge Nurse chose that time to take my pulse and temperature. After a minute or so she said, "You're excited, I'll come back later." Then, "Better get that pulse down if you want to go to the Ambulant Hospital this afternoon." She sounded stern, but she was smiling and I knew that she was happy over my progress and no doubt glad to get rid of me.

Kate came in then and the Charge Nurse told her that she too was to go to the Ambulant Hospital that afternoon. She said that we were to rest quietly until the move. It was like asking someone to rest quietly on her wedding day, but we tried. Lizzie and Mrs. Harmon were pathetically generous with their congratulations as were all the other patients who learned of our good fortune. I even had a note from Eileen, who in spite of her optimistic outlook in January, as yet had no time up.

She wrote, "I expect to get to the Ambulant Hospital some day but don't wait for me. I've got a new roommate and does she give the Old Dame a bad time. Her name's Delores and she used to be a nightclub singer. She's real good-lookin' and she's always gettin' little pains that the doctor has to look at and whenever he pokes her she half closes her eyes and says, 'Ohhhhhh, Doctah!' That new young doctor don't mind it at all but the Old Dame just burns. . . . Jackie don't come out any more. . . . He told Gramma he don't like hospitals but I got it pretty straight that he's got a new girl, a cheap little tramp with blond hair and good lungs. Oh, well, there's more than one pebble on the beach. . . . When you come up on washwater be sure the water's hot and there's plenty of it. . . ."

Of course I couldn't sleep during rest hours, but because I knew that I would be under close observation and would have my pulse and temperature taken as soon as I woke up, I kept my eyes shut and tried to relax. Each minute seemed like an hour, and each hour like a century but finally it got to be two-thirty and the nourishment cart came clanking in, closely followed by nurses with carts for Kate's and my belongings and bedding, and the Charge Nurse with a wheelchair for me. We took the usual route to the basement and the tunnels, then taking all turns to the left instead of to the right, which led to x-ray, we came at last to a low rustic building which housed the dining room, the examining rooms and the Ambulant Hospital Charge Nurse's office.

This Charge Nurse, according to a letter from Kimi, who had gone to the Ambulant Hospital three weeks before, was "the most terrible creature living—soft-spoken but exuding venom from every pore of her short lumpy body." Therefore I was not too surprised after the Bedrest Charge Nurse had left, to have her say, "You have been a problem, Mrs. Bard." I said, "I'm sorry." She said, "Being sorry is not enough, Mrs. Bard. We must have proof of your desire to cooperate. Proof of your trustworthiness. Proof that we will be proud to have you in our hospital."

I didn't know what she was getting at. How could I, sitting in a wheelchair in my blue woolen bathrobe, suddenly produce evidence of good citizenship? I said, "I don't know what you mean. What kind of proof?" She was acting as though she expected written references. She said, "You're going to have to change that attitude, Mrs. Bard." I said, "I'm sorry but I don't know what you want me to say." She said, "If you don't know what to say then we haven't been able to teach you very much."

I said, "I don't understand what you're talking about and I don't know what you want me to say." She smiled at me blandly and said, "I just want you to say that you intend to do your best to be an obedient, helpful, cooperative, industrious patient." I said, "I do" meekly in spite of a poignant longing to say, "The hell I will!"

The welcome over, we started for the hospital. I had a slight premonition that life from then on was not going to be any gambol on the grassy turf, so, as the Charge Nurse wheeled me to my new room, I asked about the rules. Were they the same as those at the Bedrest Hospital? If not, what were the rules of the Ambulant Hospital? The Charge Nurse said, "We do not tell the patients the rules, Mrs. Bard. We find that the trial and error method is the best way to learn them." I said, "But how can I be obedient, cooperative and helpful if I don't know what I'm supposed to do?" She said, "We do not allow arguing, Mrs. Bard. I am in authority and I do what I think is best for the patients."

We entered the Women's Ambulant Hospital. The building,

brick and of modern architecture, was two stories high, had gentle ramps instead of stairs and was designed like an ocean steamer with all the accommodations outside cabins, opening on screened promenade decks about ten feet wide. The Charge Nurse wheeled me into an apartment on the south side, first floor, facing a cherry orchard, told me supper would be at four-thirty, that a nurse would call for me with a wheelchair, that I was to be ready, and left.

My bed had already been made and my belongings were in cartons on the floor. My new roommate, Sigrid Hansen, the unsmiling blonde from the Bedrest Hospital, said, "You are to have the two bottom drawers in the bureau, the right-hand locker in the bathroom." I said, "You mean we have our own bathroom?" She said, "Yes, over there. It is warm and we dress in there." I went over and opened the door. The dressing room was deliciously warm and contained two large metal wardrobes and a wash basin. At the end there was a little lavatory. "No more bedpans, wheee!"

I put my clean pajamas and sweaters in the bureau drawers, the rest of my stuff in the bedside stand, and got into bed. The bed was very cold. I asked Sigrid if we were allowed hot-water bottles. She said, "Sure, fill it yourself in the bathroom. Fill it every ten minutes if you want to." I immediately got up and filled my hot-water bottle with scalding water. What bliss!

The front wall of the room was one huge steel casement-window facing the cherry orchard. The individual panes, about eighteen inches square and hinged, opened to form glass shelves for flowers. As in the Bedrest Hospital, all the windows were open at all times. The door, part of the same steel casement, was also glass and open. The walls were cream plaster, the furniture, consisting of two beds, two bedstands, two chairs, a bureau and a table for books and magazines, was deep turquoise, the floor terra cotta and black tiled linoleum.

The room was well arranged and attractive, the view into the cherry orchard was lovely, the air was fresh and smelled sweetly of earth, new leaves and sunwarmed grass, but most wonderful of all was the freedom. No nurses patrolled the promenade, occasional voices or moderate little trills of laughter could be heard on either side of us, eight-hour patients walking past the door, arm in arm, stopped to smile and talk to us, and Sigrid and I exchanged pleasantries without first listening carefully for the soft rubber-soled steps of a nurse. I filled my hot-water bottle with fresh hot water about ten times during the next hour and each time my skin prickled with the delight in this small free act of comfort. In spite of the Charge Nurse's hateful reception, I thought her Ambulant Hospital was pure heaven.

At four-fifteen Sigrid told me to get up and get ready for supper. She said that I could wash my face and put on makeup; that I would be taken to the dining room in a wheelchair for the first week, then I could walk one way one day, two ways the next day and so on. In two weeks I could walk back and forth to all meals.

As I washed my face and dressed, Sigrid sat on the floor of her locker and told me a little about the hospital, a little about herself. She was twenty-two, had been at The Pines almost nine months, had been born on a farm near Oslo in Norway, had a husband who had gone North to fish, loathed the Charge Nurse as much as Kimi did but was completely matter-of-fact about her, as she was about everything.

She said, "She is crazy so I keep away from her. She walks slap, slap, slap and can be heard for blocks. I either close my eyes and pretend to be asleep or go into the toilet when I hear her coming. That way she cannot trick me into one of her arguments."

Sigrid's sister had died at The Pines the year before but she was not sad about it. She said, "She should have had sense enough to go to a doctor sooner. It was better that

she died. She would have been sick all her life." I asked
her if she was lonely for her husband. She said, "No. I
knew he was going away. We will have a whole lifetime
together, why fuss about a few months."

I roomed with Sigrid for a month and she was the perfect
roommate. Always pleasant, always courteous, never emotional. I was all jagged peaks of ecstasy, deep chasms of
depression. She could have been graphed with one straight
line. As I read a great deal and seemed contented doing it,
she asked to borrow my books as soon as I finished them.
But after reading just a few pages she tossed them all aside
as "too fanciful." For anyone who thought *The Grapes of
Wrath* "too fanciful" I didn't know what to suggest.

Sigrid had ash blond hair, large sea blue eyes, a beautiful
body and walked like a proud little queen, her head high, her
back straight, her steps graceful and slow. I remarked on
her beautiful carriage. She said, "You'll walk the same way.
It comes from lying in bed and resting your back." She was
right. All the women patients walked beautifully. As I
waited for the nurse to come for me I watched them go by
on the promenade on their way to supper, moving slowly and
gracefully and as though they had books on their heads, but
not one of them had the proud grace of Sigrid. It must have
been something Nordic.

The nurse who called for me, a nice friendly little old
woman, stopped on the covered rustic walk that connected
the Women's Ambulant Hospital with the dining room and
pointed out the miniature golf course, the fountain, the Children's Hospital, the Men's Ambulant Hospital, the Bedrest
Hospitals, the Isolation Hospital. She said that in June the
walk would be covered with roses and that in just a few
weeks all the walks would be bordered with flowers, the
grounds alight with flowering trees.

The dining room, large and rustic, had a beamed cathedral
ceiling, a stone fireplace—without a fire, of course—open

casement-windows on two sides, open French doors on either
side of the fireplace and rows and rows of brown oblong
tables for four. The tables for the men were on one side, for
the women on the other, a no man's land in between. The
men and women were not allowed to speak to each other in
the dining room; in fact no communication of any kind, including winking, waving, smiling or note writing, was allowed
between male and female patients, I was informed by the
little nurse as she deposited me at a table at the front of
the room near the serving counter. She also informed me
that the dining room was run like a cafeteria; that the patients lined up to be served (males and females on opposite
sides of the room), carried their own trays, stacked and
scraped their dishes and returned the trays to the counter;
but that for the first week I would be served by nurses.

She left to get another patient and I sat at the table and
watched the patients file into the dining room. Some wore
robes, some were dressed, all were plump, clear eyed and
healthy looking. I found that I knew most of the women
patients as they had either been in Bedrest with me or I
had met them on their washwater or flower duty. Everyone was very friendly and came to my table to congratulate
me. I couldn't get used to the strange delightful sound of
talking and kept flinching and looking for nurses whenever
anyone spoke to me. Voices were kept low and there was no
loud laughter or other mark of hilarity, but it was wonderful
beyond belief to contemplate eating with an accompaniment
of conversation instead of cold silence and a reproving eye.

Also seated at the front table with me was Sylvia, still as
thin as a sparrow but shining with happiness over her time
up. She had been at the Ambulant Hospital for two days
and for this accomplishment I thought the Medical Director
should have the Congressional Medal of Honor.

Then came Kate, smiling but a little grim. She told me
that she had been put on the north side of the hospital, in a

room with a big, fat, sorry-for-herself who complained constantly. "She even thinks her eyeballs are hardening," Kate said, "and she . . ." "Shhhh," Sylvia said, as a stout older woman, with gray hair and a mouth turned down so far at the corners it looked as if she had put it on upside down, was helped to a chair at our table.

The stout lady settled herself with a great deal of wiggling of the table and spilling of Sylvia's and my tea, then removed from her bathrobe pocket and lined up in front of her place, two cod liver oil capsules, two round peppermint-flavored discs of calcium, some black oval pills, and some little red pills. "The doctor tells me to take these medicines," she said sighing, "but with the nurses so careless I always think I'm taking a terrible chance. How do I know these are the right pills? How do I know that some of them are not filled with poison?" She took them all, however, rolling her eyes and gulping as each one hit bottom. It reminded me of dropping stones into a well.

As she took the last pill, Sheila and Kimi, the last ones into the dining room, came enthusiastically up to the table. They were still wearing robes but told me that they had each been given six hours' time up and expected to wear their clothes in a week. While we were talking, the stout woman's tray was delivered to her. On it was a small glass of medicine, which the nurse told her to take after she had eaten her supper.

Kimi reached over and picked up the medicine, lifted it to her nose, sniffed and said, "This smells like something labelled with a skull and crossbone. Demand to see the bottle from which it was taken, Leila. Remember there is a long waiting list to get into The Pines and an empty bed is a helpful bed." Leila, looking exactly as if she were going to cry and in a voice midway between a whine and a wail, said, "Now, Kimi, don't make me laugh, you know how I cough."

Sheila informed me that after the first week I would have to be invited to sit at one of the tables. I asked where I would sit if no one asked me. She said not to worry as nobody in the history of the sanatorium had ever been that unpopular. Kimi said, "But if there should be a first time I will stand by you. There will be two pariah to share that one lonely table."

The Charge Nurse was motioning with her spatula for Kimi and Sheila to get in the food line, so they scuttled away and the rest of us ate our supper to the accompaniment of Leila's complaints. At last Sylvia said, "Leila, nurses do not make mistakes. I have been in hospitals and sanatoriums for twenty years and I have never once heard of a nurse giving the wrong medicine." Kate nudged me and said quite audibly, "I can hope, can't I?"

After supper I was wheeled back to bed; at five-thirty the Charge Nurse and the House Doctor made rounds; at six-thirty we were served hot or cold milk; and at seven the radio was turned on. The radio was loud enough to hear all the words and there was a control switch just outside our door to raise or lower the volume, according to our pleasure. This would have been the ultimate in luxury back at the Bedrest Hospital, but now it mattered not a whit to me.

I had so much else to think about, so many other joys. I could lie in bed, my feet nuzzling a hot hot-water bottle, and listen to the frogs screaming a welcome. I could breathe the sweet spring-scented air and watch the evening creep through the cherry orchard. I could see a small moon hanging like a splinter of mirror above a straggly black fir tree. I could think about a bath in a bathtub the next morning. I ached all over from the unaccustomed activity, I knew the Charge Nurse had singled me out for the object of her venom, I hadn't had nearly enough supper—but I fell asleep before lights out.

➤➤➤XV➤➤➤

Eight Hours Up

The next day, I had a bath in a bathtub, my first in exactly six months! The bathroom, just around the corner from our room, was a series of small spare wooden rooms smelling strongly of disinfectant and dampness. There was a reception hall containing large hampers for soiled towels and pajamas, a rack of newspapers to be used for bathmats, and printed instructions prominently displayed and carefully framed in glass to protect them from the steam. The instructions read: "Do not lock the door. . . . Do not gossip about nurses and doctors. . . . Do not leave bathroom in a mess. . . . Do not have the bathwater too hot. . . . Do not steal from other patients. . . . Do not cough without putting a napkin over the mouth. . . . etc., etc., etc., etc., etc." At the bottom of the list in the boldest type was, "Patients who cannot obey the rules should be sent home!" Opening off the reception room were two shower rooms with wooden-slatted floors, a broom closet, a toilet and two narrow rooms containing one large white bathtub each.

A nurse had already prepared my bath, a service performed only for three-hour patients, and I hurried to the bathroom expecting a steaming tub. What I found was a tub gingerly wet on the bottom with, apparently, equal portions of lukewarm water and sheep dip, for a pungent odor of disinfectant arose from the tub in gray swirls. I callously locked the door, let out the water, rinsed out the disinfectant, substituted several handfuls of bath salts and filled the tub to the lip with warm water. Nothing ever again will equal my exalted sense of well-being as I slipped into the warm scented water, nor will anything ever again equal the unexpectedly informal note supplied by the janitor who bustled in and out of the reception hall, emptying hampers, exchanging brooms and mops and tossing pleasantries to me over the alarmingly low door of my bathroom.

"Nothing like a bath in a bathtub," said the janitor. "This your first one?" "Yes, it is," I said soaping my washcloth and afraid to look up for fear I'd find him peering interestedly over the door. I washed my left thigh. "Whatever you got in there sure smells good," said the janitor sniffing loudly, much too close to the door. "It's carnation," I said reaching for the newspapers just in case. "I prefer showers myself," said the friendly janitor from behind the thin wall just back of my head. "I don't care whether it's a shower or a tub bath, I just like to be alone in it," I said meaningly. It was wasted effort. "Gosh, when we was kids," the janitor said, between counting towels, "they was eleven of us and my maw used to put three, four of us into the tub at once." It began to sound ominously as though I were going to have to move over. "I don't care what your mother did—" I had begun testily when a new bather entered the reception room. "Well, hel-lo, Janet," said the keeper of the bath, "I thought Thursday was your day." I wouldn't have been surprised to have him add, "And I see you got the same old birthmark." The three of us finished my bath in a volley of conversation and I returned to my bed enlightened by more than my cleanliness.

Two days after my first bath I had a shampoo in the beauty parlor. The beauty parlor, in the basement of the

Ambulant Hospital, was operated by ambulant patients except for the three-hour patients who were shampooed by nurses. Unfortunately my shampoo in the beauty parlor differed from other shampoos only in location, as Gravy Face, who had been transferred to the Ambulant Hospital, did the washing and, when she had finished, my hair was as dirty as before and so full of green soap that running a wet comb through it left a wake.

I was warned by Sigrid that the next step in the Ambulant Hospital routine would be a trip to the Charge Nurse's office for a little talk. The Charge Nurse said, "We do not encourage any friendships between the men and the women, Mrs. Bard. In tuberculosis, sex is the worst complication, Mrs. Bard. Infractions of the rules are punished by taking away visiting or show privileges, not granting requests for town leaves or sending you home, Mrs. Bard. I hope you will like it here and continue in your splendid recovery." I said nothing and we parted friends.

My first visitors, Mother and Madge, were as delighted as I with the new surroundings.

Mother brought me a dozen cans of fruit juice and a large box of cookies, all of which Sigrid stuffed in my old stand bag and hung under the robes and sweaters in my locker. We were all starving all the time but were not allowed to keep any food in our rooms, which were searched regularly.

Mother also brought a very glamorous pair of turquoise satin lounging pajamas which I had had before coming to The Pines. I tried them on but they were skin tight and very uncomfortable. The insidious piling up of superfluous flesh was the penalty I had paid for my well-encased t.b. germs. The first time I walked to the dining room with my visitors my sister Alison screamed when she saw me upright and said, "You're the biggest thing I've ever seen." Mother said, "But see how straight her back is." Alison said, "Nothing about her is straight. I've never seen so many curves in my life."

At the end of the first week I was asked to sit at Kimi's table. Our other tablemates were Pixie, Kimi's former room-mate who still ate like "the mouse," and a dour black Scots-woman who had been at The Pines for seven years.

Sunday morning at five o'clock I heard the sweet-faced, gentle Catholic Fathers going softly from room to room on the promenade, blessing their people. I used to see them in the Bedrest Hospital and hear the soft murmur of their voices and even though I am an Episcopalian I often wished that one of them would stop at my bed, often thought that the Catholic Church alone has the true feeling of religion. The other ministers came too, but only on occasion and usually during visiting hours. No doubt their intent was good but to attempt to make contact with God during visiting hours was as futile as trying to pray at a cocktail party.

Monday I went to fluoroscope. Six- and eight-hour pa-tients walked but I was wheeled by Henry, the x-ray man, who took advantage of the Charge Nurse's day off to ignore the dark tunnels and to wheel me through the grounds so that I could see the freshly dug perennial beds with their clumps of sharp green spikes, thick red shoots, and grayish green leaves, and the full blossoming wild cherry tree down by the Children's Hospital. Willy, the other x-ray man, brought me back the same way and I filled my good lung with the heady bouquet of earth, new leaves and manure.

Tuesday after rest hours I was peacefully engaged in lis-tening to the drowsy sound of the gardener's lawn mower outside my window and watching the white foam of the cherry orchard undulate slowly in the breeze, when the Charge Nurse came in bearing a small box of index cards listing reading courses and books available on each. There was a small library at The Pines and through the librarian (a very trusted patient) we could order books from the city Public Library. At Bedrest, the librarian took orders for books one week and the next wheeled in a cart of books and told you that yours was not among them. At the Ambulant Hospital it appeared that only the Charge Nurse was trusted enough for this responsibility, for she waved her little box of cards at Sigrid and me and told us that we must choose a subject and FOLLOW IT THROUGH! The cards embraced such subjects as philosophy, psychology, history, music, art, architecture, etc., but I chose economics, not because I was in the least interested in economics but because it sounded hardest and was, I knew, the one the Charge Nurse had not expected me to choose. The book she recommended for me to start on was called *Economics* Anyone *Can Understand*. After rest hours the librarian came breathlessly in to tell me that they were going to have to send to the Public Library for *all* my books. I told her I hoped it would take months and continued to gaze languidly at the cherry orchard.

When I had been at the Ambulant Hospital a month, Sigrid and I were given chest examinations. We were very excited as these chest examinations were important and could mean six hours' time up, wearing our clothes, working in the occupational therapy shop, going to the Bedrest Hospital on flower duty and other forms of pleasant activity, but we had to await the whimsy of the Charge Nurse to learn the results.

After rest hours Sigrid was informed that she had six hours. The Charge Nurse said nothing to me so I asked about my time up, which for some strange reason turned her livid with rage and produced a long garbled lecture on "Patients should not take the burden of the cure on themselves." As all the lessons so far had instructed me to take the burden of cure on myself or be sent home I was confused.

The Charge Nurse slapped off and I pulled a lounge chair onto the promenade deck so that I could watch the little children come through the orchard on their walk. There were about twenty-five of them ranging in age from two to fifteen years and all except the two oldest girls dressed in nothing but very brief shorts, shoes, socks and hats. They were all as brown and round as hazel nuts. The nurse led the way and they came straggling along, the smallest and largest holding hands and bringing up the rear. A small fat little girl slapped the little boy next to her, then jumped and broke off the end of a branch of cherry blossoms before the nurse could stop her.

Sigrid called to me that May twelfth was Hospital Day and that my children would be allowed to come at eleven o'clock in the morning and stay until four in the afternoon.

Two days later I was told I was to have eight hours and to increase my time half an hour a day instead of the usual fifteen minutes. I would have six hours and wear my clothes the next Tuesday; eight hours a week from the following Saturday and I would be eligible for a town leave on June third. Eight hours at home with my loved ones and good coffee!

When I told the family of my eight hours and impending homecoming they seemed uneasy. I could see them holding worried conferences over what to do with a large fat member soon to be released and too delicate to do anything but eat.

Mother brought me new underclothing—everything marked LARGE—and Katherine Mansfield's *Journal*.

Reading of Katherine Mansfield's tragic and lonely struggle against tuberculosis made me see The Pines as such a paradise that I could even place a small golden halo around the head of the Charge Nurse as she sidled in our door like a giant hermit crab to warn me that from that moment on anything I did, including breathing, would be cause for removing my town leave.

On the following Monday, at ten-thirty, Sigrid left for

home. Outwardly she was cool, calm and Nordic but inwardly there must have been some emotion because her hands were shaking so I had to button her blouse.

The moment she had gone a corps of nurses came in with scrub brushes and buckets of disinfectant to remove all trace of her. Her bedding and all her things were dumped into large cardboard cartons marked FUMIGATION, and wheeled away. Everything she had touched or used was scrubbed. The faint scent of violets she left behind was replaced with lysol. Her spilled violet bathpowder was wiped away with a rag dipped in sheep dip. Her name was added to the list of "Outgoing" and I smelt the air and looked at the empty bed, the hollow locker, the freshly lined bureau drawers and wondered if she had ever been here at all.

Eileen's roommate, Delores the nightclub singer, arrived at the Ambulant Hospital and I felt reasonably sure that the Charge Nurse would be too busy to bother with me any more. Delores had a large mouth, perfect, flashing white teeth and bold blue eyes. Her every movement had a purpose and increased weight had given her very delectable curves which she showed to advantage by pulling her flimsy purple kimono tightly around her. Her first entrance to the dining room was late and dramatic.

Arranging herself in the doorway, slightly sideways so that what lay beneath the tightly pulled kimono was prominently displayed, Delores looked the dining room and the diners over slowly and carefully. Then, when it was pretty well established that every single eye in the room was riveted on her, she put everything she had into a great big dazzling smile and slowly undulated to a seat at the front table. One of the men was so carried away by the performance that he began to clap and was rewarded with a 240-volt look from Delores' blue eyes and a raised beef stew ladle and a warning shake of the head from the Charge Nurse. Kimi said,

"For the first time I feel pity for the Charge Nurse. Her worst fears have been realized. Sex has entered her Ambulant Hospital and she has no weapons to combat it but the removal of small privileges, which when compared to Delores' no longer seem like privileges."

Pixie said that she was in the cubicle next to Delores for a month up at Bedrest and that Delores quite unintentionally used to torture the Charge Nurse by discussing her ailments so that the whole ward could hear, and by flagging down every doctor who went by and saying in her husky, penetrating voice, "I have a little pain right here, Doctah. No, a little lower down, if you don't mind, Doctah. No, a little lower down, Doctah! No, it doesn't hurt very much, Doctah, but if I thought it would make you come to see me oftener I could make it hurt moah." Pixie said that the doctors quite evidently enjoyed Delores but frost formed on the Charge Nurse during these little tête-à-têtes.

As the dour Scotswoman had gone back to Bedrest, Kimi, Pixie and I unanimously agreed to ask Delores to make a fourth at our table and I stopped on my way out of the dining room to welcome her to the Ambulant Hospital and to extend our invitation. She gave me a nice firm handshake and said through her beautiful teeth, "Jesus, honey, I'm glad to know *you*. I've heard about you since the day I came heah." I said, "Jesus, honey, I'm glad to know *you* and you'll never know how pleasant you are going to make life for me from now on."

When I had achieved my eight hours up, I was moved upstairs next door to Kimi and Sheila, who were roommates. My new roommate was twenty-one years old, read the funny papers aloud, called me Kid and talked about nothing but "IT" (sexual intercourse). She was very large, had reddish hair and should have been married.

Because the dining room was crowded Delores was moved

at once to our table, which was at the end of the dining room farthest from the Charge Nurse and in the row of tables next to no man's land and the men's section. She sat with her back to the men or rather she was supposed to. Actually she sat slightly sideways in her chair, her legs crossed like one of those confidential singers who start out, "Listen folks, and I'll tell you 'bout that man of mine." There were four nice-looking young men at the table just back of Delores and they took to being the first in the dining room and the last to leave. The Charge Nurse looking completely addled began slapping up and down the promenades day and night peering into the rooms.

-»»XVI«-

A Toecover and How It Breeds

TOECOVER IS A family name for a useless gift. A crocheted napkin ring is a toecover. So are embroidered book marks, large figurines of a near-together-eyed shepherdess, pincushion covers done in French knots, a satin case for snapfasteners (with a card of snapfasteners tactfully enclosed so you won't make a mistake and think it a satin case for hooks-and-eyes or old pieces of embroidery thread), embroidered coat hangers, hand-painted shoe trees (always painted with a special paint that never dries), home-made three-legged footstools with the legs spaced unevenly so the footstool always lies on one side, cross-stitched pictures of lumpy brown houses with "The houfe by the fide of the road" worked in Olde Englishe underneath, hand-decorated celluloid soap cases for traveling with tops that once off will never fit back on the bottom, crocheted paper knife handle covers complete with tassel, bud vases made out of catsup bottles, taffeta bed pillows heavily shirred and apparently stuffed with iron filings, poorly executed dolls whose voluminous skirts are supposed to cover telephones.

A toecover is not a thing that follows economic cycles. During the depression when everyone was making her own Christmas presents, toecovers abounded. In good times toecovers are not made at home but are bought in the back of Gifte Shoppes whose main income is from the lending library in the front.

219

On May third, I made my first trip to the women's occupational therapy shop and discovered it to be a bubbling source of toecovers presided over by the most enthusiastic advocate for and producer of the toecover in this era, Miss Gillespie.

Miss Gillespie was physically and mentally exactly what you'd expect the producer of hand-painted paper plates to be. She had a mouth so crowded with false teeth it looked as if she had put in two sets, firm, obviously dyed black hair, spectacles, wide hips and her own set of rules. One of these rules was that women patients could not use the basement lavatory because "the men will see you go in there and *know* what you go in there for." Another forbade the pressing of men's trousers by women, on the grounds that such intimate contact with male garments was unseemly.

On my first morning, I was directed by Miss Gillespie to sit at a table and roll bandages. She said, "Go over THERE! No, there! No, THERE! No talking. Quiet, must have QUIET. Work, work, no need to talk! Talking is bad for the lungs. Quiet, must have quiet!" I sat down next to Kimi who said, "Pay no attention to her, Betty." As Miss Gillespie was standing directly behind Kimi I hissed, "Be quiet, she'll hear you." Kimi said, much louder, "Oh, no she won't, for she is deaf as a stone."

For three days I rolled bandages under the hysterical supervision of Miss Gillespie and found it not unpleasant for it was useful work and the occupational therapy shop was large and light with green walls and furniture and a nice view of the cherry orchard from its south windows.

On the fourth morning when Sheila, Kimi and I reported for work at eight-thirty, Miss Gillespie screamed, "Typing! Typing. Must have typists! Magazine to get out! Quiet, must have typists, must have quiet!" Kimi, Sheila and I could all type, so we were made associate editors of the sanatorium magazine which meant merely that we typed from eight-thirty to ten-thirty anything that Miss Gillespie handed us.

As the ward news often contained "I seens," "he don'ts" and "we done its," we at first attempted to make a few editorial changes. Miss Gillespie compared the copies with the original and went wild. "Right from the heart," she yelled pounding on the original manuscript with her ruler. "Right from the heart, don't change a word. Type. Type. After all everyone don't talk like you." "No, he don't," Kimi said gently, smiling at Miss Gillespie who couldn't hear a word she was saying, "but I only done the best I could. I seen the mistakes and I fixed them." Miss Gillespie said to Sheila and me, "Why don't you try to act like Miss Sanbo. She is quiet. She don't argue. Now everybody to work, quiet! Quiet!"

While we typed, the rest of the women made bandages, hooked rugs, sterilized and powdered rubber gloves, made hospital gowns, clothes for the children in the Children's Hospital and gave shampoos.

From ten-thirty to eleven-thirty was our own time but we were supposed to learn useful occupations so that there would be a place for us in the great industrial world into which we were soon to be dumped. A few of the trades offered by Miss Gillespie were the manufacture of little crocheted baskets to hang by the sink to hold wedding and engagement rings while the owner washed the dishes, clothes-pin curtain retainers, rooster pot holders, hand-painted paper plates, embroidered combing jackets, kewpie doorstops, crocheted needle books, crepe-paper lampshades, crocheted book marks, imitation crepe-paper sweet peas, holders for paper towels made out of old candy boxes decorated with forget-me-nots and marked "This looks like a towel, This feels like a towel, This is a towel, Use it," (unfortunately Miss Gillespie always made the hole in the boxes through which the towel was to be pulled too small so that "This looks like a crumpled piece of paper" would have been a more accurate way to mark her dispensers), the spleen vases, crocheted hot-water bottle covers, and decorated pillows of every type.

I asked Miss Gillespie if I could use my time to brush up on my shorthand, but she, evidently having never heard of shorthand and supposing it to be some sort of game like volley ball, yelled, "No! NO! Too noisy!" so I went on with the tatted collar. Sheila, much against Miss G.'s will, made a coat, Kimi and her mother made many lovely things, a blouse, two new skirts, a large embroidered tablecloth, even angora anklets. The rest of the women made toecovers.

On May tenth I was sent to the Bedrest Hospital on flower duty. My flower partner, a tiny little woman who wore old corsages and referred to her husband as "Big Daddy," and I walked to Bedrest at nine o'clock and reported to the Charge Nurse who was very cordial, complimented us on our time up but couldn't resist the old impulse to warn us not to talk as we took our empty carts and started up and down the wards gathering up all the vases of flowers.

I was shocked to find Eileen very thin and white and listless. She had had another hemorrhage, she told me, and was running a temperature all the time. I told her about Delores and Kimi but she wasn't very interested. I asked about Minna and she was apathetic even about her. The only time she showed even the faintest glimmer of her old fire was when she told me about the crush she had on the new store boy.

Minna was in one of the private rooms, tickled to death because one of her kidneys had become infected and the doctors were contemplating removing it. "It's an awful serious operation," she told me blinking her pale eyes, "and the doctah said he didn't see how a little old thing like me could pull through it, but Ah just told him that sometimes us little fellers ah strongah than you great big people." I found that being ambulant made Minna and her constant reference to her tininess and my gigantic size no longer irritating. I asked about Sweetie-Pie. She said, "Oh, that pooah thing is so worried about me. He cried when I told him about my kidney."

There were so many new and strange faces in the Bedrest Hospital that I thought there must be a regular epidemic of tuberculosis in the city. Marie astounded me by having time up and being very cheerful; Eleanor was on the porch being inspirational and knitting; Evalee had three hours and was to come to the Ambulant Hospital the next day; Margaretta, the beautiful Negro girl, was dying.

She was in the light room and the Charge Nurse surprised me by asking if I would go in and see her. She tried to prepare me a little by telling me that Margaretta was very ill, but nothing she could have said would have lessened the shock of what I saw. Margaretta's head seemed to have shrunk and become wizened like the dried heads of Indian mummies, her hands lay listlessly on the bedcovers like terrible little brown claws. Her voice was completely gone. Only by her large beautiful brown eyes was she recognizable as the girl who used to smile and wave at Kimi and me.

I told her that she should hurry and get time up so she could go on flower duty; I told her a little of Miss Toecover and her idea of useful occupation; I told her about Kimi and the Charge Nurse but my voice was too loud and my gaiety sounded hollow and forced. Margaretta waved one of the little brown claws when I left and I went into the utility room and wilted the flowers with scalding tears.

My first try at washwater duty was five days later and began rather unfortunately. Harassed by Miss Gillespie's screamed warnings that I was to be in the dining room at five-thirty and not a second later, I hurled myself across the lawns in the cool gray of the dawn and arrived at the dining room breathless and ready for work at four-twenty. The night nurse, glad of company at that dreary hour, fixed coffee and fruit juice and we talked until we were joined at five-thirty by my washwater partner, a small pleasant Eskimo girl named Esther.

As my first morning at The Pines was still clear in my memory, I tried to wake the patients gently and Esther and I made many trips and gave everyone a full basin of hot water. Eileen seemed better and more cheerful as she told me that she and the store boy were engaged and would be married as soon as they were well.

Minna rubbed her thick white eyelids, blinked and said, "Ah'm soooooo sleeeeeeeepy," and for a minute I was back in the four-bed ward and wanted to pound her on the head with the water pitcher. Marie was cranky and said that she didn't like so much or such hot water; Eleanor said that she had heard that Margaretta was in emergency in a coma and wouldn't last through the day, that the little thirteen-year-old girl, Evangeline Constable, had had a spontaneous collapse and was not expected to live, and had I heard about Eileen's hemorrhage; old Gazz-on-Her-Stummick asked me if I wouldn't please fill her hot-water bottle as she had so much gazz on her stummick she hadn't closed her eyes all night, so I did and she said that the hot-water bottle was too hot and wouldn't I please put a little cold in it and while I was there would I hand her her sweater and if I saw the nurse would I send her in and would I bring her a glass of fresh water as she didn't like the taste of water after it had stood and could I pour just a little water on her flowers as they seemed to be drooping and . . . I grabbed her basin and fled.

Our kind-hearted ministerings to the sick glazed Esther and me with noble feelings but made us very late to breakfast, which elicited some acid comments from the Charge Nurse as she tossed us hard-boiled eggs and cold toast.

On Saturday mornings we reported to the occupational therapy shop but were allowed to use the three hours for a shampoo, to press clothes, to manicure our nails or to work on our toecovers. I used my Saturday mornings to write letters on the typewriter and was usually very much hampered by Miss Gillespie, who chose that time to weave.

The loom was in one corner of the small typing room and each time Miss Gillespie pushed the treadles or whatever the things were that changed the warp, they stuck for a time then gave in with a terrific crash which brought forth a scream, then a wild laugh from Miss G. It was not conducive to concentration, but I enjoyed sitting behind her and writing down accurate descriptions of her rules and habits.

On the morning of my first trip to washwater she brought out a new rule. After I had been in the shop for about an hour I started to leave to go upstairs to the bathroom. Miss Gillespie came panting after me. "Where are you going?" she demanded. "To the bathroom," I said. She said, "Now, Mrs. Bard, going to the toilet is merely a habit. Habits can be broken. Not necessary. Break it. Bad habit. Control the functions of the body. Everything can be controlled. Why there are days and days when I don't go to the toilet from dawn till dark." I continued up the ramp with Miss Gillespie clutching my arm and trying to dissuade me. She never forgave me.

When I finally finished my tatted collar and washed it and brought it down to the O.T. shop on Saturday morning to press, Miss Gillespie said, "Tatting, humph! Never cared for it much myself." Sheila and Kimi, just to be irritating, for we none of us liked the great big collar, said loudly so Miss Gillespie could hear, "It's beautiful! Gorgeous! Exquisite!"

Miss Gillespie sniffed and said, "I think that too much praise is very bad for people. I am willing to get along with nothing but a little criticism, but some people have to have flattery, flattery, flattery!" "And toilets," Kimi said softly, smiling and looking directly at Miss Gillespie, who beamed back at her.

⇾⇾XVII⇽⇽

Privileges

THURSDAY NIGHT WAS library night and after supper, pulse and temperatures, we eight-hour females put on our robes and repaired to the library to choose books, silently and under the watchful eye of the Charge Nurse. The library, on the first floor, was lined with book cases, had a fireplace and leather furniture and could have been a very pleasant reading room. It wasn't. It was dark and cheerless and cold and the inside of the fireplace, like the inside of every fireplace at The Pines, had been scrubbed and waxed and never tainted by fire.

The books had been donated and *Meet Yourself as You Really Are, My Hand Is In the Hand of Jesus, Hans Brinker* or *The Silver Skates, Daddy Long Legs, Psychology and Industrial Efficiency, Black Beauty, Office Wife, Elizabeth and Her German Garden, The Magic Mountain, Away from It All, Let the People Know, Jottings from a Cruise, Fear, The Conquest of Bread, Pollyanna* and *Over the Top* by Guy Empey, were side by side and at our disposal.

Every day, no matter what the weather, eight-hour patients took a walk. At three o'clock we dressed, including hats or head scarves, gathered in the library for roll call, then were herded to the store and back. The store, about a half a block from the Ambulant Hospital and nicely situated in a little grove of trees, carried in addition to pop, cookies, candy,

226

gum and ink, lined tablets and pencils, all the necessary implements and materials for the manufacture of toecovers.

Twice while I was at the Ambulant Hospital, our walks were supervised by one of the sweet young nurses, who took us by the farms, down a winding path through a wooded grove bordered with iris and carpeted with pink star flowers, and to a large log cabin. The warm pine needles crunched underfoot, bringing back memories of camping trips and house parties, the empty log cabin smelled deliciously like an empty log cabin and the Charge Nurse and Miss Toecover seemed very far away.

Motion pictures were shown once a month but as Miss Gillespie was the judge of who among the ambulant patients was fit to go, Sheila and I were invited to only one movie while at the Ambulant Hospital. Kimi was asked to them all but out of loyalty stayed home with us.

I sat in back of Delores at my one movie, *Victoria, the Queen,* and when Victoria was shown sipping her before-dinner sherry, Delores gave me a poke and said in a very hoarse, audible whisper, "Jesus, Betty, how would it seem to be hoisting a few again?"

After the movie the male patients arose as one man and tried to walk in front or in back of Pixie and Delores, who were roommates and rivals to the death. Pixie, small and beautifully formed, wore pastel colors and her hair on top of her head and was exquisite. Delores wore her hair hanging almost to her waist, tight bright red dresses, bright red lipstick, bright red shoes and was devastating. They drove the Charge Nurse frantic but Miss Gillespie loved them. They thought all of her toecovers were "cute" and under her supervision Delores made ten of the cement-hard shirred boudoir pillows and Pixie made one of the "This is a Towel" boxes, two ring baskets, a knitted shopping bag and hundreds of the crepe-paper sweetpeas.

On Hospital Day, May twelfth, we could have as many

visitors as we liked from nine to twelve-thirty and from two to four in the afternoon. Even former patients, not usually allowed on the grounds of the hospital within a year of their discharge, could come in and visit.

The day was warm and clear, the poplars along the drive sparkled and swayed in the breeze and by eight-thirty the whole hospital was filled with expectation and the smell of new-mown grass. Anne, Joan, Mother, Alison, Mary, Madge, Cleve, Margaret, friends from out of town, everyone came.

Anne and Joan, in their dark blue coats, spent the entire five and a half hours asking me if they could have wooden shoes, and I had a strong feeling, that if I died, their chief sorrow would be not getting the wooden shoes. Just before dinner I dressed and took the children around the promenades and introduced them to my friends and after the first four or five introductions I didn't have to push so hard on the tops of their heads to make them curtsy.

Kimi had the first town leave. On May thirteenth at noon her family came to get her and Sheila and I stood on the dining-room terrace and waved and waved, the tears running down our foolish faces. Just as she climbed into the car, Kimi looked threateningly over her shoulder at us and said, "Tell the Charge Nurse not to be surprised nevair to see me again." She came back, though, promptly on the stroke of eight, reported to the office, had her pulse and temperature taken, and then staggered up the ramp her arms full of food and presents for us all.

Eleven of us gathered in her bathroom to drink tea made from hot water out of the tap, to eat hamburgers, soggy and slightly cold but delicious, and Japanese Sembi. Kimi said that her town leave was wonderful but it raised a doubt in her mind about the future of "a large Japanese creature, riddled with germ but longing for a normal life." Delores said, "Don't you worry, honey, with your looks and brains you could go on the stage." Kimi said grimly, "But only to demonstrate to the world how large the Japanese can get." Pixie said, "Look at me, I bet not one of my costumes will fit me. This morning I weighed one hundred and *two* pounds." Kimi said, "Let us change the subject at once. When is your town leave, Betty?"

My town leave was to be on Saturday, June third, if granted. I turned in my application or request, on May twenty-first. A few minutes later the Charge Nurse sent for me and in her most ingratiating manner told me that before approving my town leave the Medical Director would have to know what my attitude was toward—and she read off a list beginning with "Controlling impulses of the bladder"—result of a report from Miss Toecover—and ending with "Speaking French to roommate." I could not imagine what this last was all about and told the Charge Nurse so. She said, "It has been reported to me, Mrs. Bard, that you speak French to your roommate in the evenings." I wondered why, if this were true, it would not be considered a virtue but refrained from comment.

The mystery was cleared up when I returned to my room quivering with rage and noticed a cook book lying on my roommate's table on top of several weeks' accumulation of funny papers. I remembered how, several evenings before, roommate was studying the cook book and asking me the meaning of the terms, sauté (she pronounced it sooty), au gratin, fricasee, en brochette, mousse (pronounced of course mouse), etc. I told her of the incident with the Charge Nurse and warned her that if I lost my town leave I would not answer for the consequences. She said only, "Speaking French. Gee, kid, what a laugh!"

Three days later the Charge Nurse sent for me, kept me waiting as she always did for about half an hour, then summoned me to her office. She preceded her lecture by telling me how many times a week the Medical Director called her a damned fool. This was supposed to establish a fellow feeling between us. All it did for me was to give the Medical Director credit for being more discerning than I had thought. The crux of the visit was that my request for a town leave had been approved but with the addendum: "Tell this patient that her attitude does not warrant a town leave but I will grant this one. However, unless she changes materially she will get no further town leaves unless it be a permanent one." After reading this message from the Medical Director, the Charge Nurse gave me a short lecture on "Thrice blessed are those who forgive and forget" and "Let us admit our faults and try to do better."

I awakened on the day of my town leave to leaden skies and driving rain which I didn't mind in the least as it meant a fire in the fireplace at home. On the stroke of twelve Mary drove up and out spilled Anne and Joan followed by Mother carrying my tweed coat. I ran down the ramp and was engulfed in embraces and my old tweed, then to the car and away. The thrill of going through the gates, rounding the bend and losing sight of the sanatorium was never to be forgotten.

When we drove up in front of the house, sisters Dede, Alison and Madge, the dogs and the cats were on the steps to greet me. We all went in, Anne and Joan glued to each side, and then I had cups and cups of delicious, strong, hot coffee. I felt peaceful and content and so happy. Then Madge began to play the piano. She played "Tea for Two," "Night and Day," "Body and Soul," "Judy," all my favorites, and I was overwhelmed. It was all too wonderful. I wept and the children cried too, and the dogs barked and everyone else tried in loud voices to be cheerful. Mother hurriedly served lunch.

We all sat down at the table and everything was very gay for a few minutes. Then Joanie put down her soup spoon and began to bawl. With sympathetic tears streaming from my own eyes, I asked her what the trouble was. She gulped and said, "I was just thinking about showing you my new shoes and I remembered they have dye spilled on them." I finally persuaded her to get them anyway and she came down with a very large pair of Mexican huaraches with a pinpoint of black dye on one side. I exclaimed over the beauty and wondrous size of the shoes and everything was peaceful until lunch was over.

Then brother Cleve, his wife Margaret and son Allen, dear neighbors and their children, the "old baby" now a little boy who shook hands and talked plainly and solemnly, and neighborhood children came to see the returned invalid. The very foreign atmosphere of loving kindness proved too much and again I wept and the children chimed in. When the visitors had gone we piled logs on the fire, made more coffee and prepared to make the most of the fleeting eight hours.

Unhappily I raised the question of where I would sleep when I returned, which brought to light the fact that the-always-ice-cold but with-its-own-bath-downstairs bedroom, instead of being filled with flowers in crystal vases awaiting my return, had not been touched since I left. In fact was being used as a storeroom. "Just as though you didn't expect me to come home ever," I said brokenly. "Oh, we knew our good luck couldn't last forever," Dede said putting her arm around me. The issue of who was to clean the back bedroom before I came home ended in a tremendous and very vigorous family fight involving every injustice done to any of us as far back as we could remember. In the midst of this emotional upheaval I was horrified to find that I was weeping and TATTING!

I was in the office on the stroke of eight o'clock and rather disappointed to find that my pulse and temperature were perfectly normal. As I had returned laden with hot ham sandwiches and a chocolate cake, I was greeted by my tubercular friends with great enthusiasm.

After lights out I lay in the dark and thought about the day. I was certain that my family hadn't the least idea of the meaning of the words rest and quiet; that they thought because I looked much healthier than any of them that I must be equally strong or stronger; that it would be impossible to observe rest hours or to adhere to only eight hours' time up at home. I was very tired, quite unhappy and bewildered and didn't care that I had lost my next town leave.

The next morning Kimi and Sheila were informed that their next town leaves had also been cancelled on the grounds that the Charge Nurse thought that they thought they were superior to her. They said that they didn't care.

As there was a perfect cloudburst during rest hours and immediately before visiting hours, Mother arrived very wet and very cross. She denounced me soundly for weeping on my day at home, said that everyone had planned a happy day for me and that I was a most unsatisfactory guest. I explained that tears were brought on by joy but she merely sniffed and intimated that I was a big "saddo" and very spoiled. She said, "You have been concentrating on yourself for eight months, now it is time you began to think of someone else."

I wish that I could say that I immediately began thinking of other people and was consequently much happier. I didn't. As soon as visiting hours were over I told Kimi and Sheila how very un-understanding my family were. They retaliated with similar tales of hard-heartedness on the part of their loved ones. After supper we sat in the bathroom, drinking tea, eating cake and talking about how difficult it was going to be for delicate, emotionally frail us to get the proper care in the big cruel outside world.

⇥XVIII⇤

"Let Me Out! Let Me Out!"

THE MEDICAL DIRECTOR of The Pines made himself personally responsible for all admissions to and discharges from the
sanatorium. He never admitted as a patient anyone who
could afford to go to a private sanatorium and he never gave
an honorable discharge to a patient until he was sure that
patient was well enough to resume normal living.

Patients at The Pines paid nothing or what they could and
only the Medical Director knew who paid what. People who
can reach out anytime and touch death have little false pride
and the nothing-payers, by their own admission, were in the
great majority. The Medical Director ruled his sanatorium
and the patients with a rod of iron, said constantly that people with tuberculosis were ungrateful, stupid, uncooperative
and unworthy. Then, carefully screening himself from his
own kindness the way he screened his patients from their
operations, he loaned those same ungrateful, stupid, uncooperative and unworthy patients money, bought them bathrobes and pajamas, took care of their families and children,
listened to their problems, helped them get work and fretted
twenty-four hours a day over their welfare.

We patients at The Pines differed in color, nationality,
political beliefs, I.Q., age, religion, background and ambition.
According to the standards of normal living, the only things

that most of us had in common were being alive and speaking English, but as patients in the sanatorium we had everything in common and were firmly cemented together by our ungratefulness, stupidity, uncooperativeness, unworthiness, poverty, tuberculosis and longing for a discharge.

Discharges, announced on Mondays directly after rest hours, were (except in the very rare instance of someone like Sigrid who was so well adjusted she could have cured her tuberculosis riding on the subway, or someone being sent home to die) given only to patients with eight, ten or twelve hours' time up.

As a patient was never told anything about the progress of his tuberculosis cure and was never warned of impending dismissal, a discharge was supposed to be a complete and wonderful surprise. Actually, every Monday from five-thirty a.m. until three o'clock, all eight-hour patients were jumpy with anticipation and lay in their beds during rest hours, stiff and prickly with hope, listening for the slap, slap of the Charge Nurse's feet. When weeks, even months had gone by without a single discharge, we'd relax or rather droop and make morbid plans for our third Christmas, our fourth summer at The Pines.

During one of these depressing no-discharge intervals, I made plans to learn to read and write Japanese so fluently that I could even take Japanese dictation. Kimi said that she would be glad to teach me, but if I was planning on a career as a spy she thought it only fair to warn me that I would be wasting my time as spies were always willowy creatures able to slip through small apertures.

Sheila decided to write a book and Kimi decided on the study of psychiatry. She said, "With such rare laboratory specimens as we have right here at hand I may become famous almost immediately."

Then one Monday at two-thirty the Charge Nurse's slapping feet stopped at my door but at the bed of my roommate, who was told to report immediately to the dining room. She came back in a little while and said that the Medical Director had told her that she could go home that afternoon if she wanted to, but she didn't want to, she liked it at The Pines and thought she'd stay on for another month or two. Resisting a strong desire to slap her for this further demonstration of stupidity, I asked who else had been given discharges.

There were six of them. A very sweet woman with four small children; Big Daddy and her faded corsages; a fat little woman who wore pink-flowered sleepers and looked like a piggy bank; a woman who had had t.b. of the spine, had had the diseased piece of her spine removed and replaced by a piece of her thigh, had lain uncomplainingly flat on her back for over a year but was distinguished not for her brilliant recovery but for not having had her hair washed for fifteen months; a young newspaper reporter, and the handsome man who had escorted Eleanor to the movies. In the dining room, as each one who had been given a discharge brought his tray to his table, there was a deafening thunder of clapping.

After supper when the Charge Nurse made her rounds my roommate said, "I don't wanna go home yet. I think I'll stay on for a few months." The Charge Nurse said, "The Medical Director wouldn't have given you your discharge if you weren't ready to go home. We are very crowded. Please leave immediately." I wanted to kiss her.

After temperatures and pulse we all lined up on the promenades and watched the cars drive up and take away the lucky seven. When the young husband came for the sweet woman with the four little children, everyone cried. The husband, a rather thin, stooped young man, climbed carefully out of the car carrying the baby, then with the other children tumbling around his feet, he stood in the twilight by the dining room looking anxiously toward the Ambulant Hospital. When his healthy wife came out in her too-small shabby suit, he handed her the baby, lifted up each child for a kiss, then put his thin arm protectively around her plump shoulders and guided her to the old car.

When our tear-blurred eyes had followed the lights of the last car bearing the last free patient down the drive, out the gates and around the bend, Kimi, Sheila, Evalee and I retired to my bathroom to drink tea and to talk moodily about the long, long week that lay between us and next Monday. Evalee said, "I don't know what I'd do if the Medical Director sent me home on eight hours. With my husband away and Mama working I'd sure have to be up more than eight hours to take care of two little children." Kimi said, "You'll just have to give the little one sedative so that you can all sleep sixteen hour a day."

Sheila said, "Well, I'm not going to stick to eight hours' time up when I get home, and as long as I live I'm never going to lie down in the middle of the day again." Evalee said, "Just you wait until you have a family. You'll be tickled to death to have an excuse to take a nap." I said nothing. I came from a family that considered one a.m. early evening and afternoon naps only for little children and the senile. I wondered if the Medical Director knew of these problems and took them into consideration when giving discharges. It seemed he did, for the days went by and we remained disgruntled, unhappy but undischarged.

The next Monday was dark and dreary. The smoke from the store chimney sat sluggishly overhead and the steady beat of the rain was punctuated by the staccato drip from the eaves and the restless splash of the fountain. Nothing good could happen on such a day and nothing did. I had a new roommate. A very young girl who looked like a Madonna and told me that she was writing a book. She said, "It's about robbers and stuff like that. I don't have any trouble getting ideas, it is the putting them down that is hard."

The next Monday was beautiful and warm and the desire

to deviate from the straight and narrow path to breakfast was almost overwhelming. The perennial beds in the formal garden were gaudy with small, deep purple and blue Japanese iris, scarlet and yellow geum, large languid doronicum, pale yellow cottage tulips and blue and purple violas. Everything was drenched with dew and I wanted to bury my face in the fragrant coolness. This simple pleasure was denied me, however, for I had been advised by the authorities that wandering in the grounds before breakfast meant just one thing—s-e-x.

On the Friday before the next Monday, I was given a chest examination and spent the rest hours formulating an appropriate leave-taking of Miss Gillespie. I was torn between a well-aimed kick and a dignified and haughty exit. No word on chest examination. My longing for home was so overwhelming that in spirit I had already left the sanatorium. Only my bulky body, like an empty house with cold unfriendly rooms and dark windows, remained.

The occupational therapy shop was very crowded and Miss Gillespie's shouts for "Quiet! Must have Quiet! QUIET!" rang like a gong every minute or so. One of the innocent new patients created havoc by assuming that the WOMEN's TOILET on the door across the hall from the O.T. shop meant just that and went in. Miss Gillespie, busy painting her own likeness on a suspender button (nice Christmas gift), was not aware of what had happened until she noticed that the light was on in the lavatory. She exploded. "Who's there? Who went in there? What's going on?" She hurled herself from her seat and against the door of the women's toilet. The door was locked. "Open up! Open up!" she demanded banging on the door so loudly that all the men in the print shop next door came out into the hall to see what was going on. The poor frightened little patient opened the door and Miss Gillespie grabbed her by the arm and threw her into the O.T. shop. "Never go in there!" she yelled. "Control

the bladder. Everything can be controlled. Quiet, must
have quiet. Control everything!" She went back to her
painting. Kimi watched her for a few minutes, then said,
"She is painting her likeness on some small object. Could it
be a kidney stone?"

June twelfth was a beautiful summer morning. The per-
gola over the dining-room walk was quilted with pink roses
and purple clematis. Long ribbons of purple and blue violas
bordered all the beds in the formal garden and in every corner were clumps of great, heavy-headed peonies. The air
was moist and scented and a tender breeze gently flipped the
leaves of the poplars, now silver, now green. The brightly
robed patients moving slowly and sedately toward the dining
room were so like figures in a pageant that I expected a
chorus to come out from behind the privet hedge.

Over our morning coffee, Sheila, Kimi and I decided that
from that day forward we would maintain stoic calm and
complete indifference toward the Charge Nurse and Miss
Gillespie. Kimi said that she was also toying with the idea
of starting a rival sanatorium magazine to be called "Over
the Sputum Cups." We asked Miss West, a friendly little
nurse, if she thought there was a chance of our getting our
discharges that day, but she said that we should settle down
and forget such nonsense, as patients were never discharged
under a year. A year would mean August for Sheila and
Kimi, September for me. She could not explain why I had
received the mysterious chest examination.

In the occupational therapy shop, Miss Gillespie took me
to task over my useless tatting. She said that there were
hundreds, yes hundreds of useful articles made by former
patients and displayed on her shelves and that I was to look
them over and start to work making one of them immediately.
I said again that I would like to study shorthand. She said,
"You're no better than the rest of us, Mrs. Bard." As I
had always considered the writing of shorthand a very hum-

ble accomplishment, I was certain that Miss Gillespie still labored under the impression that shorthand was some fashionable game like badminton. I told her that I thought I would crochet a cover for my dictionary. She seemed well satisfied with this useful project.

Dinner was a frugal meal with one small chop apiece. "Chip, more appropriate name," Kimi said, dismally inspecting hers. "Until August and September," we said mournfully to each other as we parted for the rest hours.

At two-thirty we heard the slap, slap, slap of the Charge Nurse and it meant nothing to us. She turned in to Kimi and Sheila's room, then came to me and told me to report to the dining room. I was in my robe and was on the rustic walk before I noticed that I was barefooted. I ran back up the ramp to my room, grabbed my slippers but didn't stop to put them on. When I got to the deserted dining room Sheila was sitting at a table clasping and unclasping her hands. Kimi was with the Medical Director. I was the last to be called.

The Medical Director was sitting at the Charge Nurse's desk. He told me to sit down and I fell weakly into a chair. He said, "How would you like to go home this afternoon?" I couldn't answer. I just looked at him. He then told me that my sputum had been negative since October, that I was in fine condition, that I would have to take pneumothorax for from three to five years, that he had had a most difficult time teaching me that I had tuberculosis and that he still wasn't sure that I realized how serious my illness had been. I said, "If my sputum has been negative since October I must have started getting well almost as soon as I got here." The Medical Director said, "You have made a very rapid and splendid recovery and you are fortunate in having great recuperative powers. All are not similarly blessed. The important thing for you to remember is not that your sputum has been negative since October but that you had a cavity in your left lung and a shadow on your right lung. You have had serious tuberculosis, do not forget it." I asked him if I could be with the children and he said, "Certainly, you're not contagious." I tried to thank him for all he had done for me but he brushed it aside. "Take care of yourself," he said. "Show me that you have learned something about tuberculosis, that's all the thanks I want." We shook hands and I returned to the hospital where I found Sheila and Kimi sitting on their beds and looking dumbly at each other.

Miss West came in, hugged us all and offered to run over to the office and call our homes. Patients came from all sides to congratulate us and we told them all we would be packed and gone in a maximum of twenty minutes. The Charge Nurse had told me that I didn't have to send my things through fumigation so I tossed everything helter-skelter into cartons and was fully dressed and ready to leave in twelve minutes.

Sheila's family came about thirty minutes after Miss West called them. Kimi and I put on our coats and walked to the car with her. We expected our families within the next few minutes so we thought we'd just stay on the walk by the dining room. It was three-ten. At four-thirty they still hadn't come but we disdained offers of supper and returned to the promenade. I ran the gamut of things that might have caused the delay and at last came to the bitter conclusion that they didn't want me. I saw my future as a long series of trips from one sanatorium to another, a trail of enemies behind me.

The deep twilight settled down and Kimi and I could hardly see the road. A single car wound slowly around the bend. Kimi and I jumped up and began assembling our bundles. The car passed our building and went on up the drive. We sat down again. We could hear nurses calling to each other as they went off duty; the doleful splash of the fountain, the soft pad of slippered feet in the hallway. Why didn't they come? Would we have to face the humiliation of begging the Charge Nurse for just one more night under her roof? We decided to walk to the office and call again.

Kimi's mother answered the phone at her house and was so excited at hearing Kimi's voice and so bitterly disappointed not to have been home when the first call was made, that she began to sob. Kimi spoke crisply in Japanese for a few minutes then hung up the phone and translated for me. "Mama is so emotional, she is a poet you know and so of course slightly unbalanced, she began to cry when she heard my voice so I said, 'Please don't waste time crying, Mama, just get hold of Papa and drive out here as fast as you can.'"

There was no answer to many long, long rings at my house. In desperation I called a neighbor who told me that the entire family were across the lake on a picnic and she had no idea when, if ever, they would return. I left word that I would be waiting all night if necessary but they must come.

At nine o'clock the family came for me and after reaching home, we stayed up until three o'clock drinking coffee and eating left-over sandwiches. When I climbed into bed in the uncleaned back room my stomach felt like a just-hooked marlin, but I was happier than I had ever been in my life.

ᐳᐳᐳ XIX ᐸᐸᐸ

"Whom's with Who"

IT TOOK ME the whole summer to learn that you do not dispose of eight and a half months in a sanatorium just by leaving the grounds. I had had to struggle and bleed to adjust to sanatorium routine and I had to struggle and bleed to adjust back again to normal living. Certain marks of sanatorium life, like the prison pallor, disappeared with time; some, only concentrated effort erased; a few, like the scars from surgery, remained forever.

When I first came home, I dreamt about the sanatorium every night and awoke every morning when the five o'clock streetcar clanged past, expecting the washwater girls. At first I used to get up, stealthily retrieve the paper from the front porch, make a large pot of deliciously strong coffee and luxuriate in the breakfast nook until around seven when the family began seeping downstairs. After a month or so I would wake up, realize that I was at home and go back to sleep.

On my third day at home I received a letter from The Pines giving explicit instructions for care at home. It was a routine letter sent to all discharged patients but, as it was signed by the Medical Director, I thought it was a warning directed solely at me. The letter said:

1. Go back to your doctor every month for the first six months and have x-rays made as the doctor advises.

2. Do only the work the doctor approves. Ask his advice about hours and place of work.

3. Sleep at least nine hours every night, and a rest period of two hours in the afternoon is desirable.

4. Sleep alone in bed, preferably in a room alone. [Was this advice for morals or health?]

5. If attacked by slight cold, rest in bed until the cold is entirely gone. A doctor should be called if any symptoms appear.

6. Eat well-balanced meals at regular intervals.

7. If there is sputum, even though it is "negative," it should be disposed of as it was in the sanatorium. [Oh, please let me spit on the floor, just once!]

8. A woman who has had tuberculosis should avoid becoming pregnant except on the advice of her doctor. [And preferably after the marriage ceremony.]

9. Recreation and entertainment should be engaged in only in moderation.

The letter ended with a quotation on relapse, warning me that if I didn't play the game according to the rules and if I was restless, heedless or willful I would soon go to my eternal rest. I was only slightly reassured when I learned that Sheila and Kimi had had similar letters.

At first I had no inclination to resume old friendships, and I kept up an enormous correspondence with my sanatorium friends. I clung to Sheila and Kimi as though we were all lepers trying to live in a non-leper colony. Sheila disengaged herself from us after the first few weeks and became very normally interested in her coming marriage. Kimi and I clung together. She came to the house frequently and we walked in the park and talked about The Pines, Miss Toecover and the patients.

Kimi said that she was very lonely and unhappy, that her former friends treated her as though she were violently contagious, and boys, who before had been merely too short for her, were now like "mites" in comparison. I tried to cheer her with stories of my lonely, unhappy girlhood. Of how even without tuberculosis I had always been shunned. After the third chapter of "The Lone Wolf" in grammar school, high school and at college, Kimi said, "Enough of this lying. Let us face facts. I used to be full of fun and have many friends. Now I am over-sensitive. I get hurt by everything and I do not find enjoyment in anything. I am hateful to my poor mother and father and I quarrel incessantly with my brother and sister. I am only happy when I am with you discussing the old days at the sanatorium." I told her that I was sure that this was all part of the adjustment from one life to another, but I felt much less sure than I sounded for I knew that I had become big and fat and whiny and the epitome of everything the sanatorium had warned us against.

Then my sister Mary invited Anne and Joan and me to visit her at their summer camp in the San Juan Islands. We left at a little after five, one still summer morning, and drove through miles and miles of rich, well-kept farmland, deep forests and along rocky shores. The camp, a series of small silver gray cabins, was on a great curving sweep of sandy beach, sand dunes and tide flats covered with shells, sea-animals, drift wood and agates. We cooked and ate all of our meals out of doors and at night after supper we built beach fires, toasted marshmallows and watched the sun go blazing down behind the Straits of Juan de Fuca and the moon rise over the small dancing lights of the fishing fleet.

The cabins were lined with cedar and smelled of stale bacon smoke, salt air and shingles. Anne and Joan and I dressed and undressed in front of a small airtight stove that crackled and spit and turned red in the middle. The beds were hard and the mattresses were lumpy but through the windows we could hear the scrub pines complaining about

the wind, the swoooooOOOOOOSH in and out of the surf.
Inside the candle sputtered in its saucer and the children's
breathing was deep and quiet. After a day or so I stopped
dreaming of the sanatorium.

Before breakfast, small niece Mari, Anne, Joan and I
walked a quarter of a mile over the dunes to "the farm" for
the milk. As we walked along in the morning sun, the short
beach grass crunchy underfoot, the salt air fragrant with
pine, the mournful crying of the gulls accompanied by the
whirring of the grasshoppers, I held the children's hands
more firmly and quickly put aside the thought that at just
that moment only a week before I was entertaining Miss
Toecover's shop.

After ten days we returned home loaded with agates and
near-agates, vile-smelling shells, pretty stones and bright
plans for the future.

Soon after coming home from the beach I spent my first
evening among strangers and in an apartment. The evening
was not unusually warm but the room seemed suffocating
and the air smelled as if it had been rented with the apartment. Everyone looked very tired and seemed to me to be
on edge and straining to have a good time.

After the first hour I too looked tired and was on edge and
straining to have a good time for the apartment was heated
to 90°, there wasn't a shred of oxygen left in the air, I was
fat and my blood was attuned to a temperature of not over
50°. I coughed tubercularly a few times but all that got me
was another offer of a drink. About eleven o'clock as I
actually began to lose consciousness, I staggered across the
room, mumbling apologies, raised the window two inches and
opened the door into the hall. My hostess shivered a few
times, then giving me an accusing look, went in and got little
sacks and jackets for the women. The men hunched their
shoulders, looked for the draft and moved into protected cor-

ners. When I got home I sat out on the porch and breathed
in great reviving breaths of fresh air and wondered how I
was ever going to stand working in a hot stuffy office.

In July Mother left to spend a month on a friend's farm
and I took over the housekeeping. I found that with hard
work and activity my spirits soared, but I went down for
my pneumothorax overflowing with apprehension for fear I
had "overdone." The doctor collapsed my lung and told me
that I was in fine condition and that I could stay up twelve
hours a day.

Later in the week I went to a luncheon at a country club
and was dumfounded to have everyone dumfounded to be in
actual contact with a returned White Plaguer. During the
luncheon there were many questions about the exact symptoms, the location of the first pain, etc., and before the afternoon had ended I was moderately certain that I had uncov-
ered several hidden but far-gone cases of t.b.

When I got home Sheila called to tell me that two patients
at The Pines had died. One the thirteen-year-old girl, the
other a Japanese boy whom Kimi knew. Immediately my
trip to the beach, the luncheon, my household duties became
vague far-away things and I threw myself headlong into the
sanatorium. I called Kimi to give her the bad news and we
talked and talked about patients who would die, had died and
might die. That night I dreamed of The Pines again and
awakened very early with the old depression hanging over
me.

I decided that since my future was short and black, I
should spend every minute with Anne and Joan. I arranged
a crowded and gritty picnic in the park, including, in the
heat of my enthusiasm, five very young neighborhood children as well as my own two and all the dogs. Apparently
somewhere during my incarceration I had lost touch with
that carefree spirit of young things, for the dogs ran wild,

the park gardeners threatened to put us all out, the smallest children became entirely unmanageable and lay in the paths kicking and screaming, while the larger ones disappeared into the tops of trees.

I finally emerged from the park yanking in one hand, by the leashes, the three dogs who slid along on their haunches, and in the other hand, three little, red-eyed, snuffling boys tied together by their belts and led by my scarf. The four older children I had abandoned while they were still risking their necks in the trees. As I grimly headed toward home, I wondered if this was why the sanatorium was constantly warning its patients about being around young children when they got home.

As it became known that I was home, people were very kind and entertained for me, but I grew increasingly resentful of the tendency of my friends first to scream when they saw me as if I were a ghost, and then shout that I looked TEN YEARS YOUNGER BUT SO MUCH FATTER! As time passed I declined all invitations and asked Sheila, Kimi and the sweet sanatorium nurse, Molly, to dinner and to spend the evenings talking about The Pines and the inmates. I learned that Eileen still had no time up, Minna had had the operation removing her kidney and was doing very well; and that Kate, Delores, Pixie and several others were due for discharges. Kimi brought me copies of the sanatorium magazine and I was ashamed to find myself reading them avidly.

I had long letters from Kate who told me that Miss Gillespie talked about me constantly as a powerful threat of mob rule in the occupational therapy shop; that Kate was considered such a trusted patient that she was given library duty and was allowed to push the book-cart into the men's ward, which privilege had been much over-rated; that almost everyone was being strengthened for some kind of surgery; that Delores and Pixie had come to open warfare and the entire Ambulant Hospital, especially the men, had all taken sides. She said that the Charge Nurse was threatening to throw everybody out and close up the institution.

Kimi came to lunch almost every day and brought charming gifts for us all. Sembi for the children, a lovely set of bowls, little Japanese figurines, silk scarves and handkerchiefs. She was very blue and said that there was no place for her any more. She was a misfit even at home. I told her of my fragile feelings, spells of black depression and secret dread of looking for a job, of becoming so obsessed with housework that I even polished the mailbox and waxed the front porch. Of trying to get close to the children again by boring them with too much attention, too much unskilled participation in their games.

At that time Anne and Joan and Anne's best friend Ermengarde spent the lovely summer days in their room with the doors and windows shut, playing Sonja Heine. Anne and Ermengarde took turns in an old green chiffon party dress and Alison's black hockey skates, stumping around on the linoleum floor, being Sonja Heine. But Joan was always Tyrone Power. Dressed in her Buck Rogers helmet, an old pumpkin suit with bloomer legs, long brown stockings and her red rubber raincoat she pursued Sonja on a pretend roller coaster, on a pretend Ferris Wheel, on pretend horseback, then finally caught her on the ice (or linoleum rug), always posing in a poorly executed very unsteady arabesque performed to the squeaky accompaniment of the Skaters Waltz played on their little phonograph. I watched the performance one day much against their wills and made some suggestions about the costumes. The suggestions were not well received. Joan said that I had been in the hospital so long that I apparently didn't recognize the fact that she was dressed exactly like Tyrone Power. Anne said that she and Ermengarde dressed and skated exactly like Sonja Heine and they could prove it by pictures.

When Joan had other plans, Anne and Ermengarde spent the lovely, sunny, summer daytime in their room with the windows and doors shut, playing opera singer. Crouched by the little phonograph they would listen attentively while Alma Gluck sang "Lo Hear the Gentle Lark" over and over and over again. Then Ermengarde would stand up and sing the song with Anne prompting from her crouched position on the floor, then Anne would sing and Ermengarde would prompt. This was a harmless enough activity except that Ermengarde was the type of singer who had a gesture for every single word. "Lo" she sang with her index finger pointed menacingly toward the audience; "hear" (her head was bent slightly to one side, her right hand cupped her right ear) "the gentle" (stroking motions) "lark" (bouncing and fluttering of wings) and Anne copied her exactly.

Anne's voice was sweet and true and she had perfect pitch; and it disturbed me to see her dressed in an old black lace party dress, her red curls pinned to the top of her head with hundreds of old jewels, standing on her little table and spoiling her sweet singing with the corny gestures. I said as much. Anne exploded. She said, "You've had tuberculosis and you don't know anything about singing opera. Ermengarde's grandmother was an opera singer and she taught Ermengarde how to sing and she said that all opera singers used gestures all the time just like Ermengarde."

Anne continued to sing exactly like Ermengarde, even adding to her already large operatic repertoire some popular numbers such as "Boo Hoo" and "When I'm Calling You, hooooooohoo, hoo, hoo, hoo" from "Rose Marie," which required thousands of much cornier gestures.

Kimi said that she thought it would be a good idea to leave the children alone and to brush up on my shorthand. I retaliated by suggesting that she register for the University in the fall as a means of filling her idle time, occupying her mind and meeting new people. Kimi begged me to speak to her mother and father on behalf of the University idea as she feared that they thought her still too frail for such a venture.

So one evening I went over to her house and talked too much, about the University, in the high shrill voice I reserve for foreigners, but was apparently convincing for the next week Kimi obtained the permission of the Medical Director to take ten hours at the University in the fall. I registered at a business college for an evening class in shorthand.

My shorthand teacher, an old lady who wore black patent Mary Jane slippers and a hat with a long black tassel that swung when she dictated like the hand on a metronome, was very excitable and when she dictated over one hundred words a minute she ran all her words together, tore out the pages of her book and dropped her pencils. One evening, when she got up to 150 words per minute, she became so hysterical she dropped her glasses on the floor and crushed them under the heel of one of the large Mary Janes.

She was a dreadful teacher and in temperament almost a twin sister to Miss Gillespie, but I reasoned that if I could take down and transcribe her dictation, "Dissa (dear sir) Weareinreceiptofyoursofthethirdandwewishtostatethat-wedonothaveanymorehorseshoesinstockbutwewillshipthemto-youassoonaswereceivethem," I could work anywhere. Also I liked the atmosphere of the shorthand class because all of us students were obvious failures of one kind or another but I was the youngest and the prettiest or, more truthfully, the least old and the least repulsive.

In August I accepted an invitation to a bridge luncheon and had my first experience in being considered an untouchable. A friend was extolling the virtues of her new house and comparatively new baby, and I, merely as a polite gesture, made the untrue statement that I would love to see them both. When friend looked horrified and changed the subject, I thought I had blundered and forgotten that her baby was an idiot. I asked Mary what was wrong. She said, "Oh, Marjorie's such a dope. She thinks you're contagious. You didn't want to see her ugly house and her grubby little baby anyway." I didn't, but I was hurt just the same. After that I waited to be invited before going anywhere.

Early in the fall Mary and I drove into the country to buy peaches and stopped at the house of an old school friend. We had forgotten that Old School Friend had ripened into the type of housekeeper who washes off banana skins with lysol before peeling them and we greeted her effusively and demanded food and coffee. She was most unenthusiastic. "Weren't you in a Tuberculosis Sanatorium?" she asked me through a small crack in the door. "She only got out June twelfth," Mary said, looking at me proudly. Old School Friend excused herself for a minute, firmly shutting the door in our faces. The day was warm but certainly not warm enough to warrant our being kept out on the porch as long as she kept us. When she did let us in, some time later, she produced coffee and food but we ate it quickly and over such a bedlam of noise that conversation was impossible. It was not hard to determine that while we waited on the front porch Old School Friend had gathered up her children and bolted them in some back room where they kicked and screamed and pounded on the door and demanded to be let out the whole time we were there.

As we drove away Mary said, "Don't you dare go back and live with her no matter how hard she begs. You just tell her she lives too far out in the country and you must keep in circulation." I laughed but I was bothered. What if I applied for a job and somebody in the office felt like Old School Friend? I asked Kimi if she had had any such unpleasant experiences. She said, "Oh my, yes. Sometimes they do not wait until I am out of the house before producing the Flit Gun and vigorously spraying everything I have touched."

About the first of September, Pixie received her discharge and dropped in one evening at seven-thirty on her way home from the sanatorium. I made a large pot of coffee and we drank it all as we talked. She told me that the Charge Nurse returned from her vacation dripping with sweetness and understanding but that one of the sweet young nurses had contracted miliary tuberculosis and died; that Katy Morris had t.b. and was in bed at Bedrest; that Eileen had had another hemorrhage; that Kate and Evalee had also been discharged and the Medical Director was going to let Evalee leave the children in the Children's Hospital for a month or two; that Marie was at the Ambulant Hospital and Sylvia had eight hours. I asked about Delores and Pixie said that she didn't care to defile my living room with discussions of anyone so vulgar. I thought it might be interesting to hear what Delores had to say about Pixie but did not say this out loud.

Pixie looked very pretty and said that the doctor had told her that she could start working immediately. She said that she was going to see about her old job on her way home. We parted with affection and promises of an early reunion and she left.

Her enthusiasm was contagious and when she had gone I started at once to assemble an outfit to go jobhunting.

The next morning, feeling very spiritless and shabbily neat, I boarded a streetcar crowded with the ten-thirty group of smartly dressed, refined-looking female suburban shoppers. I crouched up near the front and kept reassuring myself that it wasn't printed anywhere on me that I had had t.b. Then the streetcar hit a rather bad district near town and who should get on but Coranell Planter, the Bedrest occupational therapy teacher.

She saw me immediately and screamed, "Well for Gawd's sake, Betty, you're lookin' swell! A lot better than when you left THE SANATORIUM! You're sure FAT TOO!

Ha, ha, ha!" Feeling hundreds of curious eyes on me I
cowered into the corner and mumbled, "You look well too."
Coranell yelled, "What did you say, honey? I can't hear
over all this noise." I said, "You look well too." She said,
"Feelin' grand. Just grand. Did you hear that Minna had
her kidney took out? Just eaten away with t.b. Gracie is
having the third stage of a thoro and Bill Williams just had
another HEMORRHAGE! Gawd that poor kid has had a
tough time. Eileen has had another HEMORRHAGE TOO.
You know, kiddo, I don't think that poor little Eileen is going
to pull out of it. Swell little kid, too, but she don't have any
spirit any more. She says that she's never been happy since
they moved her away from you and Kimi. Roommates are
awful important when you're on bedrest and the Charge
Nurse is a real good nurse but she don't realize that the most
important thing of all is whom's with who."

When I finally got off the streetcar five blocks after Coranell, I decided that I would put off going to the employment
office until after lunch. I was to meet Mary for lunch at an
Italian food-importing place at one o'clock and though it
was then only eleven forty-five and the restaurant was just
around the corner, I went bleakly in, sat down at the counter
and ordered a cup of coffee.

"Aren't you Betty Bard?" said a pleasant masculine voice
at my elbow. "I used to be," I said turning around. Bill
Wilson, an old friend of Mary's, was beaming at me. He
said, "Well, this is pleasant!" He leaned back in his chair
and looked me over with interest. "Weren't you at The
Pines?" he asked. "Yes," I said, looking down, fumbling
with my gloves and wishing that Bill didn't have such a loud
voice. "When did you get out?" he asked in the same carrying voice. I told him. "You look wonderful!" he said enthusiastically. "Are you all well?" "Yes," I said, "in fact
I came downtown today to look for a job." "You mean you
haven't a job and you want one?" he asked eagerly. "Yes,"

I said. "Thank God," he said. "I've been interviewing secretaries for three weeks and I'd given up hope of ever finding one who wrote both shorthand and English. Can you come to work tomorrow?" I said, "I might consider it even if it means walking twenty miles in my bare feet over old Victrola needles every morning." My new boss laughed and ordered me a roast beef sandwich. He said, "How was it out there at The Pines? I've heard it's a pretty tough deal." "Oh, not at all," I heard myself saying. "I actually enjoyed it. The discipline is strict, of course, but it has to be in the cure of tuberculosis. . . ."

From away far off I heard the gates of The Pines clang shut forever. Coranell certainly had something. The most important thing of all is Whom's with Who.

THE END

About the Author

BETTY MACDONALD was born Anne Elizabeth Campbell Bard in Boulder, Colorado, on 26 March 1908. She married Robert Heskett in 1927 and settled on a forty-acre chicken farm near Chimacum, Washington. Her experiences on the farm became the subject of her first book, *The Egg and I* (1945), which sold over a million copies in the year following publication, was made into a film starring Claudette Colbert and Fred MacMurray, and spawned the successful series of "Ma and Pa Kettle" films. In addition to *The Plague and I*, which was originally published in 1948, her other books include *Anybody Can Do Anything* (1950) and *Onions in the Stew* (1955). She died in Seattle on 7 February 1958.

THE PLAGUE AND I

Other books by Betty MacDonald forthcoming in
COMMON READER EDITIONS:

Anybody Can Do Anything

Onions in the Stew